THE POWER MAKERS

THE POWER MAKERS

The
Inside Story of
America's Biggest Business . . .
and Its Struggle to
Control Tomorrow's
Electricity

BY RICHARD MUNSON

RODALE PRESS Emmaus, Pennsylvania

Printed in the United States of America on recycled paper containing a high percentage of de-inked fiber.

Book design by Linda Jacopetti.

Library of Congress Cataloging in Publication Data
Munson, Richard.
    The power makers.

    Includes index.
    1. Electric utilities—United States.   I. Title.
HD9685.U5M86   1985   338.4'736362'0973   85-8243
ISBN 0-87857-550-2   hardcover

2   4   6   8   10   9   7   5   3   1   hardcover

To Mom and Dad

CONTENTS

As new discoveries are made, new truths discovered and manners and opinions change, with the change of circumstance, institutions must advance also to keep pace with the times.

Thomas Jefferson

INTRODUCTION

My grandmother was born in the year Thomas Edison developed the electric light bulb, 1879. The real benefits of electricity, however, would take several decades to reach my grandparents and most Americans. Gas and kerosene lamps would long provide their only illumination. Strong hands would pump the water. Wood stoves would supply the heat. Cooking, washing and other daily tasks would remain difficult chores for many years.

By the mid-1930s, my mother's parents had built the first all-electric home in California's San Fernando Valley. An early "all-electric home" still meant my grandfather had to regularly place 50- or 100-pound ice blocks in the ice chest. But innovations were arriving rapidly. Within several years, the family purchased an electric refrigerator which, because it didn't leak, could be placed in the kitchen rather than on the porch. My grandfather had enough faith in the new technologies to invest in the expanding electric utility companies, confident that the promised dividends would eventually help finance his retirement.

My father's first home lacked indoor plumbing, but by the time he entered high school, the family enjoyed running water warmed by an electric heater. His mother assembled a crystal radio set that brought entertainment and news, and his father rode Los Angeles's electric streetcars to work.

When my parents first married, their washing machine lacked a spin cycle; instead, clothes were run through a wringer by hand before being hung on the outside line to dry. By the time I arrived, the family home sported an electric washing machine, dryer, refrigerator, garbage disposal, television and radio. Today, I find it remarkable that many writers still work without electrically powered word processors.

Over the past three generations, Americans came to enjoy low-cost and reliable power, reassured by a future promising cheaper and more abundant electricity. We securely purchased blue-chip utility stocks and received healthy dividends. We confidently flicked switches to turn on lights, heaters, appliances and machines. We viewed the all-electric home as a badge of prosperity.

But the utilities' golden age has been shattered. Since 1973, electricity prices have tripled and utilities have canceled at least 180 proposed power plants—more than the combined electric generating capacity of Texas and California; several more unfinished facilities will probably soon be scrapped. A dozen power firms, including Long Island Lighting in New York and Public Service Company of Indiana, teeter near bankruptcy. And economists worry that the industry's proposed construction budget will divert massive amounts of capital from other businesses and raise interest rates throughout the entire economy. It is ironic that businesses founded by (among others) that peerless innovator Thomas Edison have failed to adjust—innovate—in the new era of higher costs and lower demand for electricity.

The utility industry's problems are hurting businesses and individuals. Today, a poor woman in Tennessee pays her electric bill with a Social Security check and faces the month of February with less than $30 left for housing, groceries and clothes. Some middle-class homeowners on Long Island confront monthly electric charges exceeding their mortgage payments. Thousands of small investors lose their life savings in worthless power system bonds. A Texas businessman is forced to shut down his crystal growing laboratory for two months because a one-day power outage contaminates the materials. A New England sportsman can no longer fish because acid rain from midwestern power plants kills all life in his mountain lake. A Pennsylvania steel executive closes his plant and lays off workers because high electric rates make his products too expensive on the world market.

Problems promise to accelerate. Consumers face "rate shocks" every time a power plant joins the utility grid. Kansas Gas & Electric customers will confront an 83 percent increase when the Wolf Creek reactor's bill comes due. Electric bills for the average El Paso industrialist will skyrocket almost $900,000 during the first year the Palo Verde plants are in operation. The Callaway 1 reactor will raise the average Missouri homeowner's annual bill $328 (and, one economist predicts, will result in the loss of 24,500 jobs in the St. Louis area alone). If the Seabrook reactor is completed, New Hampshire's rates will almost triple.

America still requires reliable, reasonably priced power, particularly those young, growing industries that offer the best hope for U.S. economic revitalization—computers, robotics and electronics. To satisfy this demand, a new generation of entrepreneurs is emerging, bringing with them innovative technologies and aggressive marketing that provide alternatives to the utility monopolies' power. In fact, independent energy suppliers have quickly become a multi-billion-dollar business, instilling competition within the electricity market for the first time in 60 years. New businesses are introducing sophisticated computers and efficient appliances to reduce the demand for utility company power. Others are producing electricity with newly designed generators; in some regions of the country, these entrepreneurs will soon supply a third of the electric power. Their rise portends a new era of diversity, with efficiency and innovation the cutting edge.

This book tells the story of a critical industry fraught with change. It explains how America's electric companies were born, flourished, became monopolized, began to founder and today are losing power—both literally and figuratively—to a new generation of entrepreneurs. In human and political terms, it traces the battles for control of the electricity market from the conflict between private and public power companies to the struggle for government support. Through personal profiles, it emphasizes today's competition between utility executives and independent power producers.

In describing the industry's development, the book concentrates on the turning points—1879, when it all began in Menlo Park, New Jersey; 1903 in Chicago; 1933 in the Tennessee Valley; 1957 at Shippingport, Pennsylvania; 1979 at Three Mile Island; and 1983 in Washington State. It also looks at the individuals—among them Thomas Edison, Samuel Insull, George Norris, David Lilienthal, Hyman Rickover and Donald Hodel—who illuminate these turning points. But more importantly, the book explains how the emergence of new electric entrepreneurs affects the utility industry's 8.5 million stockholders and a nation of ratepayers.

The shift to a competitive electricity market promises to transfer fortunes, shift employment patterns and alter the means of producing energy. The significance of these effects becomes ever more real in the book's Epilogue, which predicts the rate shocks that will soon confront consumers across the country. It also lists those power companies that will be burdened with skyrocketing cost overruns. And it catalogs timely investment opportunities with independent power producers.

To gain an inside look at this giant and crucial industry in transition, I donned the role of an inquiring journalist, attended utility conferences and interviewed more than 200 power company officials. This book does not set out to explain all the intricacies of the utility industry nor does it dwell on nuclear, solar and other energy technologies. (A brief overview of the structure of utilities and the science of electricity generation is provided in the Appendix.) Rather, it seeks to answer the question: Who will control the production and distribution of electric power?

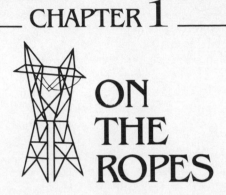

CHAPTER 1

ON THE ROPES

The 2,000 dark-suited executives seem oblivious to the world beyond the Boston Sheraton Hotel. It's mid-June 1984 and the morning papers report additional problems with the Shoreham and Three Mile Island nuclear reactors, but the power titans gathered here remain relaxed and confident. Even the weather has no effect; New Englanders swelter in a muggy heat wave, but the conferees spend four days amid plush surroundings, comforted by the air conditioners their generators power.

Though their names and faces are not known to most Americans, the participants control more assets than any other group of executives in the United States. In terms of capital investment and market value, they represent the biggest business in America. Their companies gobble up one-half of all new common stock issuances and one-third of all corporate financing. They consume the most fuel, burning 82 percent of the coal mined in the United States, and they spend almost four times as much each year for new equipment than does the automobile industry.

Electric utility leaders are not the best-paid businessmen, but they enjoy the most job security, many having worked their way up the company ranks from construction engineer to chief executive. Although they brag about the glories of America's free-enterprise system, they have been protected from competition by state regulators and swaddled in benefits by federal lawmakers. They are conservative, patriotic, male, white and middle-aged.

For this 52nd reunion of the Edison Electric Institute (EEI), the trade association of private utilities, executives fly in from all 50 states and a dozen foreign countries, bringing their wives and anecdotes about

1

their children and mutual friends. Luxury suites have been converted overnight into reception halls, complete with open bars and buffet tables laden with exotic desserts. Westinghouse Electric Corporation, a maker of utility equipment, offers free blackjack chips to entice conferees to its fabricated casino. Near the door, a company salesman spots a utility executive from his region and begins hustling Westinghouse's new generator. In the back corner, five southwestern utility planners formally discuss power pooling arrangements. Another group quietly calculates the future composition of congressional subcommittees.

It is a friendly, if insulated, fraternal gathering. The wife of a General Electric executive, seeing me alone at the company's luncheon, kindly introduces herself and welcomes me. But when I speak of my book, she stops talking, appears embarrassed and quickly returns to her chair. Throughout the conference, other participants also express their skepticism of "outsiders," protesting that utility executives are misunderstood by the media, regulators and environmentalists.

The main convention room, reeking of cigars and cologne, feels staid and sedate. A minister opens one session by asking God to "grant industry leaders the courage to make vital decisions, despite criticism, that will serve the public interest." Conservative columnist Patrick Buchanan wins the audience's applause by predicting Ronald Reagan's reelection. Tom Sullivan, a correspondent for "Good Morning America," wins their hearts by declaring that utilities "provide Americans with one of our fundamental freedoms—electricity." He urges executives to overcome the public's misperception of power companies, just as he overcame his blindness.

Lectures by utility executives seem strangely divorced from the industry's troubles. Although utilities hold more excess capacity in 1984 than at any time in their history, Charles Dougherty, EEI's chairman, warns of possible power shortages. Although entrepreneurs are supplying an array of energy-saving devices, Dougherty predicts electricity demand will soar. Although independent power producers are building more capacity than private utility companies, Dougherty fails to mention the competition. Although utilities are canceling scores of nuclear reactors, Dougherty boasts that the technology offers a "success story with unequal record." Without nuclear power and increased power plant construction, the 43-year industry veteran predicts that "civilization would regress."

Executives clearly prefer talking about their "service ethic" than their economic troubles. They proudly describe themselves as public servants providing power to modernize America and eliminate life's drudgeries. Andrew Hines, Florida Power's chairman, declares, "Electricity is the flame of life, and utilities are the keepers of that flame." When I ask about possible reforms, he responds, "Why change a giant industry that provides a real public service?"

Are bankruptcies and competition, as utility executives suggest, merely temporary aberrations? Or is electricity production undergoing a fundamental change, and are utility executives unwilling or unable to adapt to the evolutionary pressures?

A TROUBLED SYSTEM

With a single stroke of the gavel in June 1983, the Washington State Supreme Court set the stage for America's largest default, banishing to the auction block a hundred miles of pipe, a thousand miles of electrical cable and a few 500-ton steam generators. But the sale will recover less than 2 percent of the $2.25 billion debt incurred constructing a series of overbudget nuclear power plants that are no longer needed. Bondholders and ratepayers of the Washington Public Power Supply System (WPPSS, sometimes known as "Whoops") must pay the difference.

WPPSS may be the first of many electric company failures. More than two dozen "nuclear-exposed" utilities wonder if they can afford to complete partially built facilities. In January 1984 Public Service Company of Indiana decided against the gamble, halting construction of its two Marble Hill reactors (despite a $2.5 billion investment), slashing its quarterly dividend 65 percent, and asking Indiana's Public Service Commission for an emergency $105 million rate boost just to keep the utility's doors open.

These decisions seemed to unleash an avalanche of bad news for the power industry. For the first time ever, the Nuclear Regulatory Commission denied Commonwealth Edison of Chicago an operating license on safety grounds for its $4.2 billion Byron nuclear plants. The Tennessee Valley Authority temporarily shut down its $1 billion Browns Ferry unit and laid off 400 workers because of "numerous violations" of government safety rules; later in the year it canceled four unfinished reactors and wrote off about $2.7 billion in losses. Cincinnati Gas & Electric decided to convert its $1.7 billion Zimmer nuclear plant to a less-costly, coal-fired operation. Long Island Lighting Company (LILCO), already on the brink of bankruptcy because of its stalled Shoreham plant, eliminated its dividend and backed out of the Nine Mile Point nuclear project in upstate New York, leaving its partners with severe financing uncertainties. Public Service of New Hampshire, burdened by the troubled Seabrook nuclear plant, cut its dividend. In July 1984, Consumers Power of Michigan canceled its twin-unit Midland plant after sinking $3.6 billion in construction and another $400 million in nuclear fuel.

The industry's troubles translate directly into higher electric rates for consumers and lower returns for investors. Monthly utility bills have already tripled since the 1973 oil embargo and threaten to double again in many regions when utilities complete the expensive plants now under construction. Suffering investors have made money in only 4 of the last 15 years. Even EEI's chairman admits that "electric industry shareholders have taken a terrible whipping in the past decade." Unlike investors in many other industries, utility shareholders are of the mom-and-pop variety. Individuals own about 78 percent of all publicly traded utility shares, according to a study by Bear Stearns & Company. That figure is nearly 88 percent for Consumers Power of Michigan, 93 percent for LILCO and 98 percent for Public Service of New Hampshire. My grandfather, like many people of his generation, believed utility stocks would provide reliable dividends forever; in the past 2 years, he helplessly watched his shares lose 30 percent of their value. Bondholders have done as poorly. WPPSS bonds, once promoted as secure, income-producing investments, are now virtually worthless.

Utilities' rosy financial statements often camouflage bleak news. Consider Commonwealth Edison of Chicago. Despite regulatory penalties and construction cost overruns, Commonwealth Edison reports that its 1983 earnings rose 17 percent. Much of the gain, however, results from a clever accounting entry called Allowance for Funds Used During Construction (AFUDC), which utility accountants created to make up for profits the companies are not allowed to earn on money tied up in unfinished projects. Close to 60 percent of the total industry's earnings in 1983 resulted from AFUDC entries. If power plants are eventually completed and rolled into utility rate bases, this paper-income entry presents no real problems. But if facilities are abandoned or if regulators refuse to charge ratepayers for the unused plants, the huge AFUDC "profits" will probably be worthless. In February 1985, the Standard & Poor's investment rating service announced it had lost confidence in utilities' financial reporting and will reclassify AFUDC entries as bad debt.

An array of statistics partially explains today's financial crunch. Fuel-cost increases, spurred largely by the machinations of the Organization of Petroleum Exporting Countries (OPEC), raised the industry's expenses $30.2 billion in 1980 alone, almost eight times the industry's total fuel bill a decade earlier. The average cost of building a newly installed kilowatt of capacity soared from $140 in 1969 to $531 in 1979; the average cost of nuclear reactors still under construction in late 1984 totaled $2,800, while the most expensive unit topped $5,100 per kilowatt of capacity. The industry's long-term debt rose from $42.2 billion in 1970 to $105.6 billion in 1980, necessitating about $10 billion in annual interest payments. (Some utilities actually pay more in interest than they earn on their investments.) Nuclear safety regulations doubled labor and equipment costs and tripled engineering expenses. Pollution-control equipment, according to one Wall Street analyst, added 20 percent or more to the cost of a power plant, a regulatory burden that surpasses any other industry's.

But the most important cause of the industry's troubles is its own remarkable miscalculation of the future demand for electricity. Executives who had enjoyed two decades of steady and rapid expansion failed to foresee that the rising cost of electricity—caused by the oil embargo, inflation, safety and environmental regulations, and technical complexities—would motivate consumers to conserve electricity and use alternative fuels. In 1975, for example, Donald Cook, the former chairman of American Electric Power, predicted that a massive upsurge in demand would cause blackouts unless utilities rapidly built new power plants. In 1978, EEI launched a multi-million-dollar advertising campaign to declare, "The time to build power plants is now." Both Cook and the EEI were wrong, incredibly wrong. Expanding construction, combined with reduced consumption, produced a staggering and expensive capacity gap, forcing utility directors to abandon more than $18 billion of investments in 113 proposed nuclear reactors; another 67 coal-fired plants were also canceled. Despite the cutbacks, the industry's surplus generating capacity—which engineers attempt to maintain at a 15-20 percent level to

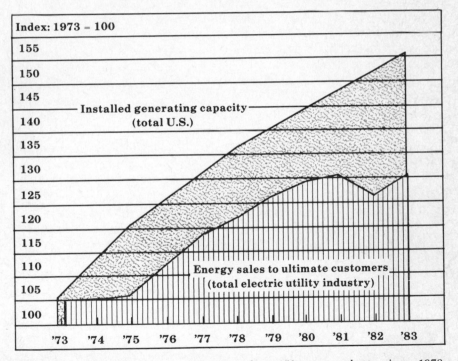

Index: 1973 = 100

Installed generating capacity (total U.S.)

Energy sales to ultimate customers (total electric utility industry)

Although utilities have canceled more than 150 power plants since 1973, generating capacity has increased 50 percent. Because demand for electricity increased only 20 percent, power companies possess huge amounts of expensive excess capacity. Some utility executives predict they will never build a power plant again.

handle emergencies—still rose from 21 percent in 1973 to almost 40 percent a decade later. Today's excess electricity has dearly cost utility stockholders and ratepayers.

TOO BLEAK TO METER

The nuclear reactor, once a symbol of so much promise, has become a financial lemon. Only two decades ago, power companies predicted that by the year 2000, 1,000 reactors would be providing electricity "too cheap to meter." The reality? Only 82 atomic plants operating in March 1985 and no new orders placed in seven years. In fact, only 2 nuclear reactors ordered since 1974 have not been subsequently canceled; no work has been done on even these 2 plants and neither plant will probably ever be completed. What has gone wrong with the way Americans produce and regulate electric power?

"The business of generating electricity has ceased to be a commercially viable enterprise," declares I. C. Bupp of the Harvard Business School. An overstatement perhaps, but soaring construction costs do plague the nuclear industry. LILCO's Shoreham reactor, if it ever operates, will cost $5,192 per kilowatt, more than 15 times the original estimate. One Atomic Industrial Forum spokesman, noting that a reactor's final price is usually more than twice a utility's original estimate, rued that "estimating capital costs for power plants is like shooting at a moving target."

More than ordinary inflation is at work here. Richard Morgan, author of four books on utilities, calculates that between 1964 and 1984 "nuclear costs have increased more than ten times faster than the Consumer Price Index. The cost of building an oil refinery has increased only one-tenth as fast as the cost of a nuclear reactor, and coal-fired plants have increased less than half as fast."

Utility executives, blaming government regulators and environmentalists, say new rules and delays accelerate costs. Safety requirements to contain radioactivity, for example, demand thick and expensive concrete walls. New modifications frequently force utilities to rebuild many of their systems, as when Northeast Utilities of Connecticut spent $5 million to add new pipes at its Millstone 2 reactor, then 50 percent complete.

The flood of regulatory changes, however, did not begin until after the large reactors ordered in the mid-1960s came on-line and began breaking down. Pipes and valves cracked under intense radiation and high temperatures. Tubes corroded, fuel rods bent and cooling systems malfunctioned. Only after a score of accidents catalyzed the public and politicians did the Atomic Energy Commission and its successor, the Nuclear Regulatory Commission, alter their habit of routinely granting nuclear licenses. Still, safety problems persist. At Wisconsin's Lacrosse reactor, for instance, investigators found that a 3,000-gallon tank of radioactive wastewater had been inadvertently connected to the plant's drinking water system. At the Diablo Canyon reactor atop a California fault line, Pacific Gas & Electric received a preliminary start-up license from the Nuclear Regulatory Commission in September 1981, only to discover two months later that the plant's anti-earthquake structures were installed backward due to a blueprint error. In 1983 alone, utilities reported more than 5,000 mishaps at nuclear power plants, 247 of which were considered "particularly significant" by the Nuclear Regulatory Commission. The *Wall Street Journal* concludes that the problems with reactors in the Midwest "tell the story of projects crippled by too little regulation, rather than too much."

Put simply, utilities misjudged the technology by initially considering nuclear power as "just another way to boil water." To understand nuclear power's complexity, consider that some 40,000 valves go into a large reactor, ten times more than for a coal- or oil-fired plant of comparable size. The temperatures within the fuel rods soar to 4,800 degrees Fahrenheit, and highly refined zirconium alloys are needed to contain the fission products. Physicist Carl Walske of the Atomic Industrial Forum, the nuclear industry's trade association, says utility executives who were "darn good at building big coal plants," didn't appreciate that nuclear technology demanded "ten times the management intensity."

Some utility analysts are even harsher. "Many of the worst problems to befall the nuclear industry have occurred as a result of its own management failures," concludes the engineering department of the Massachusetts Institute of Technology. A 1984 report by the congressional Office of Technology Assessment also finds the main factors contributing to the cost of nuclear power construction to be the lack of competence and experience of utility managers. In February 1985, *Forbes* ranked the U.S. nuclear program "as the largest managerial disaster in business history, a disaster on a monumental scale."

Many utilities virtually abdicated management oversight to outside engineering and construction firms, such as Bechtel and Stone & Webster, which had experience building complex reactors. But the independent consultants often had no incentive to keep prices low because their "cost-plus" contracts guaranteed higher profits if the project went over budget. In fact, those utilities building the least expensive reactors—such as Duke Power of North Carolina and Commonwealth Edison of Illinois—have tended to employ their own engineering and construction staffs.

Labor union officials also share some of the responsibility for cost overruns. To expand their take-home pay, welders have admitted slashing precision pipes with their torches, forcing inspectors to approve overtime work to refile the weakened tubes. At the Shoreham site on Long Island, the Teamsters trucking union insists its workers unload all trucks, although each union regularly warehouses its own materials. "To mollify all the unions, LILCO added two Teamsters to each two boiler-makers," says one union official. "The boilermakers did the work. The Teamsters watched. All got paid."

Power companies were also shortchanged on reactor reliability. General Electric, Westinghouse and other equipment manufacturers, as well as the Atomic Energy Commission, promised that nuclear plants would operate at 80 percent of capacity and close only for minor maintenance and refueling. But the nation's reactors have been out of service more than twice the expected rate, operating at only 58 percent of their capacity.

Nuclear power's total cost has not yet been calculated. Although U.S. utilities pay the government $1 for every 1,000 kilowatt-hours generated to cover the costs of safely disposing of radioactive wastes, the numerous leaks and cost overruns with initial waste disposal efforts portend much higher expenses. Another unknown cost is for the decommissioning or dismantling of old nuclear reactors. The high level of radioactivity requires that elaborate and expensive safeguards be used to limit human exposure. The radioactive sections of the small Shipping-port reactor, the first commercial plant opened in 1957, must soon be barged down the Ohio and Mississippi rivers, through the Panama Canal, to a burial site in Hanford, Washington. Cost estimates for dismantling a large reactor range from $50 million to more than $1 billion; the cleanup of the disabled Three Mile Island plant will cost well over $1 billion.

Burdened by nuclear construction programs, utilities must raise money the expensive way. In August 1984, Louisiana Power & Light, already paying $12.3 million each month in financing charges for the unlicensed Waterford III plant, issued $50 million of preferred stock at a whopping interest cost of 19.2 percent. Compounded interest expenses accelerate quickly: on a $1 billion loan, for example, the addition of 1 percentage point annually costs $10 million.

Financial damage caused by unnecessary nuclear plants is stagger-ing. Economist and industry critic Charles Komanoff estimates it could reach $95 billion, including $17 billion invested in plants already abandoned, $38 billion in reactors likely to be canceled before completion, and another $40 billion for facilities that will come on-line after sustaining such huge cost overruns that their expensive electricity cannot be sold. Not tabulated are the billions of dollars contributed by U.S. taxpayers through subsidies. For some comparison, the loss on nuclear power plants equals about half the celebrated 1985 federal deficit.

Despite accelerating costs, Commonwealth Edison (Com Ed) remains committed to the "peaceful atom." The giant Chicago utility inaugurated its eighth large unit in 1984 and has four more reactors under construction, making it the nation's paramount nuclear utility. In his plush office overlooking downtown Chicago, Byron Lee, the utility's executive vice-president, declares nuclear power plays a critical role in the region's heritage, beginning in 1942 when Enrico Fermi engineered the world's first controlled fission reaction under the University of Chicago's stadium, just a few miles to the south.

But even Com Ed, which prided itself on building reactors within budget, is being rocked by rough economic waters. Construction cost overruns helped boost the average Chicagoan's electric bill from $16.87 in 1979 to $28.60 in 1983. Com Ed expects another 50 percent jump by 1987; critics predict rate hikes will reach 110 percent. "I don't think we have a pleasant few years ahead," predicts Philip O'Connor, chairman of the Illinois Commerce Commission.

The Nuclear Regulatory Commission (NRC) also shattered Com Ed's reputation for effective management in January 1984 by denying Com Ed's application to operate the Byron nuclear station, citing "no confidence" in the plant's safety. "I don't know of any other company with this many (safety) violations in one year," noted Jerry Klingher of the NRC. The denial stunned Com Ed and the entire nuclear industry. It also provoked the Illinois Commerce Commission to postpone a rate increase, and the company's stock responded by plunging almost 20 percent.

Com Ed must raise $5.25 billion over the next five years to complete its plants now under construction. Asked why the utility continues building, Lee predicts, "Use of heat pumps will continue to grow and—who knows?—we may have electric cars." Asked if Com Ed would consider even more reactors, Lee concludes, "History will show that nuclear power is the most economic source of electricity."

Nuclear critics say the real reason for Lee's continued devotion to building expensive power plants is more ego than economics. One New England executive says, "The feeling in the industry is, if you have a plant under construction, you must get it through. It is a sign of manhood." The concept of not building, he maintains, is viewed as antiestablishment extremism. Other critics say utility executives like expansion because they want their names immortalized on power plants or substations, something not amenable to insulated walls or more efficient refrigerators. But the construction projects, utility critics warn, may become only expensive memorials to bankrupt power companies.

RATE SHOCKS

And the worst is yet to come. More than a third of U.S. households, four million small businesses, and 200,000 industries will soon face soaring electricity prices when their local utilities add new power plants to the grid. A few coal facilities now in the works will hike charges 50 percent. Nuclear plants, with higher construction costs, portend even greater shocks. Unless regulators force stockholders to pay for the overbudget Marble Hill reactors, homeowners throughout Indiana will annually pay $1,010 more for electricity, a 167 percent increase. Rates for industrialists in west central Illinois will rise more than half-a-million dollars when the Clinton nuclear power plant has been completed. And residents of Long Island in New York, already burdened by the nation's highest rates, must annually pay another $624 to finance the overbudget Shoreham reactor.

Several facilities that have escaped public scrutiny guarantee even more surprises. River Bend in Louisiana, acclaimed by the nuclear industry as a low-cost reactor, is well over budget. The Grand Gulf project in Mississippi will substitute 16-cent-per-kilowatt-hour electricity for 5-cent-an-hour power from existing coal plants. New Jersey's Hope Creek reactor has become one of the most expensive power plants, and Nine Mile Point #2 is straining the resources of several New York utilities. In late 1984, utilities continued building 49 reactors, which may cost an additional $75 billion to complete. For those power companies still building plants, rates will rise an average of 41 percent.

Rate shocks will devastate local economies. Individual consumers will be forced to spend more of their income for basic electric needs and less for other goods and services, hurting community businesses. Some industrialists, unable to compete with factories in other regions of the country or overseas, may be forced to close down or relocate. One economist predicts rate shocks caused by the Shoreham reactor will eliminate 35,000 to 49,000 jobs on Long Island, disqualify 37,000 families from the mortgage market, increase foreclosures and home abandonments by as much as 2,000 per year, and push 11,000 households below the poverty line. Similar employment impact studies show job losses of 19,000 in New Hampshire because of rate hikes caused by the Seabrook reactor, of 35,000 jobs in Michigan because of the Fermi reactor, and of 40,000 jobs in Missouri as a result of the Callaway and Wolf Creek units.

Overbudget nuclear projects have become major political issues in these communities. Several states have launched ballot initiatives to temper rate shocks, while many local politicians are organizing to take over faltering private power companies. As the public's concerns about nuclear power shift from safety to economics, the debate has lost its partisan flavor. "We're basically a conservative Republican community," says Frank Jones, the deputy executive of Suffolk County, which is the home of the Shoreham reactor. "We're not a bunch of left-wing pinkos. I've been a Republican committeeman for 20 years. I voted for Nixon twice. I'm voting for Reagan again. Shoreham for us is not a cause. It's a case."

Higher rates are needed to pay today's debts, but they may boomerang on a utility if they prompt consumers to use less energy and buy cheaper power from other producers. A lower demand for the utility's electricity will produce less revenue, forcing the power company to again increase rates to make ends meet. But higher rates, in turn, will only further depress growth, requiring still more rate increases. Theoretically, this "death spiral" will continue until consumers can find no cheaper means to satisfy their needs for warmth, light and mechanical power.

British utility executives take the problem most seriously. "We face a disturbing prospect," admits the chairman of Britain's Central Electricity Generating Board. "A vicious circle of rising electricity prices causes further reductions in demand, which in turn will push up prices still more."

Many American executives, however, reject this theory, maintaining that electricity demand is inelastic, that it does not directly respond to price changes. Arguing that electricity is a necessity of life, they claim higher prices will not encourage consumers to conserve or to use alternatives.

The day of reckoning for at least a dozen utilities is close at hand. Defaults and bankruptcies have become common topics in power company boardrooms and Wall Street investment houses. Yet any bankruptcy would be remarkable considering the industry's economic strength just two decades ago and its protection from competition by public service commissions. State regulators certainly don't want their protectorates to "go under," but they may be unable to withstand the political outcry if rates are raised high enough to save the companies. And conservative executives, who have long touted the advantages of free enterprise, may be forced to accept the consequences of their risks.

(While default refers to the failure to repay loans or bonds, bankruptcy in a Chapter 11 proceeding is a formal process of financial reorganization by which a utility renegotiates its debts to permit continued operation. During the procedure, the company saves cash by not paying dividends to stockholders or interest to unsecured bondholders. A federal bankruptcy judge appoints committees to represent different classes of creditors—preferred stockholders, common stockholders, secured and unsecured bondholders—and to reach agreement about reducing or extending the utility's debts.)

Bailing out a troubled power company will surely spark the nation's bitterest consumer struggle. Ratepayers demand investors bear the burden of management's mistakes, just as they enjoy profits when times are good. Stockholders, on the other hand, want consumers to cover all expenses, arguing that public regulators initially agreed to support the facility's construction. Utility executives quietly hope IRS deductions will transfer most losses onto unsuspecting taxpayers.

Some impacts of bankruptcy have already been felt—even without the dread event actually occurring. During 1984, for instance, LILCO's common stockholders watched their securities fall in value from $16 to a low of $4; many retirees who invested in utility stocks for the promise of secure dividends lost most of their life's savings.

The full consequences of insolvency, however, are not known. Power company executives and bankers paint a bleak picture complete with blackouts and astronomical rate increases. If a bankrupt utility can't afford to maintain reliable service, the scenario goes, manufacturing industries will leave the service area, taking jobs with them and raising rates even further for the customers who remain. Existing managers will be fired, Uncle Sam and local communities will lose tax revenues, and court-appointed bankruptcy officials will sell unnecessary facilities to raise the cash needed to continue supplying electricity. In the long run, utilities say, raising money from wary investors will be like wringing blood from a turnip.

Steven Cooper of the accounting firm of Touche Ross presents the most disturbing scenario, one privately endorsed by many Wall Street analysts. Because power companies are commonly interlinked through transmission pools or construction partnerships, the accountant predicts even relatively healthy firms that are forced to pick up the cost of other utilities' abandoned plants may falter. The result could be a domino effect, with one cash-strapped utility after another falling into insolvency. "Everyone would get hurt," Cooper explains. "It would be terrible."

Consumer-oriented experts, in contrast, maintain that a utility bankruptcy would not conform to the 1930s' image of ruined farm families packing their few goods into a rattling pickup truck while a banker auctions off the homestead. A few analysts even argue that insolvency may be healthy medicine for the utility industry if it leads to new management and innovation. Consumer activists distrust the industry's message of doom, charging that utility executives are seeking to scare ratepayers into accepting higher rates. They remember Wall Street analysts once predicted skyrocketing municipal bond rates if WPPSS defaulted; the bond market, however, has suffered no measurable setbacks, and even defaulting northwestern utilities have been able to raise money for other projects at reasonable rates. If the local impacts of the first utility bankruptcy are similarly tame—in other words, if the lights stay on—regulators in other states may deny rate relief to their troubled power companies, while consumers increase their political willingness to "stick it to investors."

IN TRANSITION

Despite regular reports of rate hikes and nuclear plant cancellations, about half the nation's power companies enjoy good financial health. Differences among utilities have never been so pronounced.

Today's most prosperous utilities abandoned unneeded power plants at an early stage, avoiding high interest loans, regulatory shifts and construction cost overruns. These power companies also benefited from a multi-million-dollar public relations campaign designed to boost rates. Beginning in the early 1980s, the Edison Electric Institute placed full-page ads in major magazines and newspapers profiling economists who argued that utilities should earn better returns on their investments.

The pleas worked. State regulators granted a record $8.3 billion in rate hikes in 1981 and another $7.6 billion in 1982.

Investment banker John Barr of Morgan Stanley claims rate increases and construction cutbacks transformed a few utilities from "cash pigs" to "cash cows." The Government Accounting Office agrees, reporting that "since about mid-1981 [the utility industry's] financial indicators have been improving." The financial outlook will brighten even further for those power companies abandoning construction projects and avoiding new ventures. Instead of rate shocks, customers of these cautious utilities should temporarily face fairly stable electricity prices.

Despite this partially rosy picture, the very ways electricity is generated and priced are being challenged. No longer can utility executives count on low-cost fuels or the promise of the atom. No longer can engineers take advantage of economies of scale to build ever larger and more efficient power plants. No longer can planners accurately predict the future demand for electricity. And no longer are utility monopolies the sole generators of electric power. In fact, an array of technological innovations may be making the central power station obsolete, while entrepreneurs are introducing competition into the electricity market.

With so many subsidies and regulations tempering its supply and demand, electricity is the energy source perhaps most vulnerable to political machinations. Power company planners argue that state regulators approve dangerously low returns on utility investments, while consumers believe rates are too high. Executives criticize commissioners for delaying the construction of new power plants, while environmentalists think too many facilities are being licensed. Entrepreneurs complain that the system retards innovative technologies. Tax experts say federal subsidies encourage unnecessary expansion and waste precious resources. In short, political confrontation surrounds electricity production and delivery, and some officials are beginning to wonder if there is not a more efficient and innovative system for getting the job done.

Utility executives are slowly learning that to survive in the 1980s they must challenge many of the industry's historic assumptions, including its "grow and build" philosophy. A few privately admit that several power companies are temporarily more prosperous than news reports indicate, but more threatened by competitors than executives acknowledge. "The U.S. electric industry," concludes one utility leader, "is in the midst of its greatest historical transition."

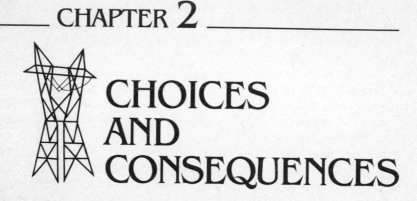

_____ CHAPTER 2 _____

CHOICES
AND
CONSEQUENCES

Defaults and rate shocks were not inevitable. Over the past decade, the choices utility executives made among clear options determined their companies' destinies. Most managers believed high fuel and construction costs were temporary obstacles that a new generation of atomic reactors would eliminate; they chose to build new power plants to meet an expected rise in the demand for electricity. In contrast, a few officials predicted skyrocketing expenses would cause consumers to dramatically cut their reliance on utility power; they opted to eliminate energy waste before adding new capacity.

Guy Nichols of New England Electric System (NEES) and Wilfred Uhl of Long Island Lighting Company (LILCO) understood the options and started from similar positions. In the early-1970s both ran well-respected companies and utilized modern equipment. LILCO and NEES engineers, for example, consistently improved operating efficiencies and had cut inflation-adjusted rates in half over the previous 20 years. The similarly sized utilities regularly offered dividends and enjoyed high stock prices. Both executives relied on petroleum, most of it imported from the Organization of Petroleum Exporting Countries (OPEC), and both were pressured by government officials and their companies' own accountants to switch to other fuels.

In the early 1970s, Nichols and Uhl chose different paths. The NEES chairman decided to switch from oil to coal-fired plants and to begin an energy conservation campaign. LILCO's Uhl elected to construct several nuclear power plants, including one at Shoreham.

LOSING THE NUCLEAR GAMBLE

Wilfred Uhl was a LILCO man, having joined the New York utility in 1949 fresh out of engineering school. Almost 30 years later, the tall, wavy-haired executive had worked his way up the corporate ladder to become president. He loved Long Island, having grown with the area, and wanted to spur its continued expansion by providing abundant and inexpensive electricity. The nuclear bandwagon lured Uhl with its promise of low fuel costs and technological sophistication. The atom seemed to be the wave of the future and Uhl jumped on board.

The story of Shoreham's roller-coaster ride is well-known: Three nuclear plants, to be completed by the late-1970s at a combined cost of $350 million, were supposed to save millions of dollars in oil costs. But by 1984 LILCO had abandoned two reactors, was confronting a $4.1 billion construction bill and teetered near bankruptcy. How was such a financial disaster allowed to develop?

From today's perspective, LILCO's decision to invest in nuclear power plants was irresponsible and dangerous. But Uhl, who had overall responsibility for Shoreham's management throughout the 1970s, claims it appeared reasonable at the time. Reactor construction costs seemed to be tumbling. General Electric had completed its first plant at Shippingport, Pennsylvania, in 1957 at a price of $950 per kilowatt; by 1960, New England's Yankee Rowe cost only $255 per kilowatt. Three years later, Jersey Central's Oyster Bay reactor caused a sensation among utility executives with construction costs totaling only $100 per kilowatt, a third less than coal and oil facilities. What Uhl and other utility executives didn't know was that General Electric had heavily subsidized Oyster Bay's construction through a turnkey contract to spur nuclear development, promising to pick up all expenses above the fixed contract price. By the time LILCO announced plans for the Shoreham reactors in 1965, General Electric had abandoned its generous (and secret) promotional incentives. Uhl, as a result, continued to use financial projections based on Oyster Bay but assumed all responsibility for cost overruns and construction management. He didn't realize the change until Shoreham's cost and LILCO's debts started escalating. "We had no reason to believe that [General Electric's early] plants weren't fairly priced and that the manufacturer wasn't fully recovering his costs," he later lamented.

At the initial stages, however, Uhl was no passive victim of forces beyond his control. The bespectacled LILCO president leaped onto the nuclear bandwagon with full force and enthusiasm, predicting, in 1970, "catastrophic" brownouts within five years if nuclear plants weren't operating. Even in 1981, with no shortages in sight, LILCO's radio and newspaper advertisements boasted that the nuclear plant "will decrease our dependence on OPEC oil and save customers like you hundreds of millions of dollars on your electric bills in years to come." The predictions never materialized.

Today, much responsibility for Shoreham's problems lies with Uhl and other utility managers, says New York's Public Service Commission. "LILCO effectively lost management control of the project immediately following commencement," concludes a commission study. "The management deficiencies . . . represent fundamental and unreasonable flaws in the application of basic principles of management."

Uhl claims the blame is not solely his. "We had traditionally built our own plants, but with nuclear [we were] concerned that we wouldn't know enough about building a nuclear power plant since we never built one on our own," he explains. Therefore, LILCO hired Stone & Webster, a Boston-based engineering firm experienced with the design and construction of nuclear plants, to oversee the project. But confusion and delays still plagued the Shoreham construction site. Some stainless steel valves arrived 21 months behind schedule; pipe supports averaged a 7-month delay, while pipes were 18 months late. Important documents would take ten days to journey from one part of the plant to another.

To save a little money, LILCO tried to cut corners. But luck, Uhl says, was not running his way and the gamble backfired. In April 1974, one of the utility's mechanical engineers warned that buying Transamerica Delaval's untested diesel generator posed a "risk" and that there would be "potential liability in accepting this engine" rather than the proven model from Colt Industries. LILCO, however, opted for a $100,000 savings with Transamerica's lower bid. In August 1983, the inexpensive diesel broke down, and a replacement had to be purchased.

In response to high electricity demand in 1968, Uhl and other LILCO executives took another gamble when they decided to enlarge the plant's capacity. Rather than simply build another small plant of the same design, utility officials chose to expand the planned reactor from 540 megawatts to 820 megawatts. The change added enormous design, engineering and building costs. "With hindsight that decision was unfortunate," Uhl admits. "We would have looked very smart to have gone ahead with the 540. And we would have probably not had the licensing delays."

While not denying his errors, Uhl blames environmentalists for Shoreham's high costs. He views the 1970 public hearings as a protracted "circus" that cost ratepayers millions of extra dollars. Protestors, indeed, tried to make Shoreham a "landmark case." Starting shortly after Earth Day, the hearings attracted widespread attention as more than 100 witnesses testified at 70 sessions lasting over 32 months. Cost estimates for building Shoreham, primarily driven by high interest rates, rose nearly $250 million during this period.

Uhl's wrath also focuses on federal regulators. He claims the Nuclear Regulatory Commission (NRC) has revised almost 300 guidelines since

1970, with each change costing LILCO time and money. A 1980 Government Accounting Office study shows new regulations did raise electricity bills about 8 percent and some changes appear superfluous: Regulators, for example, required LILCO to redesign the breakwater—at a cost of $750,000—to withstand 34-foot waves, twice the size of the highest waves ever recorded on Long Island Sound. Most changes, however, were based on new operating experiences. The 1975 fire at the Browns Ferry reactor in Alabama, for example, led to a requirement for two separate wiring routes for safety cables, an amendment costing LILCO more than $10 million. Harold Denton of the NRC defends his actions, saying, "We want the plants to be safe. If that costs a hell of a lot of money, it's somebody else's problem." The somebody else was Wilfred Uhl.

Regulatory changes, says Uhl, forced LILCO to sign "cost-plus" contracts that provided little incentive for contractors to meet target dates or to hold down costs. Stone & Webster's fee, for example, grew from $16.6 million to an estimated $347 million. Uhl explains his predicament: "When you're in an environment in which the regulations are continuously changing and the engineering is not far enough ahead of construction to give a contractor a set of drawings on which to bid, you don't really have any option but to get to a cost-reimbursement type of contract." Executives at other utilities, however, were better able to limit rising costs. Arkansas Power and Light officials, who built a reactor at the same time but at one-quarter Shoreham's cost, set incentives and penalties to encourage Bechtel, their architect-engineer, to meet the schedule.

LILCO's ratepayers and stockholders have suffered, and the worst may be ahead. According to a panel appointed by New York Governor Mario Cuomo, rates will double in the next five years to pay for Shoreham, whether the plant operates or not. The Public Service Commission staff recommends LILCO executives—and ultimately the stockholders—be charged a $1.55 billion mismanagement penalty. Investors have already seen stock prices fall from a high of $32.00 in 1965 to $3.75 in 1984, almost a 20-fold drop when inflation is taken into account. In 1984, the dividend also disappeared.

Asked in 1981 about the consequences if LILCO canceled its dividend, Uhl responded, "I'd lose my job." The 57-year-old executive's prediction came true three years later. Today, the utility's press office refuses to even discuss Uhl's presidency.

HEARING A DIFFERENT DRUMMER

Guy Nichols enjoys good publicity. The New England Council named the short, frail-looking executive its "New Englander of 1983." A leading Wall Street analyst praised Nichols's NEES as "one of the handful of utilities that has a truly creative and innovative management."

Nichols grew up in the utility business and by his own estimate remains "an old operating man." The crew-cut former chairman still carries a voltmeter when he travels to check an electric system's reliability. U.S. utilities, he boasts, "are the best in the free world."

Nichols gained fame within the industry by recognizing in the mid-1970s that higher fuel and construction costs would depress consumers' demand for electricity. When virtually all utility executives, including NEES economists, predicted electricity consumption would annually expand at least 5 percent, Nichols declared, "It's my honest opinion that growth rates are going to sink." Perhaps living near Walden Pond, where Henry David Thoreau dared to hear a different drummer, encouraged Nichols to buck the crowd. Perhaps he was a shrewd businessman. Maybe he was just lucky. Whatever the reason, Nichols rejected a headlong rush toward the nuclear promise, contracting for only small portions of two nuclear projects. His goal: diversity.

Nichols unveiled his unique strategy, heavily promoted as the "NEES Plan," in October 1979, shortly after Iran cut off its oil and the federal government denied the utility's request to build a power plant in Rhode Island. (NEES manages utilities in parts of Massachusetts, Rhode Island, Connecticut and New Hampshire.) Of the plan's main planks, coal conversion has been Nichols's most spectacular success. Throughout the 1960s and 1970s, NEES had converted most of its power plants from coal to oil in response to government campaigns against air pollution. Showing an uncanny understanding of Washington's vicissitudes, Nichols ensured that the power stations could easily be reconverted to coal use if needed. With oil prices hovering around $35 a barrel in 1979, and with the utility relying on oil for 80 percent of its generating capacity, Nichols decided the times called for another change. By converting six big oil plants to coal, NEES saved $200 million in fuel costs between 1978 and 1983. The utility's oil dependence now lies below 20 percent, far less than most utilities in the Northeast.

Nichols also adopted formal conservation and alternative energy programs to eliminate the need for expensive power plants and to abandon portions of five nuclear reactors. (The utility holds only a 10 percent share of the Millstone and Seabrook reactors, and Nichols has even tried to cancel the second Seabrook unit.) NEES, for example, can shut off the water heaters of 130,000 customers when it wants to shave electricity use during periods of peak demand; participating customers enjoy a slightly lower rate. Solar, hydro and other alternative energy projects will soon supply the utility with 328 megawatts of electricity, enough to power about 164,000 homes. NEES expects to buy one-third of its new capacity from independent power producers using such technologies. A wind turbine spins outside Nichols's office.

When high electricity rates, a recession and NEES's conservation programs dramatically cut sales, Nichols did not panic. "If you're going to have a deliberately no-growth business or a no-growth part of a business," the former NEES chairman explains, "you better for sure have some activity somewhere else." So Nichols established an oil and gas exploration subsidiary that eventually located about 18-million barrels of petroleum reserves off the California coast and in the Gulf of Mexico. And while his colleagues built power plants, Nichols launched a 665-foot-long boat named *Energy Independence* to haul coal to New England from ports in the Chesapeake and Delaware bays.

Nichols may be a maverick, but he is no radical. A Massachusetts Institute of Technology professor describes him as a very conservative, perceptive businessman. "I have great faith in a regulated marketplace for investor-owned utility monopolies," Nichols says, predicting little potential for government-owned or independent power generators.

And he is not a no-growth advocate. In fact, Nichols recently proposed a controversial plan to spur demand in recession-wracked Rhode Island by offering a 20 percent discount on electric rates to businesses that move into the state and to current industrial customers who increase their electricity use. Other utility executives, who have developed similar plans, rejoice at Nichols's supposed return to the pack of growth advocates (although Rhode Island's attorney general believes the plan is illegal because it discriminates against residential customers and small businesses in favor of large industries).

Nichols's tenure with NEES has clearly been a blessing to stockholders. In each of the past six years, he increased earnings and dividends. In early 1984, when many utility stocks floundered, NEES's hit an all-time high. Ratepayers have also benefited. Citing greater use of coal, a relative softening of oil prices and increased operating efficiency, NEES recently cut its average price per kilowatt-hour 6 percent. Within the past five years, NEES's rates dropped from the upper to the lower third among New England utilities.

What does the future hold? "Utility executives," says Nichols, "live with unknowns and must be able to react quickly to inevitable changes." Nichols hopes his Rhode Island discounts and other marketing efforts will revive electricity demand. But even if consumption rises sharply, he plans to avoid constructing 1,000-megawatt, $3 billion plants, which take 12 years to construct, in favor of less-risky, 400-megawatt, coal-fired facilities. "Utilities need to build in smaller increments, closer to the time of need," he preaches.

In early 1984, only weeks after Wilfred Uhl was forced to resign from LILCO, Nichols unexpectedly announced his retirement to form an arbitration service. "It's time to move on," he said as workmen cleared his office to make room for a new NEES executive. The utility's staffers and Wall Street analysts say he will be sorely missed as the company and the entire electricity industry face even more uncertainties in the coming decades.

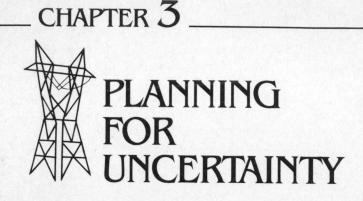

CHAPTER 3

PLANNING FOR UNCERTAINTY

Utility executives gamble billions of dollars based on judgments about tomorrow's energy demand, using data gathered yesterday. Uncertainties have multiplied dramatically since Guy Nichols chose to diversify New England Electric System (NEES) in the late 1970s. Today's questions go beyond nuclear costs to the very way electricity is generated, distributed and regulated: At no time have consumers had more choice over the amount and price of the electricity they use.

In the 1980s, the utility industry's basic assumptions are being questioned. Planners can neither believe that growth in demand for electricity will rise steadily nor continue to monopolize the decisions about when to build power plants. The industry's paramount technologies—nuclear reactors and coal-fired plants—are threatened by cost overruns and acid rain; executives don't know what to build, if anything. And perhaps most important, a utility's monopoly within its service territory is being challenged by independent power producers.

True, America's 200 private and 2,000 public utilities vary in size, use different fuels, face diverse climates and utilize an array of technologies. But all industry executives face common problems: They must select among wildly different demand projections, confront consumers who want more participation in energy planning, face changing regulations, guess the future cost of alternative fuels and meet competition from a new generation of electric entrepreneurs. Perhaps retirement allows Nichols to view these uncertainties as "difficult but fascinating issues." Most executives lack his optimism.

PLANNING FOR WHAT?

Utility executives once predicted electricity demand without difficulty, crowds or controversy. Today's planning procedures, they complain, provoke lengthy technical studies, endless regulatory hearings and heated arguments.

Throughout the 1950s and 1960s, consumption of electricity regularly advanced about 7 percent each year, doubling every decade. Forecasters simply used the proverbial ruler to plot a continued rise, confident that they could safely plan and build new generating facilities. But declining power plant efficiencies and higher fuel costs shattered the momentum in the early 1970s. The rate of electricity growth dropped to 2.9 percent throughout the decade after the 1973 oil embargo.

The North American Electric Reliability Council, a utility-sponsored organization, assumed the cutbacks were temporary and projected a return to the days of steady increases. It was wrong. In 1974, it overestimated what the consumption would be in 1982 by 58 percent. Its 1978 projection overshot the mark 23 percent. In 1982, it came closer to the actual usage for that year, but still missed by 6 percent.

Some utility executives think the trend toward slower demand growth was reversed in 1984 when an improved business climate caused a 4 percent rise in nationwide electricity consumption. Gulf States Utilities

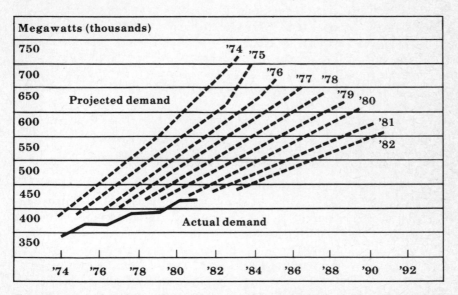

For the past decade, utilities have vastly overestimated the demand for electricity. But higher energy prices have encouraged consumers to use electricity efficiently and to find alternatives to the utility company's power.

in Texas and a few other power companies enjoyed 16 percent increases in sales to industrialists, a result of a recovering economy. The addition is "already causing some managements to reexamine their construction plans for the next five to ten years," explains Ernie Liu, a utility analyst for Goldman, Sachs & Company. But it's too soon to assess the significance of this increase, particularly because electricity sales still lagged far behind the robust rise in U.S. gross national product, something which has occurred in seven of the last eight years. Even with business advancements, utilities possessed more than a third more capacity in 1984 than they needed to meet their peak demand.

Utility planning has never been a totally reactive process. Throughout the 1950s and 1960s, executives spent millions of dollars on subsidies for all-electric homes and advertisements to encourage consumption. Legislators also facilitated electric company expansion with massive tax subsidies. After the 1973 oil embargo, the national priority reversed and a new breed of energy analyst argued that utilities must adopt "load management" techniques that save energy and reduce construction costs. How much control do utility planners have over electricity demand? Guy Nichols admits he doesn't know. "We've never really tested whether advocating conservation or promoting more use actually work," the former NEES chairman admits. Advocates of both approaches, however, plan to continue trying to "shape" electricity consumption.

Uncertainty naturally muddles the future. But for utility planners, today's volatility and the enormous expense of power plants make that uncertainty more risky than ever before. One percentage-point difference in the annual growth rate of electricity demand equals the equivalent of 100 large nuclear power plants by the century's end, costing about $400 billion. Overbuilding would bankrupt the entire industry, while underestimating would cause energy shortages. Clearly, being far wrong either way terrifies power company executives.

Predictions and management goals, however, are far from uniform. Hunter Chiles and Amory Lovins, both intelligent and opinionated energy analysts, stand at the extremes.

J. Hunter Chiles III knows the utility industry from the inside, having directed strategic planning for Westinghouse Electric Corporation, a leading seller of electrical and nuclear equipment to power companies. When the Reagan administration began to scrutinize ways to assist electric companies and promote nuclear power, officials asked the conservative and thoughtful Chiles to coordinate a $3 million study.

Supplying reliable electricity is a patriotic mission for Chiles, who believes "electricity is the locomotive of the American economy." This "magic fuel," he points out, is highly flexible and clean at the point of use, can be controlled to varying temperatures, powers an array of machines and appliances, and can be conveniently delivered over long distances.

He equates electrification with progress, fondly remembering power companies bringing modern conveniences to his parents' home. Suggesting that electric utilities are unique businesses that supply a necessity of life, he even argues that the advance of civilization depends upon additional electricity, regardless of the price. Electricity, he claims, is "the power of choice" for modern consumers and industrialists.

Technologies promising business development, Chiles says, demand electric processes. Computers and robots are only the most advertised examples. Metal workers now use electric-powered lasers to treat materials more efficiently; ten minutes under a laser can harden a metal as well as a 24-hour bath in a 1,000-degree-Fahrenheit nitride liquid. Modern plastic plants employ electrically heated injection-molding machines, while textile and paper firms utilize microwave technology for drying applications.

New electricity uses are not limited to industries. Homeowners seeking to improve indoor air quality are turning to additional fans, precipitators and humidifiers. Farmers are increasing the productivity of their poultry and livestock operations by controlling the animals' environment with electric heaters and coolers. Additional power plants, Chiles claims, are needed to support these new applications, as well as to retire aging plants and reduce America's dependence on imported oil.

Chiles and his colleagues within the Reagan administration expect electricity use to grow approximately 3 percent annually, even if aggressive conservation programs are implemented. Meeting this demand and replacing a few oil-fired burners will require 438 new power plants by the year 2000, or approximately two large stations each month. Such expansion would cost a whopping $1.8 trillion, equal to half a year's gross national product or more than four times the utility industry's existing net assets. The projected expansion would not even stop at the century's end; the "grow and build" advocates anticipate an ever-accelerating demand for more power plants and more capital.

To gain some perspective on this huge amount of money, consider saving $100 every second for new power plants. After a full day, you would have accumulated $8.6 million. By year's end, your fund would total more than $3.2 billion. Still, it would take 570 years to accumulate $1.8 trillion. Looking backward in time, you would have had to begin saving well before Columbus set sail to finance the power plants projected for the next 15 years.

Chiles derives his estimates from an extensive system of macroeconomic computer models, using broad assumptions about economic growth and technological development. Admitting that the gross national product is not in lockstep with electricity usage, he nevertheless predicts business expansion will drive energy demand ever higher.

To encourage adequate investment, Chiles advocates a variety of innovative—though controversial—federal initiatives. He would, for instance, eliminate regulation of new power plants supplying wholesale electricity and establish regional generating companies and planning authorities.

Charles Dougherty, the 1983-84 chairman of the Edison Electric Institute (EEI), endorses Chiles's predictions of an expanding utility industry, in large part because electric companies have a clear and simple incentive to grow. Regulators are supposed to guarantee these monopolies a "fair return" on their investments. The more utilities invest, the more they earn. And the higher the demand for electricity, the more they can invest.

This incentive spurred EEI in 1984 to launch an ongoing marketing campaign that includes sophisticated television, radio and magazine advertisements, as well as brochures for schools, exhibits for shopping malls and a "structured effort to make the nation's news channels more accessible to the industry." The $20 million program is also encouraging individual utilities to rebuild the marketing departments abandoned in the early 1970s when conservation was a more popular public relations theme and practice. Because opinion surveys show less than one-quarter of the American public believes electric rates are "reasonably fair," EEI hopes to "position electricity in terms of the everyday tasks it performs at low costs" and thereby remind the public of "the incomparable service it provides and good value it represents."

Dougherty and his colleagues have not limited their marketing campaign to public relations and advertising. As already mentioned, Guy Nichols of NEES offers special rates to induce Rhode Island industrialists to use more power. Philadelphia Electric, Iowa Public Service and at least a dozen other utilities plan similar promotional fees. According to a delighted executive at Pacific Power & Light, "We're back in the growth business and are stressing the promotion of sales."

Chiles and Dougherty do not dismiss conservation or alternative energy development. Conservation, EEI admits, was "a highly useful and necessary undertaking" that reduced utilities' need to spend money on more power plants. But cutbacks saddled electric companies with lower revenues and excess generating capacity. Conservation, in short, "reduced expenditures, but it also reduced income."

Chiles's report, released in June 1983 and entitled "The Future of Electric Power in America," was severely criticized by the Congressional Research Service and the Electricity Consumers Resource Council (ELCON), an association of large industrial users of power. Arguing that new plants will raise rates and injure American businesses, ELCON officials feel that "no utility capacity shortage exists now or is likely to exist in the foreseeable future." Frustrated by Washington's machinations, Chiles left the Reagan administration in spring 1983 to convert his ideas into concrete projects, taking a position with Bechtel Group, the world's largest power plant construction firm, where he will again try to convince utilities to build new generating stations.

Amory Lovins also wants reliable electricity, but he advocates alternative means to obtain it. The controversial physicist and environmentalist has provoked, irritated and stimulated utility executives for almost a decade. *Newsweek* describes him as one of "the Western world's most influential energy thinkers." Critics see him as an "anti-technologist bent on selling visions of radically different futures for electric power."

Lovins's pocket calculator rests like a gun in a holster on his belt, ever ready to supply rounds of data to shoot holes in an opponent's arguments. His favorite target is Hunter Chiles's belief that more centralized power plants are needed. Lovins calculates that full use of the best electricity-saving methods now on the world market would cost less than the running costs alone for new power stations; put another way, conservation and alternative energy technologies can eliminate the need for new plants *and* retire some existing facilities.

Lovins does not oppose electricity outright; he admits his computer would be worthless without the juice. But electricity, says the physicist, is a premium source of power. Three units of primary fuel—such as natural gas or coal—must be burned to produce one unit of electricity. Wasting such high-grade power on heating a home—when more efficient gas or solar resources are available—is like "killing a fly with a cannon."

The former Oxford don believes Chiles's expansionary plans will bankrupt electric companies and the American economy. Spending $1.8 trillion for new power plants, says Lovins, would "complete the economic destruction of this vital industry by making its product even more uncompetitive and its investments even less able to be amortized from revenues." And if utilities divert more and more money from other enterprises, interest rates will rise, severely damaging U.S. businesses; $1.8 trillion even exceeds the total federal deficit, a huge number that politicians claim is threatening our future.

Better investments—for consumers, for the country *and* for utilities, says Lovins—are efficient appliances and machines. High electricity prices have sparked a revolution of energy conservation technologies. Some of the most effective innovations—computer-controlled energy management systems for "intelligent buildings," high-pressure sodium lights, improved windings and drive trains for electric motors, superinsulation for home construction, fluidized-bed heat treatment of metals and much more—have been introduced only within the past few years. In fact, the average house that is built today is probably twice as thermally efficient as the 1974 standard. (Lovins's own home in Snowmass, Colorado, goes even further, employing adequate insulation, glazing and passive solar features to virtually eliminate the need for heating or cooling with fuel. Body heat, light bulbs and a computer keep the house warm.)

Since 1979, says Lovins, such efficiency improvements have saved 100 times more energy than all new U.S. power plants have produced.

Moreover, renewable energy sources—solar, wind, biomass and falling water—have provided more new power than all the nonrenewables—coal, oil, natural gas and uranium. He predicts these trends will accelerate, forcing utilities to confront surpluses rather than shortages of generating capacity. Conservation and alternative energy technologies will make today's large power plants so uncompetitive, he claims, that utilities, rather than spending $1.8 trillion, will be forced to write off approximately $100-$200 billion by the century's end.

Societal trends also suggest electricity demand will continue to stagnate or decline. A few demographic facts are clear: The baby boom is over and population growth has slowed. Moreover, U.S. business activity has shifted from manufacturing to services; energy-intensive industries are on the decline. Although large numbers of manufacturers are turning to electrically powered machines, robots do not necessarily increase overall consumption; they don't need, for instance, the same heated rooms, air conditioning, ready lights, coffee breaks, cafeteria meals, or flush toilets of the workers they displace.

Government could do a great deal to encourage efficiency, claims Lovins, just as it has historically promoted utility expansion. For instance, in 1975, Congress tried to adjust the market by establishing efficiency targets for appliance manufacturers. By setting an upper limit on a new refrigerator's consumption, such standards would have narrowed the spread of forecasts for future electricity demand, reducing the uncertainty of power planning. (The Reagan administration blocked the program on the grounds that targets interfere with the free market. Lovins counters by saying appliance labels and standards would supply energy at far less cost than the new power plants Ronald Reagan is willing to subsidize.) Other policy options abound. Upgrading building codes would quickly achieve dramatic energy and cost savings in residential and commercial buildings. Energy conservation "banks" providing low-interest loans would enable low-income renters to take advantage of energy reduction technologies.

Lovins believes today's utility executives must choose "between participation and obsolescence; between being obstacles to or vehicles of an historically unique transition to least-cost alternatives." Continuing to build more centralized power plants, he says, will only injure utilities and the nation. The stock and bond markets seem to endorse Lovins's logic by raising the value of conservation-oriented utilities above the industry average. The shrewdest utility executives canceled power plants and promoted conservation so as to stave off the need for future building outlays. Wisconsin Electric, for instance, decided in 1976 to halve its annual increase in demand. It has since saved $1.5 billion in construction costs.

Lovins appeals to traditional American themes as frequently as Chiles does. He puts his faith in "the genius of free enterprise to help us do the cheapest things first," and believes consumers will invest in the least expensive energy options that supply comfort, mobility and work.

Lovins and Chiles vow to continue arguing about preferred technologies and planning procedures. Chiles favors the tested resources of coal, natural gas, oil and uranium; Lovins advocates "soft" technologies employing efficiency and solar energy. Chiles employs econometric analyses that link energy demand to the nation's gross national product; Lovins uses "end-use planning" that calculates the energy required for specific purposes, such as the projected commercial floor space or the number of electric water heaters. Chiles relies on his experience within the industry; Lovins packs his pocket calculator.

Utility executives are caught in the middle. On the one hand, they distrust forecasts of rising power demand, having been financially burned over the past decade. But they also fear the possibility of energy shortages.

The debate about electricity planning is slowly gravitating from congressional hearing rooms into the marketplace. At stake are trillions of investment dollars in electrical equipment and appliances.

PLANNING BY WHOM?

The vast differences between Chiles's and Lovins's predictions— and the consequences of their estimates—have stirred diverse interest groups to demand a role in energy planning. Just as Georges Clemenceau declared that "war is much too serious a matter to be entrusted to the military," so utility critics say electricity forecasts are too important to be left to power companies alone. Wall Street analysts want assurance that their investments remain sound. Environmentalists seek clean air and water. Large electricity users demand low rates, while individual consumers want enough affordable energy to meet their basic needs. Energy planning, in short, has become a political battle.

Utility executives prefer the traditional system in which state commissioners rubber-stamp strategies developed by power companies. Multi-state utilities particularly favor this method because they can play one commission off against another to maintain their control of electricity planning. But a growing chorus is demanding change, heightening uncertainties within the electricity industry.

Consumer advocate Ralph Nader wants to help ratepayers effectively compete with power company lawyers in hearings before state commissions. Although most states fund consumer councils or public advocates, Nader prefers citizen utility boards (CUBs), which would recruit dues-paying members by including literature in the utility's monthly bill. The Wisconsin CUB, with 100,000 members and a $700,000 budget, hires organizers and researchers to challenge rate increase requests. Similar institutions exist in Illinois, California and Oregon, where voters in November 1984 approved a CUB despite a $1 million effort by utilities to defeat the initiative.

Many regulators also want an alternative, but they want one that will not lead to more lawsuits or more cantankerous hearings. Admitting they lack the resources to adequately monitor huge utilities' selling of bulk power across state boundaries, some commissioners favor regional planning. They feel that the states have become obsolete overseers of electric utilities because most U.S. power feeds into a dozen tightly coordinated multi-state pools that follow a "one-utility" planning concept. "Given the way the U.S. power pools are actually organized," one critic declares, "state boundaries make about as much sense as the African national borders drawn by European colonial powers."

A growing number of financiers and environmentalists also prefer a regional approach to electricity planning, arguing that efficiency would be enhanced if several states jointly assess the potential for conservation, alternative technologies and central power stations. Solomon Brothers, a leading investment banking firm, predicts that over the next ten years regional power planning will become more prevalent as utilities and independent power producers seek to enhance their efficiency and profits by exchanging electric power.

Thus far the only significant regional planning effort has been conducted in the Pacific Northwest, an experiment that challenged the utility industry's decision-making process and its grow-and-build philosophy. After years of legislative wrangling between industrialists and environmentalists, President Jimmy Carter signed the Northwest Power Planning and Conservation Act on December 5, 1980, ordering a Regional Council to devise a 20-year conservation and electric power plan for the area's 120 utilities. With utility executives in the Northwest stirring political passions by predicting electricity shortages and rationing by 1983, the governors of Washington, Oregon, Idaho and Montana appointed bright, able and objective planners with no apparent ideological prejudices.

Advocates on both sides of the issue mobilized quickly. Industrialists and utilities formed the Pacific Northwest Utilities Conference Committee to promote the construction of new power plants, arguing that economic development for the region required more electricity consumption and that coal and nuclear facilities offered the "least cost" options. The committee became an organizational giant, with 45 task groups addressing every conceivable issue, hundreds of staff and consultants, and a multi-million-dollar budget.

In February 1981, leaders of 38 citizen, labor and environmental groups agreed to oppose power plant expansion, to form the Northwest Conservation Act Coalition and to hire Mark Reis, a former congressional aide, as executive director. While Ralph Cavanaugh of the Natural

Resources Defense Council (NRDC) in San Francisco helped write a model plan that would "create jobs and conserve the region's financial resources," Reis organized low-budget conferences throughout the Northwest and encouraged his coalition members to testify before the Regional Council's public hearings in what became the nation's most open energy planning process.

The strong political coalition of industrialists and utilities appeared to be winning ... until May 1981 when the manager of the Washington Public Power Supply System (WPPSS) called for a moratorium on construction of nuclear Units 4 and 5, citing skyrocketing costs. The following month, WPPSS announced retail electricity rates would jump another 37 percent, and the utility coalition helplessly watched its arguments crumble. Nuclear power could no longer be considered a "least cost" energy option. The region's electricity was no longer inexpensive; from 1979 to 1983, industrial rates rose 750 percent and homeowners' electric bills doubled or tripled. Higher rates bludgeoned the region's lumber and aluminum companies and encouraged individual consumers to cut their usage, causing electric surpluses rather than shortages.

Reis and Cavanaugh rode the WPPSS crisis to victory. The thousands of residents and small-business owners demanding that "something be done" about massive rate increases made their organizing easy. A Washington county commissioner called the protests "the biggest consumer revolution this country has ever seen." Describing overcapacity as the primary cause of skyrocketing rates and conservation as the least-cost alternative to new power plants, the environmentalists convinced the Regional Council in April 1983 to support enough efficiency programs, small hydropower dams and wood-based cogenerators to defer indefinitely the need for any new coal or nuclear power stations throughout the Northwest, a far cry from the utilities' prediction of 50 new reactors made only a decade before.

After the Regional Council vote, many of the defeated development advocates retreated from the spotlight. But the controversy continues. Utilities and industrialists have turned again to Charles Luce, the Bonneville Power administrator who first promoted the ill-fated WPPSS plants in the late 1960s, to salvage the nuclear reactors. Choosing to ignore conservation measures until the region's utilities are bailed out, Luce says consumers should pay off WPPSS's bondholders and creditors, the federal government should complete two nuclear units and a high-voltage transmission line to California, and Congress should pass legislation "holding harmless" the Northwest utilities and their executives for claims arising from the $2.25 billion default. Cavanaugh, almost hidden behind piles of reports in his cramped NRDC office, complains that "Luce has learned nothing from his past mistakes and still yearns to build large power plants."

Cavanaugh and Luce will continue to disagree about the merits of conservation and nuclear power. But more important, the two stand on different sides of a growing debate about who should take responsibility for electricity planning. Cavanaugh believes stockholders and bondholders should accept the risks of their investments; Luce says ratepayers should pay whatever charges a regulated monopoly incurs. Cavanaugh feels energy planning is too important to be isolated within utility boardrooms; Luce says it's too serious to be politicized in public hearings. For the moment, Cavanaugh is winning the argument, and the autonomy of individual utilities appears to be waning.

WHO WILL STOP THE RAIN?

Those utility executives not afflicted by nuclear problems often have acid rain to worry about. Old coal-burning plants are spewing what American politicians claim is "the burning environmental conflict of the 1980s." Canada's ambassador to the United States calls acid rain "the most difficult and important issue" dividing the two countries. Power company officials fear its cleanup will demand huge expenditures and dramatically raise the cost of burning coal.

Over the past 25 years, the acidity of rainfall has increased 50-fold throughout New England. Today's showers, sometimes with the acidity of battery acid or lemon juice, are destroying lakes and forests. Perhaps 200 lakes in upstate New York and another 140 in Canada are "dead," with all fish, algae and frogs having been killed by acidic precipitation. Fifty-thousand more reservoirs are threatened and at least six species of coniferous trees in the East are disappearing. According to one Canadian official, "Acid rain is literally a rain of death."

Although the U.S. problem is worst in the Northeast, vinegarlike precipitation falls in Minnesota, northern Wisconsin, Michigan, San Francisco, Los Angeles and the Rocky Mountains. Some scientists believe forests in the Midwest and southern Appalachian Mountains are also affected. Acid rain honors no international boundaries, destroying Germany's Black Forest and eating away the Acropolis in Athens and the Parliament Building in Ottawa.

How much does acid rain cost? It's difficult to calculate. A presidential panel in 1979 predicted enormous health and insurance losses resulting from "an increase in the number of asthma attacks in susceptible individuals and ... exacerbation of acute and chronic respiratory disorders." A 1984 report by Standard & Poor's warns that acid rain presents a clear danger to the $49 billion forest products industry and cautioned that "if acid rain kills an appreciable number of trees on the millions of acres owned by the forest products companies, the companies' stock prices will die faster than the trees." The Minnesota Pollution Control Agency believes that state's "tourism and fishing economies could suffer an annual loss of $78 million." The damage caused by acid rain in the eastern United States annually tops $5 billion, concluded the

National Academy of Sciences, which recommended a "prompt tightening of restrictions on atmospheric emissions."

The costs of curtailing pollution are not cheap, either. Existing scrubber technology can remove up to 90 percent of the sulfur emissions spewed from a coal-burning plant's smokestacks. The expensive machines essentially scrub the combustion gases with a chemical solution to produce a new solid substance called "sludge," a dangerous cakelike compound that must be carefully buried in landfills. The 1977 amendments to the Clean Air Act exempted power plants completed before 1979 from scrubber requirements; environmentalists want the exemptions eliminated, but utility executives oppose adding any new equipment to old plants. An Edison Electric Institute survey of 24 utilities calculates that stringent pollution controls would cost $15 billion to install and $4 billion each year to operate; environmentalists, accusing the industry of exaggeration, believe those figures should be cut 75 percent.

Whose responsibility is it to foot the bill? The question generates strident political debate, pitting environmentalists like lawyer Dick Ayers against utility executives like the Southern Company's Alvin Vogtle. Ayers, coordinator of the National Clean Air Coalition, blames the problem on coal-fired power plants and industries, primarily in the Ohio River Valley, which spew sulfur, nitrogen oxides and other pollutants. The gases, transformed in the atmosphere into sulfuric and nitric acids, are carried by the prevailing winds hundreds or thousands of miles before falling to earth as acid rain, snow, fog or smog. Ayers estimates 200 coal plants, built before pollution regulations were approved, discharge some 28-million tons of sulfur-dioxide emissions across America each year. He and his colleagues have been lobbying for legislation that would order a cutback of 12-million tons by 1990.

Clean air has been a long-term campaign for Ayers. Shortly after the Clean Air Act of 1970 ordered government officials to measure air pollution at ground level near power plants, electric companies built 172 smokestacks over 60 stories tall to send their pollutants downwind and away from regulators. In 1972, Ayers won a lawsuit blocking such tall stacks, but the Environmental Protection Agency (EPA) never wrote effective regulations. Pressured by the coal and utility industries in 1980, President Reagan relaxed the already loose standards. In 1983, Ayers won another lawsuit, but 80 utilities appealed to the Supreme Court for a new ruling. In November 1984, the EPA released new regulations that would curtail only 7 percent of the nation's sulfur-dioxide emissions. Ayers approaches the delays philosophically: "You must come to terms as a person with the need for slogging it out over the years."

Alvin Vogtle, Jr., is no stranger to battle, either. In fact, the character played by Steve McQueen in the 1963 film, *The Great Escape,* is loosely based on Vogtle's exploits at Stalig Luft II during the Second World War. Although now retired as chairman of the Atlanta-based

Southern Company, the tough and opinionated Vogtle is determined to block new environmental regulations for electric companies.

The problem is lake acidification, Vogtle maintains, not acid rain. New England lakes were known to be acidic long before industrial development in the Ohio Valley, and Vogtle reasons today's acidity is caused by the region's natural soils rather than precipitation. He wants more research, not new legislation. Additional pollution-control equipment, he argues, "could drive electric rates to levels that may be unacceptable to our customers" and could restrict power companies from burning coal, the abundant resource utility executives want to substitute for expensive nuclear power.

Vogtle favors lake-liming programs to mitigate damage in certain "environmental hot spots." Adding lime would reduce a lake's acidity and be much less expensive for the utility than adding pollution-control equipment. According to one estimate, treating 468 of the Adirondacks' most acidic lakes would cost only $4 million a year, significantly less than the $15 billion estimate for placing scrubbers on power plants. Some utility executives even favor breeding varieties of trout and other fish that are more tolerant of acidity. Ayers scoffs at these "Band-Aid approaches" that he claims do not cure the basic pollution problem.

Acid rain also divides the nation's governors. Most agree sulfur-dioxide emissions must be reduced, but they argue about how to pay for the reductions. Northeastern and western officials tend to favor a national trust fund, underwritten by taxes on utilities, to finance either the installation of scrubbers or the use of low-sulfur coal. "Polluters should pay for what they do," declares Senator Patrick Moynihan of New York. But midwestern officials, particularly Governor James Thompson of Illinois, feel the federal government or all taxpayers should finance the cleanup rather than tax utilities.

National politicians feud as well. President Reagan has long sided with utility and coal companies, saying pollution-control measures need to be studied rather than implemented. While campaigning in 1980, he promised to "see to it that the Environmental Protection Agency has leaders who know and care about the coal industry." Democrats severely criticize Reagan's environmental record, particularly his failure to confront the acid rain problem. "If the Russians seeded our clouds with sulfur dioxide," declared the Reverend Jesse Jackson, "the Reagan administration would consider it an act of chemical warfare that requires expensive and elaborate counter-initiatives." Jackson charges Reagan with favoring utilities' financial returns over the public's health. Perhaps feeling the heat, the President's 1984 State of the Union Message focused more attention on acid rain than on the war in Lebanon. But the attention did not satisfy Canadian officials who castigated the Reagan administration for limiting spending on acid rain research to $55.5 million, less than 7 percent of a coal plant's cost.

Will anything be done to stop acid rain? Utility executives promise a bitter lobbying effort, privately admitting that the costs of litigation and advocacy are less than the expense of new pollution-control equipment. But a growing coalition of doctors, fishermen, foresters and tourists are pointing to man-made pollution as the chief culprit and demanding action. If they convince the federal government to finance pollution-control equipment, taxes will rise. If utilities are charged, electric rates will increase. Either way, utilities' coal-fired plants become more expensive to operate.

Burning fossil fuels also threatens to change the earth's climate by adding carbon dioxide to the atmosphere, creating an invisible cloud that allows sunlight to pass through to the earth but retards the cooling release of heat into space, causing surface temperatures to rise in what scientists call the "greenhouse effect."

The Institute of Space Studies of the National Aeronautics and Space Administration (NASA) recently detected an overall warming trend in the earth's atmosphere extending back to the year 1880, approximately when oil and coal burning started becoming widespread. A continuing trend, according to NASA, would melt and dislodge the ice cover of West Antarctica, eventually causing the sea level to rise 15 to 20 feet, which would flood "25 percent of Louisiana and Florida, 10 percent of New Jersey and many other lowlands throughout the world" within a century or less. Warming climates would also disrupt prime agricultural lands, perhaps dramatically decreasing the availability—and increasing the price—of food. According to the President's Council on Environmental Quality (CEQ), "farming regions might warm up, dry out, and become less productive; dust bowls could be created. These consequences could render human settlement patterns and capital infrastructures obsolete."

Carbon dioxide accumulates and can linger in the atmosphere for hundreds or perhaps thousands of years. "Once the effects of increased CO_2 concentrations are visible enough to arouse concern throughout the world," says the CEQ, "they may be virtually irreversible for centuries."

The continued spewing of pollutants from electric power plants promises to severely burden the economy and human health, causing a growing political coalition to call for new environmental regulations. Electric companies, already troubled by high nuclear construction costs, may soon face expensive requirements to clean up their old coal-burning plants. "What are utilities to do?" pleads one power company executive. "The viability of the resources we once relied upon are now uncertain."

WHAT PRICE FOR FUELS?

On top of unknown nuclear and coal costs, utility executives must confront a set of monopolies that increasingly control their fuel supplies.

Although several electric companies recently acquired their own mines and wells, most rely on coal, petroleum and uranium companies and the transportation firms that deliver these fuels.

Throughout the 1970s, the major oil companies assumed substantial ownership of the nation's energy resources. By the decade's end, they held title to more than 70 percent of all U.S. natural gas reserves, half of the domestic oil resources, half of the world's refining capacity, a fourth of our coal reserves, and half of our uranium resources. Was it enough? Not quite. Arco, Amoco, Mobil and Sohio also gained control of almost 80 percent of the U.S. solar photovoltaics industry.

Oil company diversification frightens both private and public electric companies since affordable fuels are their lifeblood. When it comes to purchasing fuels, utility monopolists prefer competition. They understand—at least when it relates to their supplies—that competition provides lower prices and better service.

The Tennessee Valley Authority and the Rural Electrification Administration advocate horizontal divestiture, forcing Big Oil to abandon all nonpetroleum ventures. And the former president of the Edison Electric Institute expresses "fears and concern about multiple fuels energy companies" because of the "apparent ability for them to withhold one fuel from the marketplace to the enhancement of the price of another fuel." Without divestiture and interfuel competition, electric power companies worry they will become increasingly dependent on Big Oil.

The world's biggest fuel monopoly, of course, remains the Organization of Petroleum Exporting Countries (OPEC). The 1973 embargo caused substantial price increases for utilities, forcing many—most notably the New England Electric System—to dramatically reduce their reliance on petroleum. Although oil prices have stabilized and decreased in the 1980s, one thoughtful executive, reflecting on OPEC's odyssey, says, "The clear and scary lesson for me is that I have no control over petroleum prices."

OPEC's story is well-known, but not so well publicized is the tale of "UPEC," the Uranium Producers Export Cartel. In 1972, several nuclear fuel producers met secretly in Johannesburg, South Africa, to "discuss ways and means of assuring an adequate price of uranium." UPEC held subsequent meetings in Paris, Toronto and Chicago. The cartel's control of uranium prices is difficult to assess, but industry executives suspect UPEC has manipulated the market to its benefit.

Utilities also fret about fuel transportation costs. Railroad companies, which control 85 percent of the coal-shipping market, have dramatically raised their tariffs to utilities since 1980. The Interstate Commerce Commission, despite the power companies' objections, allows railroads to increase coal-hauling rates 15 percent above inflation and to charge captive shippers like power companies more in order to lower rates where there is competition. Coal transportation now accounts for about half the total cost of coal delivered to utilities.

The price of hydropower has also become a political hot potato. In 1984, Congress had to reconsider its contract to sell electricity from the giant Hoover Dam, located at the Arizona-Nevada line near Boulder City. Because Hoover Dam was the first of several 50-year contracts from the Depression era to be renewed, the debate promised to set a precedent for the price of electricity generated at federal dams throughout the country.

An odd coalition of Environmental Defense Fund lawyers and Grace Commission economists wants the federal government to stop subsidizing electricity and to sell hydropower at whatever price the market will bear. Hoover Dam, located on the Colorado River, distributes power at three-tenths of a cent per kilowatt-hour, 18 times less than the market value. Continuing low-priced sales, argue environmentalists, will cost the federal government $3.85 billion by 1997, while raising the price to reflect real market rates would reduce the federal deficit, be fair to all taxpayers who underwrote the project, and curtail energy waste.

Politicians tend to follow their regional self-interest rather than their philosophical convictions on this issue. Western conservatives, who usually oppose government subsidies, enjoy the water-power benefits and want them continued. Frost Belt and northern Californian liberals, who have traditionally supported public power initiatives, do not benefit from cheap power and want the subsidies stopped. "Fifty years of bargain-basement benefits would seem long enough for the exclusive Hoover club," declares Congresswoman Barbara Boxer, the San Francisco Democrat who led the congressional fight, which became known as the "Boxer Rebellion." Congressman Donald Albosta, a Michigan Democrat, complains cheap southwestern rates give some midwestern industries "the incentive to move to Arizona and California."

Utility companies, as expected, view raising rates to market prices as a revolutionary act, claiming "the stakes are enormous." Increasing the prices charged to 700 municipal utilities and 600 rural cooperatives buying electricity from federal agencies, predicts one official, "would have a devastating effect on most of these utilities, many of which are small and do not have access to other sources of reasonably priced wholesale power." Utility executives favor sales based on the actual cost of producing power, rather than what they call "ill-defined market concepts."

In response to aggressive lobbying by power companies during August 1984, Congress rejected a move to increase prices, though by a closer margin than most expected. Despite their setback, environmentalists and some lawmakers resolve to continue their efforts to let the competitive marketplace—rather than tradition—set electricity rates. Utilities remain worried about the future cost of their fuels.

WHO GENERATES POWER?

For most of this century, electric companies have enjoyed a monopoly, accepting public regulation in exchange for freedom from competitors in their service areas. Guaranteed a return on their investments, these monopolies systematically convinced individuals and industrialists to purchase the utility's power rather than produce their own; self-generated electricity fell from 60 percent of all U.S. capacity in 1900 to only 4.2 percent in 1973.

The evolution initially made economic sense because utilities' new and larger power plants consistently generated lower-cost power. Consumers naturally preferred that the utility handle the hassles of electricity production, as long as the supply of power seemed reliable and cheap.

But by the mid-1970s, the electricity industry appeared ripe for competition. High electricity prices and innovative technologies offered enormous opportunities for independents to profitably supply electric power. Interested parties ranged from large lumber companies wanting to burn wood wastes in their own generators to individuals wanting to tap the wind and other alternative resources. Both private and public utilities, as might be expected, launched a series of rear-guard actions to block their challengers.

Ted Finch, for example, had to battle Consolidated Edison (Con Ed) of New York to install a three-blade windmill atop a Lower East Side Manhattan tenement. The giant utility refused to purchase power from the 2-kilowatt machine, saying "surges" might damage its 10-million-kilowatt system. Finch called the windmill harmless and argued that Con Ed only wanted to maintain its total monopoly over electricity generation. On May 5, 1977, Finch declared a "moral victory" when the New York Public Service Commission ordered Con Ed to buy electricity supplied by the residents' small windmill at the same rate the utility pays to generate power. Although Finch and his fellow residents saved only 46 cents a year, they had fought Con Ed and won: 519 E. 11th Street boasted one of the first electric meters to spin backward.

Finch possessed more determination and stamina than most consumers; few people want to challenge their local utility alone. If alternative energy technologies beyond such an isolated example were to be developed, politicians and energy analysts realized the barriers constructed by utilities would have to be legally eliminated. The battle for independent power generation temporarily shifted from the tenements of New York to the corridors of Capitol Hill.

Within 100 days of his inauguration, President Jimmy Carter declared the country was "running out of gas and oil" and that "we will live in fear of embargoes" that will threaten "an economic, social and political crisis." In perhaps his most memorable phrase, the new President said the campaign to solve the energy crisis must amount to "the moral equivalent of war."

Carter's first volley—the National Energy Act of 1977—sparked immense controversy between energy producers and consumers. The five-part bill moved slowly through Congress, in part because the Carter administration failed to give clear signals to its Capitol Hill commanders. The White House, for instance, initially declared energy conservation to be the legislation's "cornerstone"; but officials later spoke of raising the price of natural gas through deregulation as the plan's "centerpiece." In the early stages, Carter called nuclear power the energy source of "last resort," but as political deals were cut, Energy Secretary James Schlesinger proclaimed that nuclear power was "enshrined in the President's program."

Throughout the energy debates, energy news (most of it bad) bombarded Americans. Electricity rates rose 16 percent during Carter's first year as President. Oil imports soared to 47 percent of U.S. petroleum use, annually draining $45 billion from the nation's economy. Threats of future OPEC embargoes or price hikes demanded that utilities be weaned from oil and natural gas. Elected officials felt they had to do something.

Some of the news, however, was upbeat. On May 3, 1978, 15-million Americans, and thousands more in 31 other countries, participated in Sun Day rallies, conferences, teach-ins and demonstrations. Congressmen Richard Ottinger of New York and Jim Jeffords of Vermont led a predawn trek up Maine's Cadillac Mountain to be the first Americans to greet the day's sun. Moments later, crowds clustered outside the United Nations to hear Lola and Robert Redford and Ambassador Andrew Young extol the promise of renewable energy development. At a more civilized hour, a group of Wall Street investors attended a briefing on solar economics.

As the sun passed over the nation, it illuminated an array of bizarre and serious events. A school in New Jersey held funeral services for fossil fuels. The Washington Monument formed part of a giant sundial towering over the crowds attending a day-long outdoor concert/solar fair. Miami residents strung a "solar clothes dryer" (commonly known as a clothesline) five miles through the city as a tribute to Sun Day, while the Salvation Army "recycled" the clothes hung there. And throughout California, schools and museums organized science fairs and solar home tours.

The staid *New York Times* heralded Sun Day as nothing less than "the dawn of the Solar Age." A Harris Survey conducted in late May showed that 94 percent of Americans favored aggressive solar energy development, an outpouring of support that spurred Congress to quickly pass solar tax credits and double the renewable energy research budget.

Not everyone, of course, welcomed the Sun Day enthusiasm. Pacific

Gas & Electric spent $900,000 on advertisements to convince Californians that "until solar electricity is ready, we must build other kinds of power plants." Mobil Oil mused in its regular editorial in major newspapers that "a solar-powered economy is a lovely idea and a worthy goal, but still a long, long way off."

In this atmosphere of heightened energy awareness, Congress debated how to substitute alternative energy technologies for oil. According to the Carter administration's studies, cogenerators, small-scale hydro dams, municipal solid-waste systems and wind-energy conversion machines could save the equivalent of 200,000 barrels of oil per day by 1995. Lawmakers, fearing utilities would not aggressively promote alternative energy development, wanted to free independent power producers from burdensome state regulation, to establish a market for power generated by entrepreneurs, and to block utilities from discriminating against these new competitors.

For power companies, the most critical portion of President Carter's legislative package was the Public Utility Regulatory Policies Act (PURPA). As most bills do, PURPA had several sections or titles, although the first and second were the most important and controversial. The first called for rate structure reform, while Title II mandated incentives for cogeneration and small power production.

On one side of the debate, electric company officials worried that Washington might dictate (rather than suggest) rate reforms to encourage energy conservation. They did not want pressure to enact marginal-cost-pricing or time-of-day rates that might complicate their bookkeeping or lower their profits. And they certainly did not want to be bothered by independent competitors. As a congressional vote neared, 40 top utility executives flew to Washington and, according to one trade journal, "virtually set up camp on Capitol Hill."

On the other side of the controversy, Sun Day organizers (most of them environmentalists) formed the Solar Lobby and quickly encountered powerful political allies. Lumber companies and conservationists may have battled over expansion of federal lands or regulations against clear-cutting trees, but both wanted to promote cogeneration—environmentalists felt it would save energy and reduce pollution; timber executives believed that it could produce profits. Thus, an odd coalition formed, including representatives of Weyerhaeuser, Du Pont, several oil companies, International Paper, Solar Lobby and other environmental groups. Michigan Congressman John Dingell and New York Congressman Richard Ottinger, determined foes of monopolies, led the coalition's fight.

Most utility lobbyists concentrated on PURPA's rate reform sections rather than on Title II, never believing small power producers would flourish or compete with their markets. One congressional staff member remembers that the independent power provisions were "the most underlobbied, unsung pieces of the National Energy Act." But those provisions, he continues, are having more impact on U.S. energy policy than almost any other legislation.

Days before the final vote on PURPA, Edison Electric Institute obtained a copy of the "secret" Conference Committee's report, which included more stringent rate reform provisions than utilities wanted. Executives quickly organized a press conference to accuse Democratic staff members of a "travesty of draftsmanship" that distorted the intention of senators and congressmen. Republicans joined in to criticize the proposal for eroding states' rights and for transforming certain sections into a "happy hunting ground of litigation." Department of Energy officials scoffed at the complaints, saying "the utilities are seeing bears in the woods." Charges and countercharges flew for almost a week. Only the White House's extreme pressure for a compromise broke the deadlock. When the dust settled, PURPA's only true requirement was that utilities must cooperate with independent power producers; rate reform and conservation provisions were considered only suggestions.

The results satisfied few legislators. Republican Senator Dewey Bartlett, considered a friend of utility companies, said: "This bill will produce no energy whatsoever, though it may produce a great many lawyers and 'energy experts.'" Democratic Senator Howard Metzenbaum, considered a consumer advocate, lamented that "because the lobbyists for the utilities did their work well and because the administration decided not to support mandatory conservation measures, we wound up with legislation that is a mere shadow of what it could have been."

Independent power producers, however, were pleased. Industries and individuals could now profitably invest in cogeneration systems, windmills, hydroelectric facilities and other small power technologies; they could interconnect with the utility grid and buy back-up power at a reasonable cost; they could sell electricity to their utilities on favorable terms; and they could avoid cumbersome state regulation.

Before PURPA, the federal government's support of renewable energy sources was limited to research. The new law established a marketplace mechanism to promote alternative technologies. Specifically, PURPA requires that the rates for transactions between independent producers and utilities "shall be just and reasonable and in the public interest, and shall not discriminate against the qualifying cogenerators or qualifying small power producers." The law forces a utility to buy power at the price of its "avoided costs"—that is, what the electric company would have spent to produce the same amount of power. For example, if an entrepreneur installs windmills that provide energy the utility would otherwise have had to build a new power plant to obtain, the utility must pay the independent producer the amount (per kilowatt-hour) that it would have had to pay to capitalize, finance, fuel and operate that plant. Entrepreneurs generating power for less than a utility's avoided costs can turn a profit.

President Carter's signature in October 1978, of course, did not end utilities' opposition to PURPA. But it did eliminate their exclusive right to sell power. Title II of PURPA, an overlooked but revolutionary provision, opened the door to competition in the electricity industry. Entrepreneurs, including large businesses and individual consumers, quickly took advantage of the opportunity, placing more orders in the early 1980s for cogenerators, wind-energy machines and small hydro dams than did utilities for centralized power plants, be they fueled by atomic power, coal or petroleum. Within only a few years, independent power production has become a multi-billion-dollar industry.

CHAPTER 4

THE INVENTORS

To appreciate today's electric entrepreneurs, consider the initial struggles for control of the electricity market. In the late 19th century, scores of inventors competed to develop practical equipment, while engineers battled with the dominant gas companies for markets and investors sought new technologies promising huge profits. It was a time of innovation, falling energy prices and economic growth.

The story actually begins before the rise of electricity, when post–Civil War American homes substituted natural gas and kerosene for candles and whale oil as lighting fuels. Although new lamp designs improved illumination, the light still flickered, shed a dull yellow glow, cast mysterious shadows and caused numerous fires. Homeowners, ever bothered by maintenance, had to trim wicks, replenish fuel and wash fragile glass chimneys. Most chose to keep their residences dark after sunset.

Just as contemporary fuels helped dictate a family's routine, so did they limit a city's design. Teams of horses pulled the only form of public transportation, rendering impossible a commute from the countryside. Steam-powered elevators limited building heights to only a few stories. Moreover, factories and their workers were forced to locate near waterways where power wheels could be constructed. Inventors and investors knew fortunes were to be made with a lighting and power system that eliminated these problems.

Most Americans equate electricity with Thomas Edison, but the distinction of discovering this versatile energy source belongs to Thales. Six hundred years before the birth of Christ, the Greek philosopher and mathematician noticed that rubbing a piece of amber with cloth or fur would first attract, then repel, small objects brought near it. The experiment was repeated many times before Humphrey Davy developed a practical application for this mysterious form of energy. In the 19th century's first decade, the English chemist demonstrated the first electric-arc lamp, consisting of two carbon rods separated by a thin gap. When Davy applied an electric current to one of the electrodes, a glowing arc leaped across the gap and provided light. Such lamps were first used in 1844 for a Paris Opera production. Twenty years later, Michael Faraday, Davy's former assistant, discovered essentially all the laws affecting electromagnetic induction and built a working model of an electric dynamo or generator.

Early electric equipment was crude and impractical for commercial application. But by the late 1870s, many inventors were making marked improvements. Already a respected inventor of telegraphy, Charles Brush designed 12 outdoor arc lamps to brighten Cleveland's downtown. The outdoor lights were quickly adopted for other cities' streets although they could not capture the residential market, in part because the dangerously high electric currents had to be kept well away from people, and because the lamp's 4,000 candlepower created a glare too bright for any home. Moreover, Brush wired his systems in series, so that if one lamp failed the entire group on that circuit would go out. Needed were a 16-candlepower lamp and a parallel wiring system that would allow homeowners to independently operate their soft lights without affecting their neighbors'.

Enter Thomas Alva Edison. On the night of October 19, 1879, after years of experiments, he and Francis Jehl created the first long-lasting incandescent bulb, composed of a strong, carbonized filament set within an airless globe. When announced two months later, the New York *Herald* devoted its entire front page to the achievement.

THE WIZARD OF MENLO PARK

Proclaimed the "Napoleon of Science," the "Wizard of Menlo Park," and the "Purveyor of Light," Thomas Edison became an American hero. Fifty-thousand admirers stood for hours on San Francisco's foggy streets one evening to catch a glimpse of the great inventor. Even 50 years after his death, two-million people annually tour the Edison laboratory, carefully moved from Menlo Park, New Jersey, to Greenfield Village, Michigan, by the admiring Henry Ford.

History's most prolific inventor, Edison holds 1,093 patents. A list of his discoveries reads like a litany of modern technologies: the stock ticker, automatic telegraph, phonograph, telephone transmitter, motion picture camera, multiplex telegraph, electric storage battery, mimeograph machine and the industrial research lab. His most famous practical invention, of course, is the incandescent lamp, or electric light bulb. But more important, Edison created an entire lighting system—inventing, developing, financing and managing the generators, parallel distribution lines and meters needed to bring electric power to consumers.

At birth, Edison appeared destined to be neither rich nor famous. Called Al by his friends, he was descended from a line of rebels. His grandfather, a prosperous Tory, fought against George Washington and the American Revolution in 1776. Convicted of treason and sentenced to hang, he fled to Canada. Al's father also narrowly escaped, this time from Canada to Michigan after participating in an unsuccessful coup against the Royal Canadian government.

Born in 1847 as the seventh and final child of midwestern, middle-class parents, young Edison spent his early years dreaming, drifting and getting into trouble. One of his first experiments ended by burning his father's barn to the ground, but Al's whipping in the public square failed to deter his curiosity. A practiced practical joker, he also knocked down any friend or relative he could lure to touch his electric generator.

To earn money for himself and his family, Edison landed a job at the Port Huron, Michigan, telegraph office. Although fascinated with the technology, he proved to be a miserable transmitter and a dangerous experimenter. One afternoon his tests with chemical mixtures blew the telegraph office up and himself out of a job.

Moving to Stratford, a crossing point for the Grand Trunk Railroad, young Edison was hired to operate the track switch during the night shift. One evening, with his mind on other things, he failed to warn an approaching train of a flipped switch, causing the engine, the tender, and one boxcar to jump the tracks. Edison quickly left for Cincinnati, where he took advantage of a union's strike to grab another telegraph assignment. But his labor-busting opportunism created a tension with other telegraph operators that forced him to move on.

By the age of 24, when he drifted through Boston and Newark, Edison exhibited recklessness, a lack of discipline, stubbornness and an extreme confidence in his own abilities. Although obviously clever, he seemed no different than the many other tinkerers working in telegraph offices. Horatio Alger would not have been impressed.

But Edison's dabbling finally produced useful products that brought him to the attention of industrialists and Wall Street financiers. His stock ticker overcame many of the telegraph industry's bottlenecks by operating at 200 to 300 words per minute. And his automatic duplex allowed two messages to be sent simultaneously on a single wire. To use Edison's inventions, Western Union provided him with what he most wanted—money—although not enough for Edison's squandering ways. To escape Newark's high rent, he and his new wife, Mary, moved 12 miles south to a large lot in Menlo Park. Here the young Edison built his now-famous laboratory, where he experimented with lamps and phonographs, and where he entertained newspaper reporters and financiers.

Western Union president Hamilton McK. Twombly and banker J. Pierpont Morgan visited the Edison laboratory early on. Although they witnessed only bursting bulbs, they shared Edison's dream of making a fortune from a successful electric system. They assembled a group of financial backers to incorporate the Edison Electric Light Company, gaining control of Edison's electric light inventions for a mere $50,000 investment. Edison received the cash and $250,000 of the new firm's stock. The initial 12-member board included Edison, his lawyer Grosvenor Lowrey, representatives of the Vanderbilts (family members did not want to be publicly associated with Edison because of their gas company holdings) and members of Morgan's banking firm.

Edison, as he would on many occasions, glowed with optimism and expressed grand predictions. "The same wire that brings the light," predicted the inventor, "will also bring power and heat—with the power you can run an elevator, a sewing machine, or any other mechanical contrivance, and by means of the heat you may cook your food." This vision of a technological revolution generated no small amount of controversy. Professor Silvanus Thompson in London, for example, labeled Edison's predictions "sheer nonsense." Edison, according to Thompson, demonstrated "the most airy ignorance of the fundamental principles both of electricity and dynamics."

In a sense, Thompson was right. Edison had almost no formal schooling and neither understood nor appreciated scientific theories. "At the time I experimented on the incandescent lamp I did not understand Ohm's law," admitted Edison. "Moreover, I do not want to understand Ohm's law. It would prevent me from experimenting."

Success, however, did not come in a flash of genius, in isolation, or quickly. As Edison himself put it, "Invention is 1 percent inspiration and 99 percent perspiration." To build a long-lasting incandescent bulb, Edison and his associates needed to create a parallel circuit where lights could be operated independently of each other; they required a high-resistant lamp filament or thin thread which the electric current would heat to a glow; and they had to make a vastly improved vacuum globe within which the filament would burn.

Edison worked best when he worked with a team. Throughout the hectic years of 1878-80, he collaborated with Charles Batchelor, Francis Upton and Francis Jehl. Like Edison, Batchelor was a wanderer and tinkerer. A cotton-mill mechanic from England, he first worked with Edison at the American Telegraph Works where they designed stock tickers. Upton, five years younger than Edison, provided order and direction to the lab. Trained in mathematics and abstract science at

Princeton and Berlin universities, Upton became Edison's calculator and information system. Originally Attorney Grosvenor Lowrey's office boy, young Francis Jehl was initially responsible for developing the lab's vacuum pump. But after Batchelor fell ill from breathing mercury fumes, Jehl became the chief technician. He later declared, most accurately, that "Edison is in reality a collective noun and means the work of many men." Edison, however, remained the lab's driving force, whose will and vision prompted continual experimentation and invention.

Initial attempts with the incandescent lamp produced only failure. Edison, for instance, ordered $3,000 worth of copper to build a series of thin pipes that were to be heated by steam. Polished-copper reflectors were to focus the heat rays onto a small point to bring "vivid incandescence." The investment brought only frustration, causing Edison to smash the device with a hammer.

Attempts with a platinum filament were no more satisfying. At $5 an ounce, platinum would have raised the bulb's cost three to four times above that of a gaslight. In addition to expense, the first experiment with platinum filaments produced only a series of Roman candles as the bulbs exploded and flared brilliantly throughout the lab.

Edison persevered. He tried almost every imaginable chemical (e.g., chromium, molybdenum, boron, silicon and zirconium oxide) to coat almost every imaginable substance (e.g., fish lines, cotton, cardboard, wood shavings, visiting cards and beards). He dismissed carbon as a possible "burner" because of its presumed weakness when exposed to the 3,000-degree-Fahrenheit heat of an electric current, until he read about Joseph Swan's experiments in England where a thin carbon rod had been brightly lit for several minutes in a vacuum globe.

Building on Swan's work, Edison began in early October 1879 to bake carbonized sewing thread and to wire the charred ribbon to a stem assembly within a globe. After his new pump exhausted the bulb of its air, he turned on the electric current. The first eight attempts produced only a broken thread. Francis Upton, one of Edison's closest collaborators, grumbled that the electric light was "a continual trouble. For a year we cannot make what we want and see the untold millions roll in."

But on October 21, 1879, the mood changed, when a bulb burned for 40 straight hours. It might have lasted longer, but Edison, ever the investigator, increased the voltage until the filament expired. Uncharacteristically, he waited almost two months before publicly announcing his accomplishment, during which time he experimented with other substances, particularly strips of tough cardboard and bamboo. Over the same period, the Menlo Park lab designed an incandescent lamp generator, since existing models worked only for arc lights wired in series.

When the success was reported, the stock market went wild. Gas company stocks plummeted, with Manhattan Gas Light Company's value, for example, falling 21 percent in only six weeks. Stock in the Edison Electric Light Company, on the other hand, skyrocketed to $3,500 per share.

But not everyone was convinced of Edison's achievement. Professor Henry Morton of the Stevens Institute labeled the lamp "a conspicuous failure, trumpeted as a wonderful success. A fraud upon the public." The *London Times' Sunday Review,* suggesting Edison's results were based on trickery, declared: "There is a strong flavor of humbug about the whole matter." Even Edison acknowledged that his production, held to only three bulbs a day because most of the delicate globes broke, would not produce substantial profits.

The public, however, was intrigued, and curiosity seekers began to flood into Menlo Park. Brought by special trains from Philadelphia and New York, more than 3,000 visitors descended on the one-store village for a New Year's Eve demonstration of 60 lamps mounted on poles throughout the laboratory grounds. Edison also treated New Yorkers to a show by outfitting a 3,200-ton steamship, the *Columbia,* with 115 Edison lamps. After a two-and-one-half-month voyage around the tip of South America, the ship arrived in San Francisco with half its bulbs still working. The skeptics were silenced.

In addition to being a clever inventor, Edison was a preeminent promoter, constantly seeking media coverage and exaggerating his abilities. Even in the midst of busy experiments, he would grant interviews, always claiming to be on the verge of a revolutionary breakthrough. Noting his past accomplishments, the media increasingly considered Edison, a crusty and opinionated character, to be good copy.

More importantly, he was an entrepreneur. Although an avid tinkerer, he experimented with a clear purpose—to make money. The long-lasting incandescent bulb was a substantial achievement, but it remained only part of Edison's vision for a complete industry that would profitably produce and deliver electricity to homes, commercial buildings and industries. The monumental task required designing and constructing a vast array of new electrical equipment, including dynamos, power lines, cables, sockets, switches, insulators, meters, voltage regulators, fuses and junction boxes. In December 1880, Edison created a new firm, the Edison Electric Illuminating Company of New York, to build the first central-station electric generating plant. As usual, the promoter in him announced overoptimistic projections, and the media printed every word. He claimed a $160,000 investment would build a plant to supply electricity to a square mile of downtown Manhattan, and that within two-and-a-half years he would power all of New York City. The facts are that $160,000 only purchased two buildings on Pearl Street, that the generator supplied power to a sixth of a square mile, and that the first station alone took over two years to build.

Although he might exaggerate, Edison knew how to get attention.

He selected a service area that included the Stock Exchange, the major banking and financing houses and the city's leading newspapers. If the project were successful, brokers, bankers and editors would be the first to praise Edison and ensure his financial success.

In addition to new technologies, Edison needed to produce political miracles. The Tammany Hall political machine dominated New York, and corrupt aldermen demanded payoffs in exchange for the franchise needed to lay electrical cables. While fighting among themselves, the city's six gas companies went out of their way to hinder Edison's efforts. The inventor's influential backers, therefore, needed to flex their political muscle in order to compete in the energy marketplace. Grosvenor Lowrey, attorney for Edison, Wells Fargo & Company and Western Union, arranged a lobbying extravaganza for the city commissioners at the Menlo Park laboratory, spent money to "work up an agitation in the daily press having in view the injury of the gas interests," and made payments to legislators for a bill allowing electric companies to do business in the state. Lowrey and Edison knew the franchise was as necessary for commercial success as a well-functioning dynamo or a durable lamp.

Edison scheduled the Pearl Street station's debut on September 4, 1882, and assembled his company's directors at J. P. Morgan's office on Wall Street to witness the event. Moments before the demonstration, one director bet "a hundred dollars the lights don't go on." "Taken," snapped Edison.

Precisely at 3:00 P.M., an electrician threw the switch that fed current from a Jumbo generator (named after the great elephant brought to America by P. T. Barnum) to 106 lamps throughout Morgan's office. Fifty-two additional bulbs glowed in the *New York Times*'s editorial office. The next day's paper described the artificial light as "soft and mellow to the eye; it seemed almost like writing by daylight."

Edison, obviously pleased with his performance, declared somewhat inaccurately, "I've accomplished all I promised."

EARLY COMPETITION

Edison's rivals were legion. Other inventors of incandescent lamps, producers of arc lights, gas companies and manufacturers of isolated and centralized power stations vigorously competed for the lighting and power market.

Edison, ever the inventor, even produced opportunities for his opponents. Several of his patent applications, for example, were so slipshod and chaotically drawn that the court rejected them. In October 1883, patent commissioners ruled that William Sawyer's production of an incandescent lamp with a carbon filament preceded Edison's and granted Sawyer the legal monopoly to sell the lamp for the next 17 years. Edison tried to amend his application, but the commissioners rejected his claim. The Edison Electric Light Company appealed, lost, and watched its stock plunge.

While stubborn Edison inherently opposed using the inventions of others, other experimenters advanced by building on Sawyer's and Edison's work. To strengthen the fragile carbon filament, for instance, Hiram Maxim fired it within a Sawyer bulb filled with hydrocarbon vapor and established the United States Electric Light Company to market the adaptation. Commenting on this "flashing process," the *Illustrated Science News* predicted: "In connection with electric illumination [Maxim's] name will be remembered long after that of his boastful rival is forgotten."

While lawyers and inventors battled, arc lamp companies dominated the lighting of large cities. Charles Brush had installed 12 arc lamps in Cleveland several months before Edison developed his high-resistance filament. Over the next few years, his company and the Thomson-Houston Electric Company obtained contracts in most major urban areas, from New York to San Francisco.

Competition also existed between the builders of centralized power plants and the promoters of isolated stations. J. P. Morgan, for one, preferred the immediate profits of selling isolated equipment to individuals and businesses generating their own power rather than the uncertainty of selling electricity from central power stations. Morgan's mansion, in fact, sported a small generator, one of the 150 operating before Edison's Pearl Street Station even opened. The United States Electric Light Company, purchased by George Westinghouse in 1888, emerged as Edison's chief rival for the isolated power plant market. By out-advertising and underbidding Edison, Westinghouse won contracts to provide electricity for the St. Louis post office, the New York State Capitol building, and the Pennsylvania Railroad's eight Hudson River ferries. But Edison, benefiting from substantial publicity and financial backing, installed five times more systems than his rival at hotels, banks, mills, ironworks, theaters and other commercial buildings across the country.

Gas companies loomed as Edison's biggest threat. According to the inventor, they "were our bitter enemies, keenly watching our every move and ready to pounce upon us at the slightest failure." By 1884, New York's warring gas firms merged into the Consolidated Gas Company and lowered their prices to challenge Edison. Although gas would remain less expensive for almost 30 years, electric power became more convenient to use and eventually won preeminence in the lighting market.

With competition from all sides, Edison Electric Illuminating Company achieved steady, but not spectacular, growth. Two months after the Pearl Street Station began service, the number of customers increased from 59 to 203. A year later, there were 513, and the venture was losing money. "We were not very commercial," Edison explained about the electric company's early days. "We put many customers on, but did not make out many bills." During these times, Edison faced constant cash problems. To gain the financing needed to expand, he was forced to sell his shares in Edison Electric Light Company, which owned the lucrative rights to his patents.

Outside the Pearl Street service area, however, Edison's fortunes looked brighter. By 1889, at the age of 39, he was a millionaire and his companies' combined assets totaled almost $10 million. His construction firm had built 500 isolated and 58 central power stations, including ones in Detroit, New Orleans, St. Paul, Chicago, Philadelphia and Brooklyn. New electric companies were paying royalties to Edison's Electric Light Company for use of his lighting and electrical patents. The Wizard of Menlo Park seemed to possess a magic touch.

MISSED OPPORTUNITIES

Edison's fortune might have been much greater if he could have better managed his laboratory. In fact, credit for the order that did exist must go to Samuel Insull, Edison's personal secretary who for 12 years arranged the inventor's financial records and purchased his clothes. Stubborn and egotistical, Edison alienated many of his other clever colleagues by limiting their responsibilities and rejecting their ideas.

One of these was Frank Sprague. Academically trained at the U.S. Naval Academy, the brilliant mathematician came to New York in 1883 and provided Edison time-saving formulas to reduce the amount of copper (and thus the expense) required for electrical wiring. Sprague's calculations allowed Edison to acquire a lucrative patent but did not earn Sprague the freedom to experiment. After only a year, the mathematician told Edison that unless he was given more independence, he would resign. Edison bluntly responded, "I think it would be the better plan for you to resign." It was not the best of plans, for within a month of leaving, Sprague patented a unique electric motor that maintained a constant speed regardless of the load. Since Edison had failed to design such a practical motor, the Edison Electric Light Company's directors were forced to pay Sprague for the right to manufacture his design. A few years later, Sprague built the first electric railway, providing a large, daytime demand for electricity. By the turn of the century, the Sprague Electric Railway and Motor Company and other firms had constructed more than 20,000 miles of track, replacing 99 percent of the nation's horse-drawn streetcars.

Edison also lost Nikola Tesla, a moody electrical wizard who began his career at the Edison telephone company in Yugoslavia. Edison's European director had sent a note to the inventor saying, "I know two great men and you are one of them; the other is this young man." Despite the glowing recommendation, Edison assigned Tesla to routine electrical work. The young engineer solved many difficult problems at the Edison lab, but he continued to earn only $18 a week and Edison rejected his many requests for a raise. More importantly, Edison rejected Tesla's ideas to utilize alternating rather than direct current. "His ideas are splendid," complained Edison, "but they are utterly impractical." Two years after leaving Edison's lab, Tesla formed the Tesla Electric Company and filed for a patent on a more efficient motor and an electrical distribution system that could carry power hundreds of miles with relatively little loss of voltage. Short of cash, Tesla accepted $1 million from George Westinghouse for his patents, which would revolutionize the electric business.

BATTLE OF THE CURRENTS

A year older than Edison, George Westinghouse built his electric company by acquiring other peoples' patents rather than relying on his own discoveries. Willing to innovate and try new technologies, the bold and ambitious businessman purchased well, buying the floundering United States Electric Light Company, which owned the important lamp patents of Hiram Maxim (inventor of the machine gun) and William Sawyer. Also demonstrating an entrepreneur's knowledge of the law, Westinghouse filed suit against the Edison Electric Light Company for infringing on Sawyer's patent.

Edison fought back, but remained stubbornly committed only to his own inventions. "Though only in his early forties," a biographer writes, "[Edison] emerged in the odd position of the arch-conservative, the defender of the status quo. He became the stubborn, reactionary old man of the electrical industry." The Napoleon of Light was most pigheaded about using direct current (DC), which maintained the same low voltage or thrust from the power station to the ultimate consumer. Not strong enough to cause dangerous electric shocks, neither was DC forceful enough to be transmitted over long distances. Manhattan alone would require three-dozen DC generators to meet the contemporary demand for electricity, stirring complaints about the power plants' noise, pollution and high capital costs.

An alternating current (AC), in contrast, could be converted to higher voltages and sent several hundred miles without significant power losses, offering lower transmission costs. A successful AC system, however, required new motors and transformers.

Several inventors have been credited with development of the efficient AC motor. Italians point to Galileo Ferraris while Germans focus on Michael Osipowitch von Dolivo-Dobrowolsky. Nikola Tesla, however, receives the most credit. An eccentric genius, Tesla often memorized entire books and recited sections on call. One autumn afternoon, as Tesla quoted Goethe while walking in a Budapest park with a friend, the flash of insight struck him. The young scientist grabbed a stick and drew the design for a polyphase generator in the sand. The wind soon erased the drawing, but the complex system remained clear in Tesla's mind for five years before he filed a patent application. Tesla's motor eliminated the need to change the electric current's direction and permitted an AC system to match the capacity of the older DC system in supplying both power and light. Never bashful, Tesla maintained that Westinghouse's success was due to his invention of the polyphase system.

Credit for developing an effective transformer—which "steps up" or increases the electric current at a large power plant and "steps down" the voltage before it reaches homes and offices—goes to William Stanley, son of a prominent New York lawyer. In 1878, young Stanley wrote his disappointed father that he was dropping out of Yale University to dabble with mechanical and scientific activities. For several years, he jumped from U.S. Electric Lighting Company, to Swan Electric Company, to Westinghouse Electric. In 1886, he installed a series of transformers in houses and businesses throughout Great Barrington, Massachusetts. Westinghouse inspected Stanley's equipment, tested a similar design in Pittsburgh and began marketing commercial plants. Within two years, Westinghouse installed AC systems in more than 130 towns across the country.

Edison lashed out against Westinghouse's AC arrangement, declaring that "the first man who touches a wire in a wet place is a dead man. Just as certain as death, Westinghouse will kill a customer within six months after he puts in a system of any size." The ensuing "Battle of the Currents," although critical for the electric industry's future, became a gruesome publicity struggle.

In 1887, the New York State legislature, searching for a more humane method of capital punishment than hanging, asked Edison's opinion of electrocution. Initially avoiding the debate, Edison stated he'd "join eagerly in an effort to abolish capital punishment." But Harold Brown, a New York engineer, convinced Edison that he could use execution by electricity to damage Westinghouse's efforts. In July 1888, Brown electrocuted a dog he described as vicious; he first subjected the dog to direct current of varying voltages and then killed him by alternating current. Over the next few months, he electrocuted some 50 dogs and cats (and many larger animals), describing AC as the perfect medium of execution and Westinghouse as a merchant of death. After hearing testimony from many experts, including Edison, New York legislators voted to install an electric chair. Despite Westinghouse's vehement opposition, Brown acquired a Westinghouse generator and placed it in the Auburn State Prison. Suggested names for the new procedure ranged from "electromort" to "electricide"; Edison is said to have recommended "Westinghoused." In August 1890, William Kemmler became the first criminal to die from electric shock. The bungled operation, according to one witness, turned into "an awful spectacle, far worse than hanging."

Brown and Edison continued to lobby state legislatures against alternating current, asking, "Do you want the executioner's current in your home and running through the streets?" Despite such gory questions, many communities sided with AC's economics, as sales of Westinghouse's systems rose. The battle ended with a gradual transition to alternating current, as Edison shifted his research to motion pictures and mining. The new wiring arrangement, called a universal system, could supply incandescent lamps, arc lights, direct current motors, single-phase AC motors and polyphase motors from a common transmission line fed by a centralized large-scale generator. It ushered in an era of both electric light *and* power.

MERGERS

Electricity sparked a technological and business revolution in late 19th-century America. Consider the incandescent lamp. The average bulb lasted only 400 hours in 1883; within two years, its durability had tripled. By the decade's end more than 1.3-million lamps lit homes and offices around the country, spurring scores of entrepreneurs to manufacture the lamps and the generators needed to power them.

Such innovation created chaos as well as opportunity. Totally unique electrical arrangements overlapped each other. More than 20 systems operated in Philadelphia alone, variously based on patents by Edison, Sawyer, Maxim, Westinghouse, Brush and others. Some DC companies offered power at 100, 110, 220 and 600 volts; AC firms provided frequencies of 40, 60, 66, 125 and 133 cycles. A customer moving across the street would often find that none of his electrical appliances worked in the new home.

To ensure order and to protect themselves from "ruinous competition," executives initially tried to fix prices and production levels among themselves. The public, however, decried such secret efforts, and the Sherman Antitrust Act of 1890 rendered them illegal.

The more effective step was to merge or consolidate. After Westinghouse purchased the United States Electric Lighting Company and gained control of the Maxim and Sawyer patents, he even sought to cooperate with Edison; however, Edison would have no part of sharing his business with a rival, accusing Westinghouse of "flying a kite that will land him in the mud sooner or later."

J. P. Morgan, who had gained virtual control of the new Edison General Electric Company, envisioned the largest consolidation. He met a like-minded businessman named Charles Coffin, the president of Thomson-Houston Electric Company. Formerly a shoe manufacturer, Coffin purchased the patent rights of the Philadelphia professors for whom his company was named. By offering easy credit and by accepting the securities of local electric companies, Coffin had expanded Thomson-Houston's business and increased its value beyond that of Edison General Electric. A merger made both financial and technological sense, in part because the two companies possessed complementary patent holdings. Edison General Electric dominated urban DC stations, DC power transmission and street railways; Thomson-Houston's strength lay in arc lighting and alternating currents.

As bankers struggled to consolidate the firms' assets throughout 1892, Morgan installed Coffin as president. Naming the company, however, sparked the most controversy. Thomson and Edison, both with large egos, vehemently opposed each other's name in the title. The only solution was to simply call the new firm "General Electric." Although Edison maintained a position on the board, he was stunned and hurt by the change. The inventor-promoter had lost control to the bankers.

Edison, acknowledged as the "provider of light," virtually abandoned electrical experiments in the early 1890s to the mathematicians and physicists using complex formulas. He had grown weary of boardroom brawls and financial machinations. Eased out of General Electric, he concentrated his efforts on the phonograph and ore milling, and he dabbled with electric cars and motion pictures. Ever the optimist and promoter, Edison declared that his ore-separating process would be "so much bigger than anything I've ever done before people will forget that my name ever was connected with anything electrical." The mining venture, however, proved to be a multi-million-dollar flop. Still, Edison had become a national resource, celebrated as a practical American hero. During World War I, when Edison devoted his lab to the armed services, the White House assigned four Secret Service agents to protect the inventor.

While Edison enjoyed the laurels of his accomplishments, Samuel Insull, Edison's personal secretary, remained in the electricity business. More accurately, he molded the emerging electric companies into a giant empire. Although offered a high-level job at the new General Electric Company, Insull, ever independent and aggressive, wouldn't work under Coffin and jumped at the chance to manage the Chicago Edison Compa-

ny, one of several electricity generating companies in the Windy City. At
his farewell dinner at Delmonico's Restaurant in New York, Insull
predicted his new firm would soon be bigger than General Electric. The
comment must have sounded far-fetched to the General Electric executives who controlled almost 20 times more assets than the Chicago Edison
Company. But Insull was a recognized salesman, promoter and manager.
No one laughed.

CHAPTER 5

THE EMPIRE BUILDERS

Despite engineering advances and Edison's optimistic predictions, delivering electricity remained an infant, struggling industry at the turn of the century. Electric motors powered only 1 factory in 13. Incandescent bulbs illuminated only 1 lamp in 20.

Prospects for growth flickered, at best. Factory owners refused to abandon their steam-powered, belt-driven systems for unreliable electric generators. Most consumers favored the less-expensive light supplied by gas lamps. Even electric company executives believed electricity would remain a luxury product without a mass market. Quickly adding new customers required the construction of expensive distribution systems, which increased the cost of power and decreased the power company's profits. The favored alternative was to grow slowly by encouraging a small number of consumers to buy more power at progressively lower rates.

Smart money favored isolated plants over central power stations. Pushed by J. P. Morgan and other financiers, the new General Electric Company promoted small-scale systems that could be mass-produced and sold at a substantial profit to factories and office buildings. Fearing competition for this market from emerging electric companies, General Electric Company charged inflated prices for its central station equipment. When Insull moved to Chicago in 1892, on-site generators (operated by streetcar companies, commercial building managers and industrialists) supplied almost two-thirds of the nation's electricity.

In addition to competing with isolated electric plants, belt-driven motors and gas lamps, electric companies struggled among themselves.

Unlike today's utilities, generating firms did not possess monopoly control over a specific region. The Denver Common Council, for instance, granted electricity franchises "to all comers" as long as the companies did not block public streets. Forty-seven generating companies competed in Chicago alone.

Over the next quarter century, however, the electricity business changed dramatically. On the engineering front, larger and more efficient generators were built, a new filament constructed of tungsten produced an incandescent lamp preferable to a gas flame, and long-distance transmission lines sent power over great distances. As the cost of a kilowatt-hour from a central power station dropped from 22 cents in 1892 to only 7 cents three decades later, electricity became viewed as a "necessity of life," enjoyed by almost 13-million Americans. Urban residents turned to vacuum cleaners and other conveniences, and industrialists turned away from isolated power plants.

On the business front, electric companies raised more than $8 billion from five-million individual investors, temporarily breaking the stranglehold of New York investment banks. They also eliminated competition, formed state regulatory commissions and created monopolistic empires. By 1930, three holding companies controlled 40 percent of the nation's electricity.

These corporate giants supplied the power that reduced life's drudgeries and the dividends that provided steady income for millions of investors. Yet their political campaign contributions, their stock market machinations, and their public relations efforts increasingly generated opposition. Franklin D. Roosevelt, then governor of New York, asked of their concentration of power, "Are we in danger of the creation in these United States of such a highly centralized industrial control that we may have to bring forth a new declaration of independence?"

In the center of this revolution and controversy lay one man— Samuel Insull. Edison once told his energetic assistant, "Whatever you do, Sammy, make either a brilliant success of it, or a brilliant failure." Insull achieved both.

THE CHIEF

In February 1881, the SS *City of Chester* arrived in New York harbor from Liverpool. On-board was 21-year-old Sam Insull, ready to serve as Thomas Edison's personal secretary. Forty years later, he returned to New York from a European vacation as the wealthy emperor of America's largest electricity conglomerate. Thirteen years after that, he arrived again, this time as a prisoner charged with embezzlement and mail fraud.

Insull's journey from shop clerk to utility chief to criminal reflects the fast pace of early 20th-century America. It also marks the transformation of small and struggling electric firms into successful utility companies into distrusted corporate monopolies. Called "The Chief" by his employees and colleagues, Insull was, according to one biographer, the most powerful businessman of the 1920s and the most publicized business villain of the 1930s. But his work, more than any other's, laid the foundations of today's electric industry: promotional rates, public relations campaigns, sophisticated engineering, monopoly control with regulatory oversight and a craving for expansion.

Insull's first meeting with Edison disappointed both men. Each thought the other was too young and odd in appearance. Short and skinny, Insull possessed a formal manner, slicked-down hair and a high-pitched, Cockney-accented voice that Edison found hard to follow. Having been seasick for the previous eight days did not help his presentation. Edison, in contrast, looked dowdy, ill-shaven, and was clothed in rumpled black trousers and a dirty white shirt. With a mouth full of tobacco and a strong midwestern accent, he too was difficult to understand.

The temperaments of the two men also clashed. According to Insull, Edison had an "almost pathological hostility to any form of system, order, or discipline imposed from without." Trained as a bookkeeper, Insull possessed a computerlike memory for detail and a craving for organization. Still, each was exactly what the other needed. Insull rationalized Edison's system and made it work, while Edison introduced Insull to the wonders of engineering and business.

After the initial disappointment, the new partners stayed up all night to devise a schedule for borrowing money against Edison's patents. Insull, Edison acknowledged, "had a positive gift for borrowing money." (That gift would later ruin Insull's career and tarnish the electric industry's image.)

Born into a lower-middle-class English family, Insull began working as an office boy at the age of 14. Bright and ambitious, he learned shorthand and became the evening stenographer at *Vanity Fair,* the successful weekly journal on fashion and finance, where he gained an appreciation for the printed word's power. He later answered a classified job advertisement in *The Times* to become secretary for Edison's European representative. His hard work and widespread knowledge of the Edison businesses impressed senior executives. When Edison's personal secretary resigned, Insull was beckoned.

Throughout his 12 years with Edison, Insull performed myriad tasks. His initial work included organizing Edison's office, answering his mail and buying his clothes, for which he was paid only $100 per month, half his salary in England. As the young secretary gained experience, he arranged financing for the Pearl Street station, sold central power plants to a dozen cities across the country, and quadrupled sales at Edison's main factory in Schenectady, New York.

Convinced that supplying electricity promised more profit than manufacturing electrical equipment, Insull quickly rejected a $36,000 per year job with the new General Electric Company in favor of a $12,000 per year job with the small Chicago Edison Company. He demanded only two conditions: that he be given free reign to run the business and that Chicago Edison's rich directors raise money to build a new power station. To guarantee control over the power company, Insull borrowed $250,000 from Marshall Field, the newspaper tycoon, and purchased a large share of the company's stock.

Thirty-two years old in 1892, Insull arrived in the rough and vigorous metropolis of Chicago, home of corrupt politicians, racketeers and a small collection of entrepreneurs who built giant corporations: George Pullman with railroad cars, Cyrus McCormick with farm equipment and Philip Armour with meat packaging. Insull wanted to make his mark, too, and Chicago presented enormous opportunities. Although almost four-dozen companies competed for the city's electric business, this midwest transportation center guaranteed tremendous industrial expansion. Residential energy demand also promised to grow since less than 1 percent of Chicago's homes used electric lamps. The windy city seemed almost a frontier town, relatively free of conservative or traditional constraints. "You know Sammy," Edison had once remarked, "this is one of the best cities in the world for our line of business."

GROWTH AND MONOPOLY

Insull approached electricity much as John D. Rockefeller approached oil—to eliminate competition, expand and make money. Competition, Insull declared, was "economically wrong." His first targets were isolated power stations.

To explain the disadvantages of small facilities, Insull often discussed a block of north-side Chicago homes. The 189 apartments, he explained to whoever would listen, used a total of 68.5 kilowatts of electricity for lighting. But because the lamps were lit at different times in different apartments, the block's maximum demand for power at any one time was only 20 kilowatts. Therefore, Insull reasoned, a central power station providing 20 kilowatts would be more efficient and economical than a series of separate generating plants in each apartment with an aggregate capacity of 68.5 kilowatts. Expanding on this example, Insull argued that a centralized power facility would supply less expensive electricity than competing isolated stations, whatever the purpose. (Privately, he would admit that a single power plant supplying several users also promised lower costs and higher returns for the electric company.)

Individuals accepted Insull's arguments more easily than industrialists who already owned on-site power plants. The latter group demanded substantial subsidies to abandon their small systems for reliance on the electric company. So Insull offered subsidies. In fact, he established a 25-person sales department and ordered employees to "sell at any price." A new luxury hotel, for example, chose electricity over gas because Insull offered a "ridiculously low" rate.

Determining electricity prices was an uncharted course. When Charles Brush first sold electricity in 1879 for San Francisco's arc lamps, no meter measured the amount of power used. Brush simply charged customers $10 per week for each installed lamp.

When a meter was perfected in the late 1880s, controversies began. Edison, believing electric lamps would become more efficient, favored continuing to charge for illumination. But Insull and other electric company officials, feeling profits lay in marketing power rather than fixtures, established prices according to the amount of electricity consumed (measured in kilowatts) over an hour (thus, kilowatt-hour). The little-noticed shift from selling services, i.e., lighting, to hustling electric energy marks the industry's first move toward a "grow-and-build strategy."

Early executives possessed little accurate information about their service costs. To their shock, company profits fell despite dramatic increases in sales. One pioneer complained, "To find that too much business was undermining the stability of the company and jeopardizing its success was startling."

Insull identified and resolved two fundamental problems. First, adding new residential customers required installing expensive distribution lines, transformers and meters but produced only small increases in the company's revenue. To recoup his investment, Insull devised a dual-rate structure. A basic charge for the first several hours of electricity use covered the company's equipment costs. A progressively lower rate for additional demand financed the firm's fuel expenses.

Second, electric companies built more power plants to meet the peak demand during the early evening when consumers arrived home and turned on their lamps, but the facilities lay idle during the day. Insull realized that unless a power station's initial costs were spread among more customers, the cost of electricity would remain prohibitively high and the return on investment disappointingly low. To more efficiently utilize power stations and increase his profits, the executive sought to supply large daytime users, particularly electric streetcars and industrial motors.

Selling power became Insull's religion. He paid particular attention to industrialists with diverse demands for electricity. Ice manufacturers, for example, were perfect customers because their demand was low on

cold January days, when the demand for electric heating strained
Chicago Edison's capacity, but high during "off peak" periods. Promotion, rather than cost, became the foremost consideration in rate designs.
To his colleagues at other electric companies, Insull succinctly stated his
plan: "Sell your product at a price which will enable you to get a
monopoly." The tactics worked. Within his first 42 months, Insull
boosted Chicago Edison's sales almost fivefold, from 2.8 million to
13.7-million kilowatt-hours. Despite needing cash for expansion, the
company began early to regularly pay 8 percent dividends.

In addition to targeting isolated power stations, Insull challenged
other electric companies. At his first board meeting, Insull persuaded the
directors to buy the Fort Wayne Electric Company, Chicago Edison's
largest competitor. Several months later, he purchased the Chicago Arc
Light & Power Company and systematically acquired the exclusive rights
to use electrical equipment manufactured by General Electric and most
other U.S. manufacturers. When Westinghouse installed a small power
station in the northern suburb of Evanston, Insull quickly surrounded
the service area with his own electric facilities. Unable to expand,
Westinghouse also decided to sell out to Insull.

For years, Chicago's political machine received large payments from
executives who wanted to do business in the city. To force Insull to pay $1
million for an electricity franchise, the politicians created a dummy
corporation called Commonwealth Electric Company and conferred
upon it the right to operate in Chicago for 50 years. They failed to realize,
however, that Insull had purchased the exclusive rights to buy the
electrical equipment a new company would need. Commonwealth, therefore, remained a shell, which Insull eventually bought for only $50,000.
By acquiring the dummy corporation's only asset—a 50-year franchise—
Insull gained, according to one grumbling politician, "one of the greatest
bargains since the Russians sold Alaska." In 1907, Insull merged Chicago
Edison and Commonwealth Electric Company into Commonwealth Edison. The newly named firm, 60 times larger than when Insull arrived,
controlled virtually the entire Chicago service area. Its sales surpassed
the combined outputs of New York Edison, Brooklyn Edison and Boston
Edison. Insull had joined the small collection of Chicago entrepreneurs
who had created giant corporations.

But a cloud threatened Insull's private monopoly. Towns and cities
across the country were taking over businesses seen as supplying basic
public services, including water, transportation and electricity. Able to
gain low-cost loans through tax-exempt bonds, municipal power companies grew at twice the rate of private electric firms during the early 20th
century, expanding from 400 in 1896 to more than 1,250 a decade later.

Even towns and cities not interested in public ownership spelled
trouble to expanding private firms. Insull, supplying power to more than
100 suburban communities, was forced to deal with every local council.

To avoid public takeovers and political headaches, Insull devised a plan to establish state regulatory commissions, staffed with professionals independent of local politics. "Exclusive control of a given territory being placed in the hands of one undertaking" remained Insull's ultimate goal; but understanding the public's distrust of monopolies, he suggested a bargain: an exclusive franchise in exchange for public regulation. "In order to protect the public," Insull claimed, "exclusive franchises should be coupled with the conditions of public control, requiring all charges for services fixed by public bodies to be based on cost plus a reasonable profit." Or put more succinctly, "regulation must be followed by protection and . . . regulation and protection naturally lead to monopoly."

Not all of his electric company colleagues agreed. Many, detesting any form of public oversight, felt confident they could block public power efforts through a variety of financial and political tactics. Insull was bolstered, however, by civic reformers who feared that if urban bosses controlled electric companies, even more positions would be filled through the corrupt patronage system. In 1907, progressive governors, such as Robert M. LaFollette of Wisconsin and Charles Evans Hughes of New York, established independent regulatory commissions to oversee electric firms. By the end of World War I, 26 states had followed their lead.

State commissions transformed electricity suppliers from competitive businesses into public utilities. To eliminate the clutter and expense of duplicative transmission wires, they gave the new utilities monopoly control of electricity distribution in defined service territories and the exclusive authority to tap the economies of scale offered by large power plants. Like water and sewage disposal, electric power became viewed as a special commodity that would be regulated by public commissioners rather than the market.

Whereas John D. Rockefeller and other oil giants dominated petroleum through secret deals, marketplace warfare and attrition, Insull and his colleagues engendered electricity monopolies through government sanction. By extending previous Supreme Court decisions regarding railroads, regulators guaranteed electric companies a "fair return" on their investment. Confident of a profit, these centralized utilities sought to expand. And expand they did. Insull's customers grew from 10,000 in 1898, to 50,000 in 1906, to 100,000 in 1909, to 200,000 in 1913.

HOLDING COMPANIES

By 1907 Insull was 48 years old, a millionaire, the ruler of Chicago's electricity monopoly—and dissatisfied. Envying the national railroad conglomerates, he began to look beyond northern Illinois.

New technologies made further expansion possible. Improved transmission systems could wheel electricity several hundred miles, allowing a single power plant to efficiently and economically service both a rural area's high midsummer demand and a city's midwinter peak. At the same time, engineers designed ever-larger generators.

But new equipment was a risky investment, because General Electric and other manufacturers refused to offer their customary performance guarantees. Still, expansion-minded Insull assumed the installation costs whether the huge turbogenerators succeeded or failed. By 1911, he had created the world's largest power station by placing ten 12-megawatt machines at the Fisk Street Station along the Chicago River.

While Insull's engineers installed larger equipment, his lawyers and accountants established the Middle West Utilities holding company and a complex bookkeeping system to organize his imperialistic ventures. By selling $4.5 million of stock in Middle West Utilities, Insull gathered the capital needed to control local power companies. Although these operating firms continued to sell their own securities, Middle West Utilities, at the top of a growing corporate pyramid, could dominate many small companies with a small initial investment. By 1912, Insull's empire encompassed 400 communities throughout 13 states.

Growth at the time made economic sense because larger power plants, more efficient than early models, reduced the cost of electricity to consumers while also maximizing the utility's profit. Adding more customers also diversified the demand for electricity, allowing a single generator to be operated more consistently and efficiently. "Expansion was not simply an aggressive drive for undifferentiated size," notes Professor Thomas Hughes of the University of Pennsylvania. "It was a purposeful move to lower the cost of energy."

What Insull was to the Midwest, John Barnes Miller was to southern California. The pipe-smoking president of the Edison Electric Company (later renamed Southern California Edison) merged many community power companies into a utility empire that brought light, power and controversy to the West.

When Santa Fe completed its transcontinental railway line in 1885 and began to compete with Southern Pacific by offering cheap fares, thousands of settlers quickly converted California's huge cattle ranches into new towns and small farms, and turned Los Angeles, once ridiculed as "the Queen of the Cow Counties," into the Southland's commercial center. Miller quickly understood that electric technologies used in the East would not be sufficient for California where the best power supplies—remote rivers in the Sierra Nevada mountains—were located long distances from the populated coastal cities. Unlike Chicago or New York, Los Angeles and the surrounding region were filled with wide-open spaces that required elaborate transmission systems.

Expanding upon Nikola Tesla's AC system, talented engineers proposed building a 120-kilowatt generator alongside the San Antonio Creek and wheeling power over 14 miles of wire to Pomona. Eastern engineers doubted that oil-filled transformers could raise an electric current to 10,000 volts. But the system proved successful in November 1892, and a month later, a second long-distance transmission line extended power 29 miles to San Bernardino.

Miller expanded the technologies even further. In 1907, he completed a 5-megawatt hydroelectric dam on the Kern River and a 118-mile, 75,000-volt transmission line that wheeled the electricity to Los Angeles. Diverting the river, digging deep tunnels and stringing transmission wires across steep canyons was a monumental—and dangerous—task using contemporary construction techniques. Even today, the project is viewed as a major engineering feat.

Miller was a promoter as well as a builder. His "New Business Department" encouraged farmers to adopt electric irrigation pumps and urged homeowners to purchase irons, toasters, vacuum cleaners, washing machines and other electric appliances. He hired "cooking experts" to tour communities and promote electric ranges. And he provided the burgeoning motion picture industry with "artificial daylight," floodlighting for indoor locations.

Called the "Great Amalgamator," Miller systematically replaced inefficient local power plants with an interconnected network of modern facilities. In 1917, he acquired railway magnate Henry Huntington's Pacific Light & Power Corporation, which had controlled the "Red Car" trolley lines, the Big Creek–San Joaquin River Hydroelectric Project and several small power companies throughout the Southland. In the process, Southern California Edison doubled its assets to become the nation's fifth-largest electric company, serving 1.25-million customers in more than 100 cities and towns.

While research labs resolved the technical problems of large generators and holding companies conquered financial barriers, new institutions—multipurpose consulting and engineering firms—supervised the construction of expanding utility systems. In 1890, only two years after graduating from the Massachusetts Institute of Technology, Charles Stone and Edwin Webster offered to advise businesses investing in electrical engineering ventures, and to design and build power plants for utilities unwilling to assume the construction headaches. They soon faced competition from Bechtel, Brown & Root, Combustion Engineering, Fischbach & Moore and several other consultants.

Stone & Webster's first project was a 400-horsepower hydroelectric generator and a short transmission line to a New England power mill. The ventures became progressively larger, including the Boston Elevated Railway, the dam and power house at Keokuk, Iowa, the Big Creek-to-Los Angeles transmission system and the Conowingo hydro station in Maryland.

J. P. Morgan boosted Stone & Webster's fortunes by requesting an appraisal of all the utilities partially owned by General Electric. In addition to evaluating power companies for bankers, the young engineers gradually invested in the utilities they analyzed. After visiting the Nashville Light & Power Company, Webster wrote about his follow-up meeting with Morgan: "I was enthusiastic about [the utility] and told him that I thought, if the assets were carefully conserved and the property was wisely developed, it would result in a great property. . . . He told me that, if I felt so confident about the future of these things, he thought I ought to buy them." So Webster borrowed a few thousand dollars and bought control. After working with the utility for several years, he sold his stock for a handsome $500,000 profit.

In 1925, the engineers formally established a holding company, the Engineers Public Service Company, and acquired the Virginia Railway & Power Company (which became the Virginia Electric Power Company). By 1932, the Stone & Webster group consisted of 43 utilities, generating slightly more than 2 percent of U.S. electricity.

Empire builders flourished throughout the United States. Alex Dow controlled service across Detroit and eastern Michigan. Wilbur Foshay extended his operations into 13 states, Alaska, Canada and Central America. And J. P. Morgan built the United Corporation into the nation's largest holding company, controlling most choice utilities throughout New York, New England and the Southeast. By the mid-1920s, 16 conglomerates dominated more than three-fourths of the privately owned electricity industry.

For a nation skeptical of monopolies, these empires provoked distrust and anger. But they were logical outgrowths of emerging electric technologies. New institutions with sophisticated financing and engineering skills were needed to manage the enormous capital investments in large generators and high-voltage transmission lines. Even the Federal Trade Commission, which attacked "power trusts" for financial abuses, did concede that under holding companies "service was improved and extended, consumption increased and costs of production were reduced."

Although many of the operating companies that remained independent of holding companies wanted to maintain their autonomy, several sought the benefits of cooperation with other utilities by forming power pools. The trend was spurred by President Woodrow Wilson who, when faced with the likelihood of an energy shortage during World War I, formed the War Industries Board in July 1917 to survey electric generating facilities and to direct war contracts to areas with excess capacity. Army engineers showed that existing power facilities could be used more effectively by integrating utility operations. The board went so far as to order interconnections of private utility systems.

After the war, utilities in Pennsylvania and New Jersey developed their own regional power pool to share diverse loads and increase their efficiency. Pennsylvania Power & Light had its peak demand in the morning when the coal mines and industries in its region were active. In contrast, Philadelphia Electric and Public Service Electric & Gas Company of New Jersey experienced early evening peaks when factories still operated, streetcars carried commuters, and homeowners turned on their lights and cooking appliances. Sharing power allowed the utilities to satisfy these different needs with fewer power plants and much less investment. But it also required complex contracts among the pool's participants, who had to agree on a strict allocation of new plants to provide reliable capacity.

The utilities could also efficiently share diverse generating facilities. Philadelphia Electric's large hydroelectric project on the Susquehanna River at Conowingo, Maryland, would supply most of the power pool's base load during times of high river flow, while the other utilities' coal or oil plants would carry the fluctuating peak demand. The division would reverse during times of low water.

The expansion of holding companies and power pools demanded an increasingly sophisticated and costly transmission system, complete with steel towers, copper or aluminum lines, expensive insulators, lightning protection equipment, circuit breakers, switches and huge transformers. Historian Thomas Hughes calculates utilities spent more money during the 1920s than did the transcontinental railroads during the period of their most rapid expansion.

PUBLIC RELATIONS

Insull clearly understood the dangers of popular hostility to a publicly regulated monopoly. At best, suspicion promised time-consuming regulatory procedures. At worst, it threatened public takeover. "Unless you can so conduct your business as to get the good will of the community in which you are working," Insull warned his colleagues, "you might just as well shut up shop and move away."

Identified as a "practical liberal," Insull tried to win community support. He endorsed, for instance, mine safety laws in order to gain the cooperation of unions whose members dug the coal for Middle West Utilities. He made concessions to the International Brotherhood of Electrical Workers in exchange for an agreement to keep his operating personnel in a nonunion environment. He organized the National Civic Federation to attack urban corruption and to ensure a neutral stance from local officials on public power. Unique for his time, he hired minorities and women and offered all employees relatively generous fringe benefits.

Gaining good will, however, required more than concessions and organizations, Insull believed. He became a groundbreaker in the young field of public relations. He published, for instance, annual corporate reports 15 years before it became a standard procedure. In 1901, well before most other businesses, he created the industry's first advertising department. He also freely distributed thousands of copies of "Electric City" to Chicago stores where he rented space and provided display racks. The well-designed tabloid described the wonders of electricity and explained how consumers could save money by using it.

Insull's genius for promotion was not fully tapped until World War I. With his parents still living outside London, he unhesitatingly supported England against an expansionist Germany. Yet America's large German population (Chicago itself was the world's sixth-largest German city) threatened to keep the United States out of the war by appealing to isolationists and pacifists. Convinced he must sway public opinion, Insull spent $250,000 sending war-promoting literature to newspapers across the country.

When the United States declared war on April 6, 1917, Insull was asked to direct the Illinois's State Council of Defense, charged with policing people suspected of disloyalty. Throughout the war, Insull devoted full time to building a public relations machine and encouraging other states to follow Illinois's example. With Bernard J. Mullaney, a former newsman and brilliant publicist, he established war-support committees in almost every neighborhood and enlisted newspaper editors, ministers, mayors, business leaders and labor bosses to promote war relief. Their efforts organized 380,000 volunteers, raised $24 million, and encouraged the purchase of $1.3 billion in Liberty Bonds.

Insull's success brought public acclaim and invitations to the White House. Because he returned $450,000 from the Illinois council to the state and federal treasuries after the armistice, some admirers suggested that if Insull had run the entire war effort, he would have made a profit.

Intoxicated by his PR machine's ability to raise money and influence public opinion, Insull simply changed the war council's name in March 1919 to the Committee on Public Utility Education and sought to equate patriotism with a favorable attitude toward utilities. At a time when businesses favored secrecy, Insull informed citizens of "the social and industrial significance of the [electric utility] industry in all of its ramifications."

The renamed committee and 40 similar institutions in other states exploited, according to the National Electric Light Association, "everything but sky writing" to promote electricity and utilities. They regularly sent packaged editorials and story ideas to newspaper editors and urged employees to join civic organizations in order to make political contacts and lobby for the company. They distributed more than 25-million pieces of literature and provided speakers to clubs and groups.

Campaign slogans were carefully chosen to solicit the desired public response. "Economies and efficiencies" justified mergers. Public power was disparagingly referred to as "political ownership." Putting conglomerates in the best light, Insull suggested: "The so-called 'holding company' in the electric light and power business . . . is more properly an investment company; even more accurately perhaps, a development company. Its primary purpose is to expand and energize the facilities and resources and activities of the local or subsidiary companies that are under its wing, and to broaden opportunities for safe investment."

The committees continued the wartime fervor by hounding utility critics. An Iowa public relations director warned: "If irresponsible public speakers know that they are being watched and checked up and that they are not going to be allowed to get away with malicious utterances they are going to be more careful."

Schoolchildren—considered "the customers, the investors, the voters, and the lawmakers of the future"—were a major target. Concerned about "propaganda" from liberal and socialist organizations, Insull declared that executives "must fix the truth about the utilities in the young person's mind before incorrect ideas become fixed there." One thrust was to distribute copies of "The Ohm Queen," a 32-page color booklet on the wonders of electricity, to 400,000 kindergartners.

Insull also identified "the great need of a campaign of education in the colleges and other institutions of learning." The National Electric Light Association and its affiliated utilities regularly employed poorly paid professors to conduct surveys, give lectures or attend conferences, believing such support would encourage academics to back utility positions before regulatory commissions and other public bodies. A few executives went so far as to gain revisions in the standard textbooks for high school civics. Their pressure removed a negative reference toward Insull that aides felt was "not warranted."

In addition to seeking more customers and trying to assure docile regulatory commissioners, Insull needed investors. Ever since he and Edison had struggled to gain money from J. P. Morgan, Insull had loathed New York financiers. Learning of Pacific Gas & Electric's "customer ownership" drives, Insull realized that the best way to win supporters for Middle West Utilities was to have consumers themselves invest money in the companies. And invest they did. Insull's advertising campaigns increased the number of utility shareholders in Illinois from 50,000 in 1919 to 500,000 in 1921. Insull's name, according to Franklin D. Roosevelt, was "magic" and a beacon of trust for thousands of small investors.

What began as public relations devices became major innovations in corporate finance. Since New York bankers sold bonds to large investors rather than to the general public, Chicagoan Harold L. Stuart was able to build a market among individuals throughout the Midwest. Even in 1922 when money was tight, Halsey, Stuart & Company sold $27 million of Insull bonds at half the going rate. Utilities effectively advertised that "if the light shines, you know your money is safe." Although Insull and

Stuart temporarily broke the stranglehold New York bankers held over the nation's investments, they raised the financiers' ire and became the target for their revenge.

To his credit, Insull realized his public relations machine could backfire. "To spread 'propaganda' and to 'mold public opinion', " he warned, "is unsound. In the long run, it defeats itself." A few other executives were even more critical. "We are not community saviors," declared George N. Tidd, the square-shouldered engineer and director of American Gas and Electric, a holding company for 40 firms throughout nine states. Public relations activities, Tidd warned, were out of control and it was "high time to call a halt before irreparable damage has been done."

But the PR machine was already upsetting powerful politicians. In the 1932 presidential campaign, Franklin Roosevelt denounced utility advertisements as "a systematic, subtle, deliberate and unprincipled campaign of misinformation, of propaganda, and, if I may use the words, of lies and falsehoods."

WILD DAYS ON WALL STREET

Samuel Insull became a business hero in a hero-worshipping era. While Babe Ruth hit home runs, Jack Dempsey scored knockouts, and Charles Lindbergh crossed the Atlantic in a small monoplane, Insull successfully challenged New York's bankers and Chicago's social elite. Rich and powerful, the self-made tycoon was a ruthless bargainer but gave much of his income to charities and to the opera, his greatest love outside business. Insull even financed the construction of a 42-story building to house Chicago's Civic Opera and regularly sent young singers to Europe for study.

But from the beginning of the 20th century, Americans were also hearing a growing chorus from reformers and muckrakers, who criticized America's largest corporations and monopolies. Ira Tarbell exposed John D. Rockefeller's greed and far-flung control of the petroleum industry. Upton Sinclair vividly described the jungle within Chicago's meat-packing houses. And utility "power trusts" did not escape critical review. Senator George Norris of Nebraska protested that "practically everything in the electric world is controlled either directly or indirectly by some part of this gigantic trust." Moreover, state regulatory commissions, he declared, "can no more contest with this gigantic octopus than a fly could interfere with the onward march of an elephant."

Although Insull admitted electric companies "have been hampered less than some other public utilities by political and kindred demagoguery," he and other executives created powerful political machines to enhance their images and protect their interests. Georgia Power Company, for example, employed battalions of lawyers to monitor state regulations and legislation. Southern California Edison and Pacific Gas & Electric formed "taxpayer leagues" to promote their campaigns. Utility critics maintained that through campaign contributions and lobbyists, power companies—particularly Duke Power Company in North Carolina, Public Service Corporation in New Jersey, the Roraback machine in Connecticut, and Alabama Power Company—virtually controlled their state legislatures.

Nothing seemed to curtail the electric giants. By the late 1920s, ten holding companies manipulated approximately three-fourths of the nation's light and power business. Banks fanned the expansionist fever by wildly extending loans to almost any business that seemed prosperous. Insull's empire, which served more than four-million customers and controlled more than $3 billion worth of property, was owned by 600,000 stockholders and 500,000 bondholders.

Flush with cash, holding companies drove up prices for utility properties. In 1925, New England Power Association, in a contest with Associated Gas and Electric, paid $223 per share for Worcester Light Company, even though the book value totaled only $70 a share. Associated Gas, meanwhile, paid 159 times more for General Gas and Electric Corporation than the utility was worth on paper.

Cyrus S. Eaton of Cleveland acquired two Mellon holding companies in 1926 and quietly began buying shares of Insull's firms. He claimed no interest in control, but Insull feared a raid from Eaton and the Morgan group. In self-defense, Insull further pyramided his companies by forming an investment trust. When trading of Insull's Utility Investments Corporation began in January 1929, the stock market was rising wildly, and the security quickly skyrocketed from $12 to $150 per share. According to Forrest McDonald, Insull's biographer, the Chief's securities "appreciated at an around-the-clock rate of $7,000 per minute, for a total rise of more than one-half billion dollars."

The pace couldn't continue. On "Black Friday," October 29, 1929, stock prices plummeted. Insull, believing the Depression would be short, continued to freely spend money. Four days after the crash, he opened the Chicago Civic Opera House and began advancing his employees the cash necessary to cover their margin brokerage accounts. Continuing his craving for expansion, Insull spent a whopping $197 million for capital investments in 1930, including the construction of a natural gas pipeline from Texas. He even spent $1,580,000 for power plants in Harlingen, Texas, which were valued at only $800,000. According to Insull, the electric utility industry would remain strong.

The deception lasted for several years, despite the economy's collapse. The stock prices of Insull's companies, for example, were higher in the first quarter of 1930 than during the same period a year earlier. Earnings rose 15 percent in 1930, and total sales of electricity for the first six months of 1931 set an all-time record. Part of the good news was real: Electricity demand from residential consumers soared, even as industrial businesses collapsed. In 1929 and 1930, more than 2.36-million Americans purchased refrigerators, often doubling their power usage. But part of the industry's higher earnings resulted from fraud. A Federal Power Commission report, citing an "apparently flagrant lack of compliance with the law," revealed extensive inflation of utility assets and earnings. Holding companies, for example, created fictitious income by selling property to their subsidiaries at high prices and taking payment only in the subsidiary's overvalued stock.

Despite the Depression's advance, Insull continued expanding and defending himself against takeovers. He bought out municipal power plants in North Carolina, purchased his own securities at ever-mounting prices, and arranged to buy Cyrus Eaton's holdings for $56 million, nearly $6 million above the already inflated market value.

But the Depression was drying up investment capital for utility expansion, forcing holding companies to dramatically extend their borrowings from banks and to juggle funds among their numerous operating firms. To purchase Eaton's shares, Insull had to offer his utility properties as collateral for a $20 million loan from the Morgan group and other New York bankers. The deal proved to be a tragic mistake. By protecting himself from Eaton's takeover, Insull guaranteed that the banks would control his companies if stock prices ever crumbled.

The electric industry had become a fragile house of cards by September 1931 when England went off the gold standard and American investors launched a selling stampede. Finally utility stock prices plunged. Middle West Utilities' shares dropped from $570 to the equivalent of only $1.25; Insull claimed a personal loss of nearly $15 million. Shares in Central Public Service plummeted from $80 to only 25 cents. After receivership, bondholders of Tri-Utilities Corporation's $1,000 debenture received only 30 cents; stockholders got nothing. And one power tycoon left only a 32-story monument in Minneapolis that carried the ironic inscription: All Your Money—All the Time—On Time.

By December, Insull had given his two investment trusts as collateral to the bankers. Still, he struggled to acquire funds. He even arranged an unsecured loan from Commonwealth Edison to save his brother's brokerage firm, an act later considered embezzlement. The end came in June 1932, 20 years after Middle West Utilities was formed, when the Morgan investment house blocked other bankers from covering Insull's $20 million note. The New York financiers also convinced Insull's directors to ask for his resignation. At age 74, Insull, broke and broken, fled to Europe.

Ironically, many individual utilities performed relatively well throughout the Depression. While gross income for manufacturing companies plummeted 63 percent, the utility industry's revenue shrank only 6 percent. According to the Department of Commerce, "the stability of the industry's operating revenues due to the rigidity of its rate structure [set by state regulators] prevented the decline in income . . . from going very far."

But higher electricity demand and stable regulation could not protect the fragile corporate pyramids that had been built on inflated assets and tricky bookkeeping procedures. Nineteen Insull companies eventually declared bankruptcy. Investors lost between $500 million and $3 billion, depending upon how unrealized paper profits were tabulated. The federal official overseeing these receiverships called Insull's financial failure "the tragedy of the century." He described the individual investor's calamity: "One day I stood and watched those holding securities and obligations of these companies coming in and filing them [to receive a refund]. They were just the average run of people—clerks and schoolteachers there in Chicago, small shopkeepers in Illinois, farmers from Wisconsin—and what they brought in, of course, was worth nothing. They had lost every penny."

CHAPTER 6

THE PUBLIC DEFENDERS

While most urban Americans enjoyed the wonders of electricity by the 1920s, rural Americans were not so lucky. The absence of electric power in the countryside, wrote historian William E. Leuchtenberg, divided America into two nations, "the city dwellers and the country folk." Farmers, he said, "toiled in a nineteenth-century world; farm wives, who enviously eyed pictures in the *Saturday Evening Post* of city women with washing machines, refrigerators, and vacuum cleaners, performed their backbreaking chores like peasant women in a preindustrial age."

Country folk certainly tried to "go electric." Time and again they begged the power trusts for service, only to hear utility executives decry rural electrification as too expensive, costing $5,000 per mile to build lines to individual farmers. Privately, power company officials believed profits would be low because farmers couldn't afford appliances that used substantial electricity. Although rural politicians published studies to disprove the company statistics, the utility controlled the switch and lighting farms remained a dim hope.

Life without electricity was drudgery. Those farm families unable to use wind-powered pumps had to carry water from a stream to the house or lift it from a well, bucket by bucket. A federal study showed that the average rural household used 200 gallons, or four-fifths of a ton, of water each day. The study also found that the average well was 253 feet from the house, and that pumping and carrying water required a farmer (or more often his wife) to put in 63 eight-hour days and to walk 1,750 miles—just to supply the family with water for a year!

Without electricity, boiling water was a task. Wood had to be chopped, stacked and carried to the house. Wood stoves were difficult to start up, could not be regulated easily, and produced unbearable temperatures in the summer. Lacking refrigerators, the women were forced to start every meal from scratch. They canned vegetables and fruit the very day they ripened, often spending every autumn day boiling water and canning. "You'd have to cook for hours," recalls one wife. "I wore loose clothing so that it wouldn't stick to me. But the perspiration would just pour down my face. I remember the perspiration pouring down my mother's face, and when I grew up and had my own family, it poured down mine. That stove was so hot. But you had to stir, especially when you were making jelly. So you had to stand over that stove."

Wash days and ironing days were even worse. No washing machine's agitator substituted for hands that scrubbed and wrung the dirty clothes. Loads of water had to be carried to vats outside the house and more wood was needed to boil the water. A typical large farm family required eight loads, often taking all day to complete. Ironing would consume another full day. More wood was needed to heat the seven-pound wedges of iron that tried to eliminate wrinkles. The hauling, bending, wringing and lifting destroyed women's backs and made them old before their time.

Even lighting the kerosene lamp was difficult. If the wick was too high, the lamp would smoke; and after every few moments, it had to be readjusted. Vacuum cleaners, waffle irons, toasters and hot plates remained only pictures in the magazines. Indoor plumbing, too, was an impossible dream for rural families because running water required an electric pump.

Senator George Norris understood firsthand the drudgery of rural life: "I had lived the hard boyhood of a primitive Ohio farm, and the possibilities of electricity for lightening the drudgery of farms and urban homes, while revolutionizing the factories, fascinated me." Norris, who moved to Nebraska and became the leading advocate of publicly owned utilities, spent most of his long government career trying to bring power to those without it.

MR. DEMOCRACY

George Norris and Sam Insull agreed on only two theories. First, both the senator from Nebraska and the power tycoon from Chicago believed greater electricity use would dramatically improve the quality of life. Electric power, declared Norris, "relieves men and women of drudgery which cannot be discharged in any other way; it drives the machines of production."

Second, both men assumed electric power would be produced by a monopoly. Physical laws and inadequate batteries required electricity to be manufactured, delivered and used in the same instant; storage, according to Insull, "is a practical impossibility." Both men felt power plants capable of delivering adequate electricity to customers with diverse demands must be so large that only huge enterprises unburdened by competition could build them. Insull declared that competition was "economically wrong," while Norris predicted electricity would be generated by "a gigantic monopoly, bigger than any we've ever known."

Whether that monopoly should be privately or publicly controlled, however, divided Norris and Insull and sparked vehement public debates throughout the first half of the 20th century. Insull and other businessmen felt that America's strength depended upon the marketplace allocating resources and production; they ridiculed public ownership as "socialism." But Norris and a growing group of progressives and conservationists believed that a privately owned monopoly would "eventually . . . come to tyranny," and that America's power development must "be under public control, public operation and public ownership."

The youngest of 12 children, George Norris grew up in a dilapidated old house in the Black Swamp section of northern Ohio. The family's only other son was slain while fighting in the Union Army; his father died of pneumonia when George was only three. In addition to assuming farm chores and family responsibilities, young Norris sought an education at Ohio's Baldwin University and Indiana's Valparaiso, considered "the Poor Man's Harvard." At 16 he began traveling throughout the northern Midwest as an itinerant schoolteacher, living with farmers and trying to eke out a living.

Many of his students' parents, having mortgaged their 160 acres to buy farm equipment and seeds, were battered by the economy and the weather. During good seasons they watched their surplus harvests fetch low prices, and when hot winds blew up from the South, their crops were destroyed. In either case, farmers constantly increased their indebtedness; many lost their farms.

Moving to Nebraska, Norris established a law practice and began to dabble in politics. After losing his first election for prosecuting attorney, at the age of 34 he won a judgeship by a mere 7 votes. Norris's staunch conservatism and his success in "breasting the Populist tide" attracted Republican leaders who convinced him to run for Congress, a seat he won in 1902 by only 300 votes.

Norris entered the House of Representatives feeling "sure of my position, unreasonable in my convictions, and unbending in my opposition to any other political party." But Washington politics, controlled by party machines, soon shocked the young idealist. By 1908, he "had thrown off the cloak of bitter partisanship," realizing that his party "was guilty of all the evils that I had charged against the opposition." His initial political battle targeted the enormous power of Republican Speaker Joseph Cannon. Boss Cannon, according to Norris, stifled democratic procedures by totally dominating House actions through his control of patronage and appropriations. By leading a successful campaign to strip the Speaker of power, Norris established himself as a leader of the Progressive movement within his party and Congress.

Memories of childhood rigors provoked Norris to advocate leniency for farm debtors and alternatives to the private power trusts. "I knew what it was to take care of the farm chores by the flickering, undependable light of the lantern in the mud and cold rains of the fall, and the snow and icy winds of winter," Norris remembered. Electricity was a blessing he wanted to extend throughout rural areas.

LEASING THE RIVERS

After the Civil War, Americans seemed to be constantly moving westward. Miners followed trappers and were succeeded by cattlemen and farmers. The Homestead Act provided the land, and transcontinental railroads the transportation for this massive wave of settlers. The migration between 1860 and 1890 could be measured by the doubling of the number of farms and the addition of nine new states to the Union, including Norris's Nebraska. By 1890, the western movement was so pervasive that the superintendent of the census announced that the "frontier" had disappeared.

To stimulate economic growth and conserve the nation's riches, President Teddy Roosevelt favored a scientific approach to resource management rather than private exploitation. His Inland Waterways Commission, for instance, concluded in 1907 that "streams of the country [are] an asset of the people" that should be protected from monopolies but developed to enhance irrigation, navigation, flood control and power production.

Utility executives and government planners enviously eyed the Tennessee, Columbia, Colorado and other mighty rivers, sparking heated debates about whether hydroelectric dams should be privately or publicly owned. In 1917, President Woodrow Wilson sided with public power advocates by suggesting that a new federal commission administer 50-year leases and that preference be given to municipalities. Because private power companies vehemently opposed some of Wilson's provisions, Congress did not approve a compromise bill until 1920, well after the armistice. The final bill, the Federal Power Act, satisfied the conservationists by confirming federal government control over rivers, but it charged private power companies extremely low rates for water use.

The most heated hydropower controversy focused on a site near the town of Sheffield in northern Alabama, where the Tennessee River becomes shallow and falls rapidly. As World War I began, President

Wilson decided to build a dam at this prime hydroelectric site to power an air nitrate factory. This Muscle Shoals facility, said Wilson, would help make munitions during the war and fertilizer during peacetime.

By the 1918 armistice, the federal government had spent $100 million on the Muscle Shoals venture, including $13 million for a 100-foot-high, mile-long dam. The facility, to be known as the Wilson Dam, remained only half complete and would spark a 15-year struggle for control of electricity production.

The political climate changed dramatically in 1920 as Warren Harding's smashing victory launched a decade of open and unashamed support for capitalism. The Republican creed promised lower taxes (especially for the rich), higher tariffs and support for private business. Foremost among Harding's advisers were Secretary of Commerce Herbert Hoover, who used his department to promote the interests and enlarge the markets of America's corporations, and Secretary of the Treasury Andrew Mellon. A multimillionaire from Pittsburgh who controlled the aluminum monopoly, Mellon slashed government spending and taxes. His motto, Less Government in Business, stimulated a public weary of war-caused inflation, civil rights advocacy, labor strikes and radical protests.

The new political environment perfectly suited Sam Insull and the National Electric Light Association (NELA). With the watchword, They Shall Not Pass, NELA attacked public power with what a subsequent Federal Trade Commission described as "the greatest peacetime propaganda campaign ever conducted by private interests in this country." Muscle Shoals, although initially only a local problem, came to symbolize the debate between public and private power interests.

Harding initially offered the nitrate plant and dam to the highest bidder. Alabama Power Company, believing no other firm would submit an offer, publicly stated it could not finance the purchase, but privately hoped a delay would encourage the government to accept a low bid. But Harding and the utility were both shocked in early July 1921 when an offer to purchase the Muscle Shoals facilities was submitted by Henry Ford.

Ford, who began his career as an engineer at a Detroit Edison power plant, had become a living American legend. His Model Ts, which outnumbered all other cars on the road, provided mobility and convenience to the middle class. His profit-sharing plan and his minimum wage, at the then unheard of rate of $5 a day, enhanced his reputation as an industrial innovator and a humanitarian. His dream of building industries throughout the Tennessee Valley, which would employ one million workers (preference given to veterans), sparked the public's imagination.

But Ford was more a businessman than a humanitarian when it came to Muscle Shoals. A close examination of his bid revealed what one observer called "the most wonderful real estate speculation since Adam and Eve lost title to the Garden of Eden." Specifically, Ford offered to buy the nitrate factory for less than 5 percent of what it had cost the government, and to lease the hydroelectric facilities for a hundred years at less than 10 percent of what Washington would spend to simply complete the facility. And to finance his $5 million purchase, Ford suggested the government loan him the money at less than 4 percent interest. Although he hinted that the project would provide fertilizer at half the going rate, Ford ignored the Federal Power Act's 50-year-lease limitation and failed to explain how he would use the vast amount of excess power.

Ford's offer worried not only public power advocates. By proposing to build transmission lines in competition with private utilities, the industrialist also frightened the power companies and the investment banking houses that supported them. Twelve days after Ford's submission, the Alabama Power Company corrected its initial mistake and offered $5 million for a 50-year lease as a challenge to Ford's offer.

Norris was asked by the Senate to organize extensive hearings on nitrate and power production to determine if Ford could deliver cheap fertilizer using the outmoded and costly cyanamide process. He listened to scores of conflicting claims before declaring that Ford's offer "would turn back the clock of progress and open the door wide for the use of natural resources by corporations and monopolies without restriction, without regulation, and without restraint." The senator also sifted through a bewildering flood of propaganda before scorning the Alabama Power Company's $5 million offer for property worth almost $100 million. Distraught with the alternatives, Norris introduced his own measure for government control of the whole project.

While the heated debate dragged on, the Harding administration tainted unrestrained capitalism with the Teapot Dome scandals. In late 1923, Senator Thomas Walsh of Montana discovered that Secretary of the Interior Albert Fall had secretly leased federal oil lands to the companies of Henry Doheny and Harry Sinclair in exchange for political contributions. The investigation eventually sent Fall to prison, making him the first American cabinet member to be jailed. Many lawmakers compared the scandal to Muscle Shoals; one suggested that giving away the Tennessee River properties would "make Teapot Dome look like bagatelle."

Two years passed before the House of Representatives finally approved Ford's proposal. The delay, however, had irritated the industrialist and he abandoned the project rather than confront Norris in the Senate. Alabama Power Company was not so easily dissuaded, and it helped organize a public relations campaign to ridicule George Norris. The *New York Commercial,* for instance, suggested Norris drew his "inspiration from the teachings of Marx." The National Electric Light

Association charged that Norris's statements were "unwarranted and unfair, originating with predatory politicians and demagogues." Sam Insull branded Norris as an "agitator."

In response to critics, Norris and other progressives stepped-up their attacks on the power trusts, protesting their high electric prices. New York Governor Franklin D. Roosevelt led the charge by stating, "We have permitted private corporations to monopolize the electrical industry and sell electricity at the highest rates they could obtain." Launching the "waffle iron campaign," FDR argued for more electric power at low rates so that all Americans could afford the conveniences of washing machines, vacuum cleaners, and even waffle irons. With electricity becoming viewed as a necessity rather than a luxury, reformers argued that consumers needed a great deal more power for their money.

To prove public companies provided lower rates, Norris visited Canada's Hydro-Electric Power Commission of Ontario, which supplied wholesale electricity to 248 municipal firms and farm districts. Knocking on doors in the service area, he met Mrs. J. Cullom who had used 334 kilowatt-hours of electricity the previous month. Norris discovered that with this power, she "swept the floors by electricity. She cooked all of her meals upon an electric stove. She washed by electricity, she ironed by electricity, she had twice as many electric lights in that eight-room cottage as are usually found in similar cottages in the United States. She heated the water for kitchen and bath by electricity." The price for these conveniences: only $3.55 per month. Equivalent power from private utilities in the United States was at least six times more expensive. In Washington, D.C., for example, 334 kilowatt-hours would have cost $23.18; in Birmingham, Alabama, it would have been $32.00; in Nashville, Tennessee, $40.00; and in Florida, approximately $60.00.

Norris also compared the costs of lighting the Canadian and American sides of the International Bridge at Niagara Falls. The same number of lights, the same bridge, the same river and the same method of production; the only difference was the price: Ontario's Hydro Power charged only $8.43 per month for the Canadian half of the bridge, while the private U.S. corporation billed for $43.10.

The contrast became most relevant to the congressional debates when the Wilson Dam at Muscle Shoals began producing power in September 1925. Because Alabama Power Company owned the only transmission line from the dam, the War Department had no alternative but to sell the government's power to the private utility at the ridiculously low price of two-tenths of a cent per kilowatt-hour. The power company, meanwhile, sold that same electricity to residents of Florence, Alabama, within sight of the dam, for ten cents per kilowatt-hour, or 50 times the company's cost. Such a discrepancy in rates between private and public utilities was becoming a major political issue.

CONTROVERSY

By the mid-1920s, a new class of Democrats and Progressives began to focus increased attention on the power companies' political contributions, their attempts to bribe academics and their campaigns to mold public opinion. The Hearst newspapers fanned the flames by characterizing Insull as "the embodiment of avarice, the fat plutocrat of capitalism defiled, who had ruined the innocent and smeared the image of holy free enterprise."

In 1928, despite a massive lobbying effort by power companies, Congress voted to investigate the utility industry's political activity, propaganda and finances. Although concerned, the private companies ensured the research would be done by "professionals" at the Federal Trade Commission (FTC) rather than politicians in the Senate. Moreover, they were confident President Calvin Coolidge would appoint a conservative supporter of business to be general counsel. They had not expected Robert Healy.

A lanky Vermonter, Healy had been a lawyer for bankers and a member of the state's Supreme Court. He supported business development and expansion, but questioned the methods of the giant utility holding companies. Healy said he "sweated blood" for four years in the examination of the power trust's complex and shadowy accounting practices. His methods were undramatic; his findings, however, made front-page news.

The FTC's 486-page report carefully indicted the utilities for misuse of political power, outrageous self-promotion and unfair attacks on public power. The document's most hard-hitting criticism, however, was reserved for the power companies' efforts "to mold the thoughts and beliefs of the present and future generations in conformity with the utility interests."

The FTC's criticism of public relations and the Hearst papers' attacks on enormous political contributions began to turn the tide of public opinion against private utilities, allowing Norris to finally pass his bill to keep Muscle Shoals under public control. But Herbert Hoover's election in 1928 kept the White House firmly in the hands of private power supporters.

Hoover, known as "the Great Engineer," had long been a friend of utilities and often spoke at the National Electric Light Association's annual conventions. Before establishing a power bureau at the Department of Commerce, Hoover directed the Northeastern Super Power Committee, which cleared the way for private utilities throughout New England to interconnect their lines and pool their power. Like utility executives, he supported "strict regulation" but opposed public ownership.

Holding everyone's attention during the Hoover administration, of course, was the stock market crash and economic Depression. The President tried to reassure Americans by declaring, "The fundamental business of the country . . . is on a sound and prosperous basis." But he was wrong. Thousands of companies, farms and banks filed for bankruptcy and 11-million workers searched for jobs. Bread lines filled the cities; despair engulfed the country.

Recessions inevitably damage the party in power, and Hoover's Republican Party was no exception. In the 1930 congressional election, it lost control of the House of Representatives and its Senate majority fell to a single vote. Although the economy, the threat of war and social issues dominated the campaign, the Scripps-Howard newspapers declared that "never in recent years has there been such a strong expression on the subject of power." Candidate John Bankhead, for example, assailed Senator Tom Heflin as a friend of utility interests and defeated the fiery Alabama incumbent. Congressman B. Carroll Reese of Tennessee, the most outspoken opponent of public power, lost to a Republican utility critic. And Julius Meyer, an anti-utility independent, won Oregon's governorship over both regular party nominees.

Utility companies and Republicans embarrassed themselves by paying a grocery clerk, also named George W. Norris, to run against Senator Norris, and to hopefully confuse the balloting and counting of votes. But the tactic backfired and Senator Norris won a landslide victory.

Although the election results strengthened Norris's hand on Muscle Shoals, he still needed to gain Hoover's signature. In an attempt at compromise, Norris offered to resign from the Senate if Hoover would appoint him to a commission overseeing the Muscle Shoals project. Removing Norris from Congress must have been an attractive offer, but Hoover, ever the business supporter, could not accept public power. In March 1931, he vetoed Norris's bill with a vehement and pointed message. "I am firmly opposed," Hoover concluded, "to the government entering into business the major purpose of which is competition with our citizens."

Norris attacked the veto, labeling it cruel, unjust, unfair and unmerciful. Although the override vote in Congress received a majority, it did not obtain the necessary two-thirds. Norris and other public power advocates were forced to wait until the 1932 election.

FDR AND TVA

The American public, tired of all of Hoover's promises, welcomed Franklin D. Roosevelt's pledge to assist the Depression's victims. Even George Norris, a Republican, could no longer tolerate Hoover, whom he described as "always two-faced, always equivocal, except when he champions big business." Although the economy dominated the contest, the power trusts became a major election issue. Campaigning against the "Ishmaels and Insulls whose hand is against every man," Roosevelt claimed the nation was confronting a menace of "highly centralized industrial control." FDR went on to win 57 percent of the popular vote and a virtual sweep of the electoral college.

En route to his country cottage in Warm Springs, Georgia, immediately after the election, Roosevelt stopped at Muscle Shoals, where he talked with Norris about the Tennessee valley's plight. Poverty engulfed the region, recurrent floods had washed away valuable topsoil, and lumber companies had overcut the thin forests. Residents enjoyed only half the national average income, and only 2 percent of the farmers utilized electricity. The best promise for economic revitalization seemed to be the region's abundant hydroelectric sites.

A child of the progressive age, Franklin D. Roosevelt understood the importance of resource conservation and the potential for regional economic development. As governor of New York, FDR held "turkey cabinet" sessions in the executive mansion that convinced legislators to approve statewide public development of water power resources. In early April 1933, only one month after his inauguration as President, FDR sent a message to Congress that made Norris believe his dreams were answered. The proposed Tennessee Valley Authority (TVA) was to be "a corporation clothed with the power of Government but possessed with the flexibility and initiative of a private enterprise." The independent government body would bring to the entire river basin a comprehensive program of flood control, power development, navigation, reforestation, diversification of industry and soil revitalization. It would be, according to FDR, a cornerstone of his New Deal and "the widest experiment ever conducted by a Government."

FDR, adamant about passing TVA legislation, called congressional leaders to the White House to demand speedy action. A compromise bill gave Norris almost everything he wanted, including authority for TVA to construct its own transmission lines. A proud Norris, bedecked in his trademark bow tie, stood beside President Roosevelt on May 18, 1933, when the bill was signed. A 35-year legislative battle was over and a strengthened government, rather than discredited private power monopolies, controlled the nation's best hydroelectric sites.

Washington professionals know that a struggle is never over when a bill is signed. While Norris acclaimed TVA as "the greatest step toward freedom and greater happiness ever undertaken by this country," 19 utilities called it an "unconstitutional competitor with private businesses." Despite the continuing controversy, this grass-roots democratic experiment cleared the rivers, replenished the soil, rebuilt the forests, delivered electricity, and brought new life and hope to the depressed

Tennessee valley. Within weeks of TVA's creation, Director David Lilienthal announced that residential customers would pay only three cents per kilowatt-hour, half the rate charged by the region's private utilities.

The power struggle then went local, as political leaders in cities and rural communities fought to gain control of their electric utility. Cleveland mayor Tom Johnson, for instance, argued vigorously for public control: "Municipal ownership will work betterment in service, reduce the cost to the people and purify politics by extinguishing a power interest hostile to good government." For his efforts, Johnson was branded a "socialist" and targeted by the private utility for political attacks. But after a 12-year struggle, the fiery Populist convinced the city council to approve the construction of a $2 million municipal power station. With a great deal of pride, he also announced that the new public utility would cut rates approximately 75 percent. Cleveland remains one of the few U.S. cities where private and public power companies compete directly against each other, often with two different sets of utility wires running down each street.

In rural South Dakota, Virgil Hanlon created a public utility district to purchase power from private companies and redistribute it to farmers throughout the state. Unfortunately for Hanlon, the investor-owned utilities refused to cooperate. Not deterred, he formed the East River Electric Power Cooperative, gained federal loans and construction assistance, and built publicly owned dams in the Missouri River basin.

Norris, however, remained proudest of the dam named in his honor, built eight miles above where the Clinch River empties into the Tennessee. Stopping there on his final trip back to Nebraska after 40 years of congressional service, he remarked, "Much of what I had long dreamed has taken place."

REFORMING THE EMPIRES

When Franklin Roosevelt became President, urban Americans had powered their factories, lit their streets and run their appliances with electricity for more than a generation. It was hard to remember what life had been like without electric power. Rural Americans were less fortunate. As late as 1935, more than 85 percent of America's farms lacked electricity.

Change began on May 11, 1935, when FDR signed an executive order establishing a Rural Electrification Administration (REA) to provide low-interest loans to public cooperatives that would build their own power lines and generate their own electricity. The REA enabled farm organizations to purchase power at wholesale rates from either private plants or government dams and wheel it to their customers. Private utilities stalled Congress's endorsement of the executive order for a year. But within the next 18 months, rural co-ops brought electric power and some prosperity to half a million American farms. Farm wives, weary from scrubbing laundry by hand, brought coffee and doughnuts to work crews stringing line, and many wept when they could switch on a light and enjoy what city folks took for granted.

In addition to providing social relief, FDR sought to break up big business and restore competition to the economy. The President and his New Dealers created the Securities and Exchange Commission to monitor and prosecute deceit within the stock markets. A series of banking acts separated commercial banks from their investment banking affiliates, destroying Morgan's stranglehold on the American economy. (Ironically, the move also fulfilled Insull's dream of requiring competitive marketing of utility bonds.)

Perhaps the most controversial proposal sought the destruction of utility holding companies. As if waging a crusade, government leaders portrayed themselves as brave knights challenging a mighty and corrupt political power, while industrialists viewed their enemies as malicious destroyers of the widows and orphans who had invested in efficient power systems.

Bankers who had gained control of the holding companies during the Depression used the power industry's public relations machine to flood Congress with more mail and telegrams than was received on any other legislation. But elected officials, distrusting the utilities' propaganda, approved the Public Utilities Holding Company Act of 1935 (PUHCA), including a "death sentence" provision that forbade pyramiding and limited each holding company to a single integrated operating system. Utilities, however, were able to have eliminated those provisions that would have converted their grids into "common carriers" which must transmit the electricity generated by independent companies.

For years, utility executives challenged PUHCA with lawsuits and refusals to register before the Securities and Exchange Commission. Although all ultimately complied and reorganized their operations, several holding companies eventually received exemptions allowing them to own several utility systems.

The new breed of politicians also wanted Insull extradited from France, where he had fled after Middle West Utilities' collapse, for a publicized trial that would discredit the past age of rampant corporate expansion. Needing a "scapegoat for the sins of capitalism," they sought a Justice Department investigation and a grand jury indictment.

Insull stood virtually alone. Despite his 40-year leadership among utilities, he was abandoned by the industry that desperately sought to wrap itself in Thomas Edison's trusted image. General Electric, for example, quietly expunged Insull's name from its official company history. And the National Electric Light Association altered its name to read "Edison Electric Institute." One critic complained the industry had changed its clothes but forgot to take a bath.

Insull fled from Paris to Greece where the United States shared no extradition treaty. U.S. authorities tried every means to force Insull's return, including threats to prevent Greeks living in America from sending money to relatives in their old homeland. The Greek government finally capitulated and ordered Insull to leave the country, which he did on a chartered ship. Congress then approved a special bill authorizing Insull's seizure, which occurred in Istanbul's harbor, despite not having an extradition treaty with Turkey.

The former utility tycoon arrived at New York harbor in May 1934, 53 years after his first Atlantic journey. He read a statement prepared by his son and lawyers: "I have erred, but my greatest error was in understanding the effect of the financial panic on American securities and particularly on the companies I was working so hard to build. I worked with all my energy to save those companies. I made mistakes, but they were honest mistakes. They were errors in judgment, but not dishonest manipulation."

After a night in Chicago's jail, Insull spent the summer writing his memoirs and preparing for his trial on charges of mail fraud. Expanding on his dockside statement, he portrayed himself as an aged and infirm public benefactor who was being persecuted for his generation's sins. The jury believed him and after only two hours of deliberation declared all defendants innocent. (Jurors later admitted the decision was reached in less than five minutes, but they dawdled to avoid giving the impression they'd been bribed.)

Feeling vindicated, Insull moved to Paris, where he died in 1938. His passing closed the era of huge power trusts. He and the other empire builders were neither devilish businessmen nor financial geniuses. They had constructed efficient power facilities and modernized an essential American industry. But they also built a financial house of cards that initially brought great wealth to a few and eventually delivered financial ruin to thousands.

Despite the controversy surrounding utility executives, support for electricity development became almost universal by the late 1930s. On one end of the political spectrum, Socialist leader Norman Thomas declared electricity to be "the slave on which mankind must depend to conquer poverty." At the other extreme, Herbert Hoover explained that "mankind has never before grasped such a tool."

In their own ways, Edison, Insull, and Norris stimulated this support and ushered in the modern electric age. But each experienced frustration as well as success. Edison created the basic electrical devices, but he was hounded by lawsuits and corporate takeovers. Insull built the power industry's engineering and business structure, but his career ended in exile and disgrace. And Norris's victories for public power would not stop the advance of private utilities.

The three leaders disagreed about who should control this new necessity of life. In one opinion, however, they and almost all Americans were unanimous: Electricity's golden age lay ahead.

Thomas Edison, "the Wizard of Menlo Park," in his laboratory.
Photograph courtesy of Library of Congress

A replica of the first successful incandescent lamp, developed by Thomas Edison in October 1879.
Photograph courtesy of Edison Electric Institute

An early power plant in western New York.
Photograph courtesy of New York State Electric & Gas Corporation

The first central power station, built by Thomas Edison on Pearl Street in New York City in 1882.
Photograph courtesy of Con Edison

Brooklyn's emergency electric service crew, 1906.
Photograph courtesy of Con Edison

Samuel Insull, "the Empire Builder," controlled electric service in 6,000 communities in 32 states during the 1920s. Photograph courtesy of Samuel Insull, Jr.

In 1927, when this Chicago Tribune cartoon was drawn, Insull was at the pinnacle of success and power. Cartoon by McCutcheon, courtesy of Chicago Tribune

George Norris, a Republican senator from Nebraska, believed privately owned utility monopolies would "eventually come to tyranny" and that America's power development must "be under public control, public operation and public ownership." In the early 1930s, Norris joined President Franklin Roosevelt to create the Tennessee Valley Authority and the Rural Electrification Administration, bringing electric power to millions of poor and rural Americans.
Photograph courtesy of American Public Power Association

The Wilson Dam at Muscle Shoals in eastern Tennessee sparked three decades of controversy about whether the nation's waterways should be controlled by the government or private corporations. In the 1930s, it finally became part of the Tennessee Valley Authority, a public agency that brought electric power and economic development to an impoverished region.
Photograph courtesy of Tennessee Valley Authority

David Lilienthal was director of the Tennessee Valley Authority and first chairman of the Atomic Energy Commission. About the atom he wrote: "No fairy tale that I had read in utter rapture and enchantment as a child, no spy mystery, no horror story, can remotely compare."
Photograph courtesy of American Public Power Association

Admiral Hyman Rickover was father of the nuclear navy and the dominating force in the nuclear power industry throughout the 1950s and 1960s.
Photograph courtesy of American Public Power Association

An aerial view of the Shippingport Atomic Power Station, the first commercial nuclear reactor. Designed by Admiral Rickover in 1954, the plant is located along the Ohio River near Pittsburgh.
Photograph courtesy of Edison Electric Institute

Aunt Eve has found a new friend. Mr. Atom.

Mr. Atomic Electric Power, to be formal about it. And he's one of the most promising fellows to come on the energy scene since Aunt Eve was a girl in pigtails. For the atom is the newest of the fuels used for producing electricity.

Already, in areas where it's economical, Mr. Atom is helping Aunt Eve—and a lot of other ladies—do their housework, cook their meals, enjoy the pleasures of electric living. And surely he'll be doing more and more of the hard and heavy work as time goes on, and atomic fuel becomes more economical to use in more sections of the country.

America's investor-owned electric light and power companies are now working on 25 projects which will help atomic electric power do its stuff. It's a $1,000,000,000 program!

And this billion-dollar program is just one part of the investor-owned companies' constant search for new and better ways to go on bringing people the benefits of electric life, for work, for play, for whatever good things there are to do.

Investor-Owned Electric Light and Power Companies*
People you can depend on to power America's progress
*Names of sponsoring companies available through this magazine

One of the many pronuclear advertisements placed by private power companies throughout the 1960s. Nuclear electricity, promised some promoters, was soon to become "too cheap to meter."
Photograph courtesy of National Rural Electric Cooperative Association

In 1965, utilities promoted their vision of an electrified future.

Photograph courtesy of National Rural Electric Cooperative Association

Edwin Vennard, leader of the utility industry throughout its golden age in the 1950s and 1960s, was a master of public relations and advertising. He encouraged consumers to use more electricity and to oppose public or government-owned power systems.

Photograph courtesy of Edison Electric Institute

A 1958 advertisement equates prosperity with electricity use. Utilities were also subsidizing the construction of all-electric "Gold Medallion Homes."

Photograph courtesy of Environmental Action Foundation

Elderly couple turned back into East Berlin by communist guards at Berlin wall.

FREEDOM IS NOT LOST
BY GUNS ALONE

The greatest threats to personal freedom may come from guns and terror outside our borders. But there's also a quiet threat within. It is the steady expansion of federal government in business—and into our daily lives.

For 30 years this threat has grown. Today the federal government owns many thousand businesses, from shoe repair shops to rope factories. In the field of electricity alone the output of federally owned plants has risen from less than 1% of the industry's total in 1935 to more than 15% today. And advocates of government-in-business press constantly for more.

They advocate a dangerous course. When government owns business, it can control both goods and jobs. It adds economic powers to its vast political powers. When it does that, it can tell you where to work and live, even what to do or say. Then freedom has slipped quietly away.

A quiet threat can be the deadliest. You may not know it's there until too late.

Investor-Owned Electric Light and Power Companies . . . *serving more than 140,000,000 people across the nation*
Sponsors' names on request through this magazine

An early-1960s advertisement by private utilities compares the Tennessee Valley Authority and public power to the Berlin Wall and the East Berlin police.

Photograph courtesy of National Rural Electric Cooperative Association

The utility industry's golden age was shattered on "Black Tuesday," November 9, 1965, when more than 30-million northeasterners, including New Yorkers, lost electric power because faulty switches near Niagara Falls failed to curb a cascade of power. Hollywood dramatized the experience with Doris Day's comedy, Where Were You When the Lights Went Out?
Photograph courtesy of Wide World Photo

Air pollution over Chicago in 1970. Citizen protests forced utilities to install pollution-control devices on their coal-burning power plants.
Photograph courtesy of United Nations

The Three Mile Island nuclear reactor near Harrisburg, Pennsylvania, suffered the worst nuclear accident in history on March 28, 1979, when coolant was lost and its radioactive fuel overheated.
Photograph courtesy of Nuclear Regulatory Commission

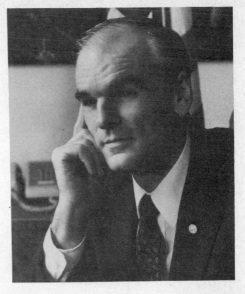

Donald Hodel, former energy secretary for the Reagan administration, directed the Bonneville Power Administration during the mid-1970s. Arguing that the demand for electricity would grow and that nuclear power was the least expensive option, Hodel encouraged the Washington Public Power Supply System (WPPSS) to build a series of reactors.
Photograph courtesy of U.S. Department of Energy

WPPSS Unit #4, in foreground, has been canceled and placed on the auction block. Construction cost overruns and a declining demand for electricity led to a $2.25 billion default, the nation's largest.
Photograph courtesy of WPPSS

Wilfred Uhl was president of Long Island Lighting Company (LILCO) during the construction of the Shoreham nuclear power plant. Cost estimates soared from $261 million to $4.1 billion. Uhl has retired and LILCO now teeters near bankruptcy.
Photograph by Jim Peppler for Newsday

Guy Nichols diversified New England Electric System's holdings and concentrated on conservation rather than construction. Nichols retired with praise from consumers for keeping rates steady and from investors for keeping the utility's stock price high.
Photograph courtesy of Energy Daily

John Bryson has seen all sides of the utility industry, as critic, regulator and executive. As Southern California Edison's senior vice-president, Bryson represents a new generation of utility executives committed to innovation and efficiency.
Photograph courtesy of Southern California Edison

Jan Hamrin, executive director of Independent Energy Producers in Sacramento, California, represents electric entrepreneurs before utility commissions and state legislatures.
Photograph by Deborah Goldstein

Joe Kennedy directs Citizens Energy Corporation of Boston, which provides low-cost fuel oil to poor people and energy conservation services for hospitals and other institutions.
Photograph courtesy of Citizens Energy Corporation

Roger Sant manages Applied Energy Services of Arlington, Virginia. The former energy official in President Gerald Ford's administration now builds, operates and owns cogeneration facilities that supply both heat and electricity.
Photograph courtesy of Applied Energy Services

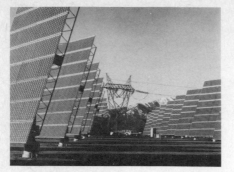

A one-megawatt photovoltaic power plant, which converts sunlight directly into electricity, was dedicated in February 1983 in Hesperia, California. Arco Solar owns the facility and sells electricity to Southern California Edison.
Photograph courtesy of Southern California Edison

A few of the 2,500 wind-energy machines that lined Altamont Pass in northern California in late 1984. These wind farms, owned by independent power producers, sell electricity to utilities. Each machine in the foreground, developed by U.S. Windpower, produces 100 kilowatts of electricity, enough to supply a mid-sized apartment building or commercial complex.
Photograph by Ed Linton

The cogeneration facility at the Great Western Malting Company in Vancouver, Washington, supplies the heat needed to dry and roast malted barley and enough electricity to heat and light 8,000 homes. The electricity is purchased from Great Western by the local utility.
Photograph courtesy of General Electric

In 1980, more than 15-million Americans weather-stripped or caulked their homes. Another 6 million added insulation. The typical new U.S. home in 1985 uses about half the energy of the 1975 prototype, and many more low-cost efficiency options still exist.
Photograph courtesy of Solar Lobby

A new industry of energy service companies guarantees savings to businesses by installing and monitoring efficient lights, boilers and other appliances. Computers at the headquarters of Time Energy Systems in Houston monitor more than 700 buildings throughout the country.
Photograph courtesy of Time Energy

102

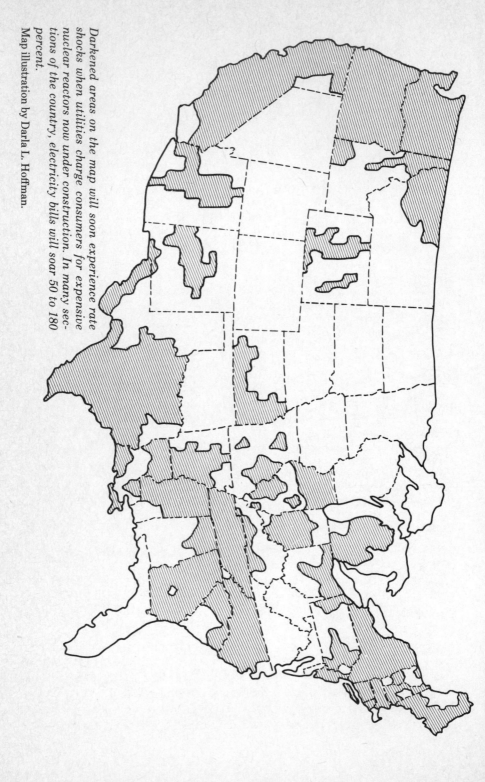

Darkened areas on the map will soon experience rate shocks when utilities charge consumers for expensive nuclear reactors now under construction. In many sections of the country, electricity bills will soar 50 to 180 percent.

Map illustration by Darla L. Hoffman.

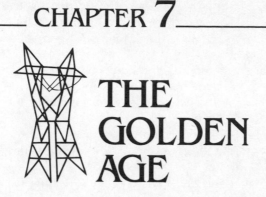

CHAPTER 7

THE GOLDEN AGE

A hit movie in the 1950s, *The Day the Earth Stood Still*, dramatizes America's post-war dependence on electricity. A man from another planet warns humans to live together in peace or suffer his destruction of the world. At the urging of a scientist from Earth, the alien demonstrates his power by shutting off all electricity for half an hour. The effect is clear—the world very nearly stands still.

Electricity had transformed America. Consumers could no longer imagine living without radios, vacuum cleaners and sewing machines, symbols of prosperity that lightened their daily burdens. Electric lights lengthened days and directed traffic. Air conditioners made it possible to seal building windows in favor of electrically powered temperature controls. Refrigerators broadened a family's food options, allowing New Yorkers to enjoy California oranges in the winter, and they decreased diseases by retarding food spoilage. Electric-powered irrigation opened more land for cultivation.

Electricity moved our world faster and filled it with abundance. Automated assembly lines curtailed dangerous and menial jobs, giving us that most precious gift—time. Electricity also multiplied the number of products available, while television urged us to buy them.

Engineers dreamed of electrifying almost every function imaginable. Automobiles would soon be plugged into an outlet in the garage for their nightly recharging. Giant glass bubbles would enclose urban areas, allowing electric filters and air conditioners to maintain constant temperatures. Futurists foresaw people rarely using their muscles since modern appliances would perform most tasks, including compacting the trash

103

and brushing teeth. *Popular Mechanics* predicted "a power plant the size of a typewriter" would allow families to enjoy low-cost, limitless power. The future, optimists proclaimed, offered "universal comfort, practically free transportation and unlimited supplies of materials."

Utilities, of course, fanned these visions of an electrified future. Electric lamps had virtually saturated the market and most labor-saving devices, such as washing machines, consumed little power. Popular radios used even less. To grow and prosper, the Edison Electric Institute declared that "electric cooking and water heating must be vigorously pushed." And pushed they were. Power companies spent millions of dollars convincing consumers they would "live better electrically."

Targeting the residential market, utilities packaged electric appliances into a "Gold Medallion Home," which their sales machine labeled a badge of prosperity. Outright payoffs supplemented advertising, with some builders receiving $1,000 to construct all-electric homes. For commercial buildings, power companies paid even more. Commonwealth Edison, for instance, gave the developer of Chicago's John Hancock Center $1.5 million to go all-electric, doubling the gas company's offer. Electric companies also aggressively encouraged farmers to adopt electric-powered irrigation.

Although advertising and payoffs helped, utilities possessed a reliable and reasonably priced commodity that sold itself. Technical improvements in generators and transmission lines enabled the price of electricity to fall steadily. Arguing that a big power station was cheaper to build and supply with fuel than a series of small generators with the same capacity, utility engineers increased the average plant size sevenfold from 1945 to 1965. Thus, power companies could build more and larger equipment to meet a growing demand for electricity—and still be able to lower their rates.

The cost of electricity, in fact, dropped steadily until the late 1960s. According to David Morris of the Institute for Local Self-Reliance, a nonprofit research group located in Washington, D.C., "Given the devaluation of money in that period and the rise in the average worker's wages, it follows that the average factory worker in 1915 would have had to work for 20 minutes to light a light bulb all day, while his 1968 counterpart would have had to work 4 minutes."

State regulatory commissions, perhaps inadvertently, also encouraged expansion. To guarantee power companies a fair return on their investments, regulators approved rates sufficient to pay for operating expenses, all construction costs associated with power plants and other equipment, and a percentage profit on these fixed investments comparable to the profits earned by competitive businesses with similar risks. The size of a utility's profits, in short, rose with the size of its investments. Protected by regulators from failure and competition, power companies possessed a built-in motive to expand and adopt expensive technologies.

Until about 1965, these incentives proved to be economical and efficient.

In the two decades after World War II, electric power usage expanded at a compound annual rate of 7.8 percent, doubling every ten years. The vigorous and predictable rise allowed utility executives to accurately plan for the future, while technical improvements assured lower prices and higher profits. It was truly a golden age for electric companies.

PRIVATE POWER ENDURES

By the early 1940s, private utilities appeared battered. George Norris and Franklin Roosevelt successfully pushed several bills designed to cripple the power trusts. They defeated Alabama Power's initiatives and built public dams at Muscle Shoals and throughout the Tennessee valley. They gave preference for inexpensive federal power to municipalities and public cooperatives. And they broke up Insull's Middle West Utilities and the other utility holding companies.

As Norris and FDR wracked up legislative victories, public power gained ground in several major cities. In late 1936, Los Angeles's Bureau of Power & Light paid $46 million for the private Los Angeles Gas and Electric Company, preventing the investor-owned Southern California Edison Company from monopolizing the entire Southland. A few years later, Memphis residents voted 17 to 1 for public power.

Political controversies continued to dog the private utilities. They were accused of bribing local officials, blocking federal power projects, conniving to fix high prices, and preventing the sale of federal power to public systems. A 1955 Senate investigation discovered "fairly consistent abuse of the monopoly position which private utilities enjoy." As a result, opinion surveys revealed strong popular support for government-produced power; 63 percent of those polled favored replicating the Tennessee Valley Authority's (TVA) model in other areas of the country.

Private companies also faced stiff price competition from public firms. David Lilienthal, for example, cut TVA's rates to half that charged by Alabama Power. And, as mentioned earlier, Cleveland mayor Tom Johnson introduced the new municipal utility by slashing prices 75 percent under the rates levied by Cleveland Electric Illuminating, the city's private power company.

Despite these barriers and attacks, investor-owned utilities (IOUs), as private utilities were now called, maintained dominance within the electricity industry. The percentage of power supplied by municipalities increased from 7 percent in 1939 to only 9 percent in 1984. While the contribution from federal power projects rose to 10 percent of the nation's capacity, the output from self-generating industries fell. Thus, although some of the investor-owned conglomerates were destroyed, private firms maintained control of 75 percent of the nation's generating capacity and serviced approximately the same percentage of ultimate electricity customers.

How did IOUs achieve this remarkable victory? A variety of factors came into play. Cold war fervor, for one, stimulated values associated with entrepreneurs and capitalists. Swept up in contests against the Soviets, Americans embraced alternatives to socialism and equated patriotism with private businesses.

General Dwight Eisenhower's presidential election in 1952 symbolized the resurgence of conservatism and furthered the private utilities' interests. TVA, according to the new President, was an example of "creeping socialism." Republican members of Congress went so far as to try to remove from the Norris and other public dams the inscription, Built for the People of the United States. They feared the wording would encourage favorable attitudes toward public ownership.

Eisenhower translated his probusiness attitudes into valuable leases of hydroelectric resources for private utilities. He gave the Idaho Power Company, for example, three dam sites at the Snake River's Hell Canyon, an area President Truman had reserved for public development. When dedicating the McNary Dam on the Columbia River, Eisenhower expressed his opinion of additional public power projects: "The federal government should no more attempt to [supply all the power needs of our people] than it would assume responsibility for supplying all their drinking water, their food, their housing and their transportation."

Although regulated utilities avoided the free enterprise system, they wrapped themselves in the American flag and branded their public power opponents Communists, Socialists, or worse. They effectively played to the conservative tide.

The genius of the private utility's public relations campaign was Edwin Vennard. When only 26 years old, the distinguished-looking engineer became general manager of the Southwestern Gas and Electric Company. Five years later, he joined Insull's holding company as a vice-president and would later lead the conglomerate through bankruptcy and divestiture procedures. Vennard revealed his most memorable talents, however, through the Electric Companies Advertising Program and the Edison Electric Institute, which he directed from 1956 to 1969. An indefatigable patriot and business booster, Vennard perfected the role of private utilities' chief promoter.

On behalf of the "business-managed, tax-paying" utilities, Vennard regularly published advertisements arguing that "tax money shouldn't be spent on socialistic federal power projects that this country neither wants nor needs." One red-baiting announcement in the October 1951 issue of the *Saturday Evening Post* pictures a proud father with his arms around his two children, the clean-cut daughter looking up admiringly at her brother in an army uniform. The father is quoted to say, "Sure, I used to think it wouldn't do any harm to have the government run the electric business. But I've changed my mind. Because when government meddles too much in any business, you get socialism. And who'd want to leave a socialistic U.S.A. to his kids?"

A scientist more than a huckster, Vennard understood the potential to monitor and mold public opinion. At a time when polling was virtually unknown, Vennard tapped George Gallup to discover what Americans felt about public power. (Gallup had gained some fame by accurately predicting the extent of FDR's massive victory over Alfred M. Landon in 1936.) Using survey data, the two experts designed magazine ads to heighten the public's distrust of municipal utilities and federal power projects. The campaign's effect on public opinion was extraordinary: Support for public power plunged from 70 percent to only 30 percent after placement of 40 advertisements.

Mindful of the importance of phrases and labels, Gallup discovered that the public preferred the concept of an "investor-owned" company rather than a "privately owned" firm. Likewise, the public disliked the sound of "government-owned" utilities more than "public power." Vennard, therefore, pushed his private utility colleagues to call their firms "investor-owned" and their opponents "government-owned." He even fined company officials who forgot the name changes. (Today, some investor-owned power companies try to portray themselves as the real "public utilities," noting that their stocks are traded in open securities markets.)

Vennard also possessed a "go-for-the-jugular" approach to debates. A particularly hard-hitting advertisement, appearing in the early 1960s, pictures armed guards stopping an old couple from crossing the Berlin Wall to freedom. The headline reads: "Freedom Is Not Lost by Guns Alone," and the text associates communist takeovers with public power: "When government owns business, it can control both goods and jobs. It adds economic power to its vast political power. . . . Then freedom has slipped quietly away. A quiet threat can be the deadliest. You may not know it's there until too late."

IOUs also used their equipment to block competitors. Because only large utilities could afford large power plants, they alone enjoyed the economies of scale. Small private and municipal firms were forced to abandon their more expensive small generators and to buy power from their giant neighbors. Municipalities' self-generation dropped from almost 50 percent in 1935 to only 10 percent in 1975. At the same time, more and more industrialists abandoned their on-site cogenerators for the utility's inexpensive and reliable power.

Private utilities also effectively employed their transmission lines to force public systems to buy their power. According to 7 Illinois cities

Illinois Power Company so restricted the supply of wholesale power that the towns had to purchase all their electricity from the utility. And 12 Michigan towns accused Consumers Power Company of refusing to offer power-supply coordination and transmission service.

Regional power pools further concentrated control in the hands of private utilities and stifled efforts for decentralization. The first contract to share electricity among investor-owned companies was signed in 1927 by Public Service Electricity and Gas Company of New Jersey and Philadelphia Electric Company. By the late 1960s, 17 regional pools represented 50 percent of the nation's electric capacity.

Most of today's top utility executives apprenticed during this golden era, a satisfying if not very challenging time to be in the power industry. A steady growth rate made long-range planning easy; engineering improvements allowed both expansion and lower costs; consumers remained relatively satisfied; and environmentalism was not yet a major national issue.

Today's $400 billion dollar electric industry is a monument to the faith of these executives in growth and expansion. U.S. utilities became the world's most sophisticated deliverer of power and the nation's largest business in terms of assets. Its size is remarkable considering Thomas Edison built the first power plant, the tiny Pearl Street Station, only a little over a century ago.

The industry's stability, however, produced a handicap: The brightest business and engineering students, seeking adventure and dynamic opportunities, avoided regulated utilities. Power companies became dominated by the cautious and the conservative, executives who were ill-prepared for the challenges of the atomic revolution and the industry's shattered momentum.

CONTROLLING THE ATOM

Like falling water in the 1930s, the atom promised an enormous supply of inexpensive energy. Visionaries boldly imagined splitting nature's basic building block to run factories, heat homes, desalinate seawater, irrigate deserts and launch space shuttles. Because only a pound of enriched uranium fuel could produce as much electricity as 1,500 tons of coal, the new resource seemed limitless. And unlike dirty coal-fired plants, atomic power offered less air pollution. The nuclear reactor was to be the golden era's crowning symbol.

The struggle to control this power source—which would involve many of this century's greatest scientists, military men and business leaders—begins at a squash court under the University of Chicago's football stadium, a site now marked by a Henry Moore sculpture that combines the images of a mushroom cloud and a human skull. Until December 3, 1942, Albert Einstein's prediction that large atoms of uranium could be broken apart to release tremendous energy remained only a theory. But on that day a few miles south of downtown Chicago, Enrico Fermi, an Italian-born physicist, placed a "pile" of graphite block, in which uranium was embedded, into a rudimentary oven. At 3:25 P.M., he and other scientists removed the main control rod and began monitoring sensitive instruments measuring the pile's temperature. Exactly as Einstein and Fermi had predicted, elements of uranium produced a self-sustaining destruction of the atoms. Fermi allowed the nuclear chain reaction to run only 28 minutes and to produce only a few watts of heat. But the physicists celebrated with a bottle of Chianti, wrote a coded message to the War Department and dreamed of the atom's great potential.

This message, "The Italian Navigator has landed in the New World," convinced President Franklin Roosevelt to sponsor a $2 billion secret operation, known as the Manhattan Project, to build an atomic bomb, considered the ultimate weapon to end World War II. Led by J. Robert Oppenheimer, a brilliant team of American, British and Canadian physicists and engineers tackled the complex scientific and technical problems involved in the weapon's production. To conduct their research, they built new and isolated "cities" at Hanford, Washington, near the Columbia River; at Oak Ridge, Tennessee, near the the Norris Dam on the Clinch River; and at Los Alamos, on a mesa in northern New Mexico. The project was so secret that even TVA director David Lilienthal, living within view of the Oak Ridge Laboratory, had no idea why the scientists needed unlimited access to TVA's power.

Three years of research on nuclear reactions, bomb assemblies and detonators culminated in a test on July 16, 1945, at a desert area within the Alamogordo bombing range in New Mexico. An experimental plutonium bomb sat atop a 100-foot metal tower, while scientists and military men filled observation dugouts six miles away. At precisely 5:29:45 that morning, a blinding flash pierced the desert darkness from the top of the tower. Within a fraction of a second, a fireball vaporized the tower and turned the desert sand into glass. Several seconds later the scientists felt the shock waves and saw the rising mushroom cloud. Enrico Fermi, ever ready with his slide rule, measured how far pieces of paper were blown by the shock wave and calculated the blast to be equivalent to 10,000 tons of TNT. The scholarly Oppenheimer sighed with relief at his team's success, but recalled the prophetic words of the Bhagavad Gita, the sacred Hindu text: "If the radiance of a thousand suns were to burst at once into the sky, that would be like the splendor of the mighty one. . . . I am become death, the shatterer of worlds."

Now that the atom bomb had been demonstrated, what should be done with it? Many of the immigrant physicists from Europe were

motivated to build the weapon before Hitler did. But within months of
the Alamogordo test, Nazi Germany's defeat seemed imminent. The war
with Japan, however, still raged, and military leaders felt a timely
bombing would speed an Allied victory. When Franklin Roosevelt died
on April 12, the decision on the atom's future passed to Harry Truman,
who until then had known almost nothing of the secret Manhattan
Project.

Scientists at the University of Chicago led the opposition to America's bombing of Japan, arguing that killing thousands of civilians would
brand Americans as barbaric and destroy the post-war effort to gain
international control of the atom. Led by Nobel laureate James Franck,
several scientists tried to meet with Truman; Einstein even wrote a letter,
but the new President passed the buck to a committee chaired by
Secretary of War Henry L. Stimson. Virtually ignoring Franck's suggestion to frighten the Japanese by demonstrating the bomb's power on an
uninhabited island, Stimson decided "we could not give the Japanese any
warning, and . . . that we should seek to make a profound psychological
impression on as many of the inhabitants as possible."

"Little Boy" exploded over Hiroshima on August 6, 1945, killing
78,000 people. Three days later "Fat Man" burst over Nagasaki, killing
50,000. Thousands more would die over the next several decades from
cancer caused by the bombs' radioactivity.

The post-war era was a heady time for Americans. Showing little
remorse over the bombs' destruction, military men boasted of their
victories, scientists bragged of their technological achievements, and
politicians predicted U.S. dominance of international affairs. The atom,
promising unlimited strength and energy, sparked visions of a glorious
future. Only two weeks after Hiroshima's bombing, *Newsweek* reported
that "even the most conservative scientists and industrialists were
willing to outline a civilization which would make the comic-strip
prophecies of Buck Rogers look obsolete."

The atom enthralled David Lilienthal, who wrote in his diary: "No
fairy tale that I had read in utter rapture and enchantment as a child, no
spy mystery, no horror story, can remotely compare." Appointed to
establish nuclear priorities, the thoughtful and articulate TVA director
quickly wrestled with the ancient question about energy sources: who
should control? U.S. military leaders, believing communist Russia had
replaced Nazi Germany as the national enemy, demanded more and
bigger bombs. Diplomats, fearing nuclear proliferation, sought to control
U.S. atomic secrets. And industrialists, dreaming of huge profits in a new
industry, pressed for commercial development of nuclear power. Congress's Atomic Energy Act of 1946 temporarily settled the conflicting
claims by creating an Atomic Energy Commission (AEC) to "conserve
and restrict the use of atomic energy for the national defense, to prohibit

its private exploitation, and to preserve the secret and confidential character of information concerning the use and application of atomic energy."

As the AEC's first chairman, Lilienthal may have dreamed of the atom's promise, but the lawyer returned to reality after examining the nuclear program. After the war, top scientists had left the Manhattan Project for university positions. Reactors built during the war were falling apart. Even the U.S. supply of uranium from the Belgian Congo was almost depleted. And to Lilienthal's shock, no nuclear weapons were stockpiled for immediate use in case of war.

Prospects for nuclear-generated electricity also disappointed the AEC. According to Oppenheimer, enormous technical and economic problems blocked the development of viable reactors. His July 1947 draft report bluntly denounced the popular visions of an atomic paradise: "It does not appear hopeful to use natural uranium directly as an adequate source of fuel for atomic power." Scientists at the AEC gave only token attention to reactor development, preferring to test bigger bombs at the Bikini atoll in the South Pacific's Marshall Islands.

Confident of their technical superiority and ability to maintain the atom's secrets, American scientists and policymakers were shocked when Truman announced on September 22, 1949, "We have evidence that within recent weeks an atomic explosion occurred in the U.S.S.R." The Russians had broken the atomic monopoly, heightening cold war hysteria. Lilienthal, unable to retard the arms race, left the AEC before Truman ordered the construction of a hydrogen bomb, a weapon many times more fearful than "Little Boy" or "Fat Man."

U.S. officials quickly sought strengthened relations among their European allies in order to retard the Soviet enemy. In 1951, Congress amended the original Atomic Energy Act to allow the sharing of certain nuclear information with members of the newly established North Atlantic Treaty Organization (NATO). Although the amendment's objective was military strength, industrialists questioned why foreign countries, but not U.S. companies, should receive atomic secrets.

The 1952 election inaugurated a new era in power politics. While Truman had considered nuclear energy "too important a development to be made the subject of profit-seeking," business-oriented President Eisenhower wanted nuclear power commercialized. State Department officials argued that the industrial atom, which Russia and Britain were developing, could be parlayed into real foreign policy gains around the world. The AEC, under the direction of investment banker Lewis Strauss, promoted civilian nuclear programs as its top priority and tried to encourage cautious utility executives to adopt an unproven technology. At hearings before the congressional Joint Committee on Atomic Energy, AEC scientists testified that the government was "vitally interested" in nuclear power "because our potential in military nuclear explosives and, ultimately, in general economic strength, would be greatly increased if we had a large-scale economic central nuclear power industry."

Eisenhower expanded the concept of nuclear commercialism in his famous "Atoms for Peace" speech before the United Nations General Assembly on December 8, 1953. After reviewing the bomb's terrible destructiveness, he pledged the United States would seek ways "by which the miraculous inventiveness of man shall not be dedicated to his death, but consecrated to his life." Moreover, Eisenhower redefined the purpose of atomic energy: "It is not enough to take this weapon out of the hands of the soldiers. It must be put into the hands of those who will know how to strip its military casing and adapt it to the art of peace." His promise of bringing energy to the power-starved world was translated into ten languages and delivered to thousands of newspapers and public officials around the world.

Eisenhower's public relations coup rekindled congressional amendments to "unleash the genius and enterprise of American business." Leading Democrats viewed the proposal as a "giveaway" to utility monopolies who would stifle nuclear development and overcharge for nuclear electricity. The better alternative, they claimed as if echoing George Norris's arguments, was for the AEC to construct and operate the reactors. But business leaders carried the day: The 1954 Atomic Energy Act encouraged private corporations to build and own reactors, to conduct nuclear research and to use uranium fuels.

THE ADMIRAL

Hyman George Rickover was an unlikely admiral. The son of a Polish-Jewish tailor, he struggled in the heart of the U.S. Navy, dominated by white Anglo-Saxon Protestants. A competent engineer with a master's degree from Columbia University, he received bad marks for military protocol at the U.S. Naval Academy. A qualified submariner, Rickover chose to avoid a ship command, the normal route for navy promotions, to focus on atomic engineering. He was supported less by his naval superiors than by congressional backers of a strong nuclear program, particularly Senator Henry Jackson of Washington.

The short, slender Rickover was also an unlikely father of the U.S. nuclear power industry. But throughout the 1950s and 1960s, the admiral maneuvered within the Washington bureaucracy to become one of the most powerful government officials and an architect of industrial policy.

Although excluded from the army's Manhattan Project, navy officers dreamed of nuclear-powered submarines. World War II vessels were notoriously slow and awkward, needing to surface frequently to recharge their batteries with diesel engines. Atomic submarines, Rickover maintained, would make the navy a viable independent fighting force.

In June 1946, only a few months after the war, the AEC invited Rickover to the Manhattan Project's Oak Ridge Laboratory, where he stayed for several months absorbing technical information. The hardnosed engineer, rejecting the common euphoria of the atom's magic, understood the practical difficulties of building a shipboard reactor. But the promoter within Rickover rode the nuclear bandwagon to a position as chief of AEC's Navy Reactors Branch, where he organized an elite team of engineers to plan and monitor the nuclear navy. By controlling lucrative government contracts, he also dominated commercial nuclear development.

An organized perfectionist, the admiral demanded strict oversight of all nuclear power operations. His representatives, monitoring the work by subcontractors and universities, sent daily progress reports. Every afternoon his secretaries delivered a pink carbon copy of everything they typed for his staff; in the morning, Rickover returned the "pinks" to his assistants with comments and corrections.

After seven years of frenzied work, Rickover delivered the world's first nuclear submarine on January 17, 1955, only 16 days behind schedule. Named after Jules Verne's fantasy ship, the *Nautilus* broke all navy records by traveling 1,300 miles under water, ten times farther than any previous submarine.

Despite Rickover's success with nuclear ships, the congressional Joint Committee on Atomic Energy and some businesses grew impatient with the AEC's slow progress in developing commercial reactors. To assure continued funding and acceptance by nervous power company officials, AEC officials knew they had to quickly demonstrate a reactor that would supply electricity to a utility grid. Cost and technological breakthroughs were less important than building something that worked. Since Rickover had demonstrated a reliable design, his "light water" reactor was chosen for an AEC-supported joint project between Westinghouse and the Duquesne Light Company of Pittsburgh.

Work began with an elaborate ceremony that would have pleased a public relations connoisseur like Sam Insull. In September 1954, President Eisenhower, delivering a speech in Colorado, waved a "magic wand" over an electronic remote-control device that started the first bulldozer at the Shippingport construction site along the Ohio River, almost 1,500 miles away. The media broadcast the event across the country, fueling the expectation that nuclear energy would soon be "too cheap to meter."

THE PRODDING

Despite public enthusiasm for nuclear power, conservative utility executives remained skeptical of the unproven technology. Their fears were logical: Reactor construction costs were much higher than those for coal-fired stations; nuclear plant reliability was unknown; supplies of uranium fuel were not assured; and atomic safety risks were potentially great. Noting nuclear power's many practical problems, *Business Week* lamented, "You can find a great many more buyers for the Brooklyn Bridge than businessmen interested in doing something about atomic power."

To overcome this cautiousness, the AEC launched a Power Reactor Demonstration Program in January 1955 that would provide data on nuclear costs and engineering problems. The government also promised free nuclear fuel and research grants to utilities and equipment manufacturers. But most power company executives continued to view nuclear power as a subsidized, but nevertheless expensive, sideshow. And although the AEC's official pronouncements remained rosy, government officials privately admitted reactors could be 60 percent more expensive than conventional power stations.

Utility executives also worried about their liability with a reactor, especially because nuclear power's first product was a bomb of enormous destructive force. Although scientists declared that the diffuse uranium within a power reactor would not explode, company officials feared mishaps or sabotage could cause the "China Syndrome," a euphemism for the melting of the reactor's overheated uranium fuel through the plant's basement into the ground in the direction of the Orient. Without vital cooling liquids, the power plant could release deadly radioactivity into the atmosphere or groundwater. Charles Weaver, a Westinghouse vice-president, described the industry's nervousness: "We cannot exclude the possibility that a great enough fool aided by a great enough conspiracy of circumstances could bring about an accident exceeding available insurance."

Trying to assuage these fears, the AEC asked researchers at the government's Brookhaven National Laboratory to calculate the statistical probability of a nuclear power accident and the possible damages from such an occurrence. The long-awaited report described at length why a nuclear accident was highly unlikely. Still, the lab's analysis of a "worst case" accident startled even atomic power promoters. Immediately, 3,400 people would die. Forty-three thousand more would be injured. Property damage would extend over 150,000 square miles and total $7 billion. Although the odds against such an accident were high, insurance companies and utilities refused to accept the gamble.

Nuclear advocates, therefore, turned to the federal government. In 1957, Congressman Melvin Price and Senator Clinton Anderson, members of the congressional Joint Committee on Atomic Energy, successfully pushed a measure that absolved utilities of most liability, irrespective of any carelessness or recklessness on their part that might have caused an accident, and provided a $560 million fund to cover any damages. Senator Anderson later admitted $560 million was an arbitrary figure, high enough to provide confidence to potential victims but not so large as to "frighten the country and the Congress to death."

In the rush to promote commercial nuclear development, the government also eliminated regulatory burdens that might slow a power plant's licensing. It became increasingly clear that the AEC and the Joint Committee on Atomic Energy preferred promoting nuclear power to regulating it. Officials who questioned safety procedures were decried for standing in the way of the government's effort to bring "kilowatts to the people." Consider the Enrico Fermi reactor. Unlike the first reactor at Shippingport, the southeast Michigan plant used highly concentrated plutonium fuel that actually could explode. Engineers at the AEC's Advisory Committee on Reactor Safeguards examined the reactor's blueprints and concluded that "there is insufficient information available at this time to give assurance the reactor can be operated at this site without public hazard." AEC commissioners, ignoring this admonition from what they disparagingly called the "Brake Department," issued the license in 1956 and kept the committee's recommendation secret. (Only after the Fermi reactor suffered a major accident in 1963 was the warning revealed to the public.)

Because domestic utilities rejected the nuclear option, President Eisenhower subsidized an international market for nuclear equipment as part of his Atoms for Peace program. The United States, for example, offered $475 million to Euratom, a consortium of European countries, for the construction of 1,000 megawatts of nuclear capacity. Such bilateral agreements required friendly countries to purchase supplies from U.S. companies (such as Westinghouse and General Electric) and to rely solely on U.S. fuel and enrichment facilities. The deal had U.S. taxpayers providing Europeans with reactors and American equipment manufacturers gaining precious experience and revenue.

By 1962, the AEC admitted spending nearly $1.3 billion on research and development for nuclear power plants, more than twice the investments made by private companies. The government figure, however, understates the total subsidy by excluding funds used in both weapons and power production, such as uranium mining and enrichment services.

Most utilities remained unwilling to gamble on nuclear reactors, despite government benefits and insurance coverage. Equipment manufacturers, realizing they could expect no further grants from Washington without risking government ownership, finally decided to jump into the nuclear business by making utilities an offer they couldn't refuse.

Westinghouse and General Electric needed nuclear power. Both companies felt reactor sales offered them a chance to expand their utility supply business into heavy-pressure vessels that boiled water into steam, a market previously controlled by Babcock & Wilcox and Combustion Engineering. Both also needed a new business outlet to raise stagnant corporate sales and to boost morale after executives from both firms had been sent to jail for conspiring to fix prices on electrical equipment. Westinghouse, which had long played second fiddle to the giant General Electric, also viewed nuclear power as its ticket to become "number one."

New chief executives at General Electric and Westinghouse decided that utilities would purchase reactors only if equipment manufacturers initially assumed all the risks of constructing this unproven technology. Utilities, working with an assortment of subcontractors and regulatory agencies, normally paid for construction delays, workplace accidents, labor strikes, material shortages and the countless other problems that can cause cost overruns. But in 1963, General Electric guaranteed delivery of a complete nuclear power station at a set price to the Jersey Central Power & Light Company. The arrangement required General Electric to manage all subcontractors, to prepare the reactor for operation, and to charge a fixed fee that was competitive with coal-fired plants. Because Jersey Central had to simply start up the generating equipment, the arrangement was called a turnkey contract. According to General Electric's John McKitterick, "Our people understood this was a game of massive stakes, and that if we didn't force the utility industry to put those stations on-line, we'd end up with nothing."

The Oyster Bay reactor, the first to be built without government subsidies, was a technical success and a public relations triumph. The 515-megawatt reactor, three times larger than any existing nuclear power plant, performed close to expectations. Jersey Central published reports "proving" the economic competitiveness of nuclear power, while General Electric and Westinghouse salesmen rushed to sign up other utilities.

The turnkey gamble, in one sense, worked. Because General Electric and Westinghouse offered another 12 such contracts, while Babcock & Wilcox and Combustion Engineering decided against the risks, the giant equipment manufacturers acquired 80 percent of the nuclear market by the end of 1966. But the strategy was expensive. Oyster Bay's construction, described as the "greatest loss leader in American industry," cost twice General Electric's initial estimates. A RAND study found Westinghouse and General Electric lost an average of $75 million on each turnkey contract, for a total of almost $1 billion.

The equipment manufacturers look back on the experiments with pride. General Electric's Bertram Wolfe says, "The turnkeys made the light water reactor a viable product. They got enough volume in the business that we could build an engineering staff, standardize our product, and put up facilities to mass-produce things so that the cost went down. That way we got over this tailor-made, one-of-a-kind, high-cost plant."

Encouraged by what they thought were low prices relative to coal-fired plants, utility executives leaped on the "great nuclear bandwagon." Reactor orders jumped from 7 in 1965 to 20 in 1966 to 30 in 1967. The sudden shift from skepticism to frenzied development is remarkable considering the almost total lack of operating data on large nuclear power plants; only 8 reactors supplied electricity in 1967.

Electric companies enjoyed their best times in the mid-1960s. Stock prices peaked. Demand for power grew steadily. Rate costs drifted lower. Public support remained high. Reliable service seemed assured. Therefore, most private utility executives, firmly in control of nuclear power and most other generators, confidently predicted prosperity and stability would continue.

But warning clouds were on the horizon. When equipment manufacturers quietly ended their turnkey contracts, a few executives began to realize the nuclear gamble's true costs. Some economists questioned utilities' ability to finance ever-larger construction projects. And a couple of industry officials worried about possible transmission failures and growing protests from a new generation of conservationists.

CHAPTER 8

SHATTERED MOMENTUM

If the previous two decades were the power industry's golden age, the mid-1960s marked the beginning of an "Era of Shocks." Blackouts, protests, embargoes, nuclear accidents and economic disasters shattered the utilities' momentum.

Electricity's prominence certainly did not disappear: Time-saving appliances, computers and robots continued to reform homes and businesses. But the deliverers of electric power suffered a series of setbacks. No longer could utilities assume reliable service was assured, that new power plants would be more efficient than older models, that nuclear power would be "too cheap to meter," and that the demand for electric power would grow regularly. The industry's basic beliefs, in short, were questioned. Staid executives, unprepared for the new challenges, would exacerbate their problems by planning for continued growth rather than accepting the new realities.

THE BLACKOUT: NIAGARA FALLS, NOVEMBER 9, 1965

United Airlines pilot Dale Chapman was flying his regular route 33,000 feet above southern New England during a clear November twilight when suddenly "the whole city of New York was missing." According to Chapman, "it looked like the end of the world."

On the ground, flickering lights startled utility engineer Edwin Nellis and 30-million other northeasterners. They watched bulbs fade into only a scintilla of orange, surge for a brief instant, and then fall into darkness. Stalled elevators trapped hundreds of unfortunate New Yorkers. Powerless subway cars stranded 800,000 commuters, while millions of motorists confronted traffic snarls at dark intersections.

On "Black Tuesday," November 9, 1965, more than 80,000 square miles—an area slightly smaller than Great Britain—lost electric power. It was not the first blackout, but it was the most extensive, the longest and the most publicized.

Trouble began at 5:16 P.M. at the Sir Adam Beck electric station near Niagara Falls. High-voltage power lines passing through the facility normally wheeled power between New England and Ontario, Canada. As commuters returned home from work, electricity demand began to rise to its usual peak. But suddenly, one line automatically "tripped out" to avoid being overloaded. Four others—with a total capacity of 1,500 megawatts—immediately followed suit. The electric current, having no other option, surged into upstate New York where faulty switches failed to curb the cascade of power. Within a total of 12 minutes—less time than it takes a Russian missile to reach the United States—protective relays promptly shut down the overloaded systems, sending eight states and Ontario into darkness for almost 13 hours.

Most of those who spent the night without power "reacted sportively," said one participant, "as if it were all a gigantic game of blindman's buff." Hundreds of volunteers directed traffic. Rescue workers found the occupants of several stalled subway cars singing and dancing. And many restaurants offered free food and drinks to the stranded.

Millions, learning the full extent of their dependence on electricity, creatively devised alternative means to accomplish their tasks. Students at New York's Fordham University, for example, studied by car lights. Farmers powered their milking machines by tractor motors. A barber completed a haircut when an obliging motorist focused his car lights on the store's front windows. Residents at the New York Hilton burned 30,000 candles. And doctors devised makeshift operating rooms to deliver five-dozen babies. Not everything was cheerful, of course. A rampaging group of 320 maximum security prisoners caused $75,000 of damage to the Walpole State Prison outside Boston. But police reported only one-quarter the normal arrests for the night.

The media networks, headquartered in New York City, shared the experience with the entire nation. And Hollywood later added to Black Tuesday's legend with Doris Day's comedy, *Where Were You When the Lights Went Out?*

But utility executives did not laugh about the bewildering accident. They had claimed interconnected power pools were reliable deliverers of electricity. Although subsequent investigations showed that an uninspected relay, about the size of a shoe box, initiated the power cascade, executives and politicians feared more accidents would occur throughout the increasingly complex transmission systems. A subsequent Federal Power Commission investigative report could give "no absolute assurance" against a similar massive failure in the future.

New York's Consolidated Edison (Con Ed) spent over a decade investigating the accident. But only three days after the utility's chairman "guaranteed" that a power cascade would not recur, another small malfunction spiraled into a widespread blackout, this time affecting nine-million people for as much as 25 hours. The Big Apple's July 13, 1977, blackout, unlike its first experience, was no carnival. In fact, chaos reigned as rioters and looters destroyed over $50 million of property.

The power outages shocked utilities out of their complacency, forcing them to redirect expenditures from building new power plants to improving the operation of existing facilities. Specifically, executives had to upgrade the fragile distribution system in order to efficiently handle larger power pools and more frequent sales among utilities. New transmission lines and expensive image advertisements, however, would not stall the public's growing criticism of utility monopolies.

THE PROTESTS: WASHINGTON, D.C., APRIL 22, 1970

Edmund Muskie's quiet demeanor masked his commitment to fundamental change in the nation's industrial practices. After years of quiet struggle, the Maine senator received a standing ovation from the thousands of citizen activists assembled at the Washington Monument for Earth Day in April 1970. He was, according to one columnist, "Mr. Clean of the environment crusade."

"My land was a place of great beauty," Muskie would say. "It was also a paper mill town where pollution seemed an inevitable, if ugly, reality." Muskie rarely accepted the inevitable. Just as he bucked political traditions to become Maine's first Catholic governor, so he rejected pollution as a necessary by-product of civilization, declaring that "if you were born in Maine, you got interested in doing something about it when that beauty was threatened."

Muskie also rebelled against the "Democratic machine." In 1959, when the independent new senator rejected then-Senate majority leader Lyndon Johnson's initial request for support of a piece of legislation, he was punished by being assigned to the lackluster Public Works Committee. There Muskie gained little attention because environment was not a national issue and legislative opportunities seemed minimal. As one political commentator noted about the environment, "there was no political mileage in it."

Rachel Carson's publication of *Silent Spring* in 1962, however, began stimulating Americans to analyze the health and environmental hazards of industrial practices. People became increasingly critical of the smog that irritated eyes and limited visibility in Los Angeles, Chicago, New York and other cities. More troubling, doctors linked particulate matter in the air to such illnesses as emphysema, lung cancer and heart disease.

Muskie built on Carson's work in 1963 when, as chairman of the new Air and Water Pollution Subcommittee, he held public hearings across the country to publicize pollution problems. He lectured extensively on the environment, claiming that automobiles and electric utilities befouled the nation's air and water. Power plants, Muskie declared, poured heated water into lakes and rivers, causing temperature changes that killed certain fish and organisms. Utilities' demand for coal led to the strip mining of an area larger than the state of Connecticut, while power-line swaths covered an area about the size of New Jersey. Muskie was particularly critical of air pollution, calculating that fossil-fuel power plants discharged about half the nation's sulfur dioxide and a quarter of its particulates (commonly known as soot) and nitrogen oxides, a dangerous, invisible gas. The respected National Academy of Sciences predicted sulfur-dioxide emissions would triple over the next 30 years unless utilities installed pollution-control equipment.

Auto manufacturers in Michigan and electric companies throughout the country stridently opposed strict environmental standards. Detroit officials claimed that no correlation existed between auto exhaust and air quality. Utility executives predicted the addition of "scrubbers" to a power plant's smokestack would double the price of electricity. If Washington wanted environmental protection, they claimed, the federal government should pay for it.

Earth Day—April 22, 1970—observed one major newspaper, was "the largest single expression of public concern in history over what is happening to the environment," and marked the turning point in the popular mood against polluters. With a small staff and hundreds of volunteers, Denis Hayes, a Harvard University graduate student, encouraged thousands of schools, colleges and civic groups to sponsor debates, sit-ins and demonstrations. Events ranged from mock burials of automobiles to serious lectures by leading scientists. New York mayor John Lindsay closed Fifth Avenue to automobiles most of the day to demonstrate the city's concern about air pollution. A Gallup Opinion Index, conducted shortly after Earth Day, revealed public support for environmental protection had increased dramatically over the past five years; of major domestic concerns, pollution moved from ninth to second place.

Earth Day also increased the political muscle of environmentalists. The event moved President Richard Nixon to announce in his 1970 State of the Union Message: "The great question of the '70s is, shall we surrender to our surroundings or shall we make our peace with nature and begin to make reparations for the damage we have done to our air, to our land and to our water?" It also allowed Muskie to rush the National Air Quality Standards Act through Congress with strong restrictions on ten major pollutants, including a requirement that Detroit reduce auto emissions 90 percent within the next five years.

Rather than being the culmination of protests, Earth Day catalyzed environmental and consumer activists across the country to focus more extensively on electric companies. In 1974, for example, the Environmental Action Foundation (EAF), a nonprofit research organization in Washington, D.C., published *How to Challenge Your Local Electric Utility,* a step-by-step handbook explaining ways to oppose rate increases and power plant construction. EAF still serves as a clearinghouse of information for hundreds of citizen groups.

Sam Lovejoy needed few lessons. The organic farmer and self-avowed "hippie" from Montague, Massachusetts, knocked down a weather-monitoring tower that Northeast Utilities of Connecticut had erected in preparation for construction of a new nuclear plant. He turned himself in to the police, saying his civil disobedience was needed to protect the public from nuclear power's dangers. Acquitted on a technicality, Lovejoy helped make a movie about his exploits and became a hero among antinuclear activists.

Disruptions at reactors accelerated throughout the 1970s. The Clamshell Alliance, a collection of New England protesters, marched onto a construction site in Seabrook, New Hampshire, on August 1, 1976. Three weeks later, police arrested 179 of the campers, giving Clamshell organizers modest fines, valuable publicity and more recruits. Seven months later, a larger march against construction of the reactor led to the arrest of 1,414 protesters. The event received heavy national media coverage, sparked the creation of other "alliances" across the country, and troubled utility executives.

Antinuclear activists, however, were not the only protesters. In 1978, farmers in Minnesota's Stearnes and Pope counties challenged the plans of two rural electric cooperatives to build high-voltage transmission lines from western coal fields to eastern cities. The lines, according to power industry executives, were to reduce electricity prices by avoiding the rail costs of shipping coal. But the "coal by wire" proposal, according to the farmers, threatened to destroy 8,500 acres of prime farmland and lower the milk and calf production of cows. "These damn lines, on a wet day, can throw shocks all over the place," complained one farmer. To block the 420-mile, 800-kilovolt power line (proposed to be the biggest in the United States), the normally conservative farmers organized an illegal bonfire demonstration, blasted the patrol cars of arresting officers with makeshift slingshots (they called them "wrist-rockets"), and toppled an $80,000 transmission tower.

Many environmentalists took to the courts, rather than the fields, to stop utility construction projects. Attorneys indefinitely postponed Con

Ed's pumped-storage reservoir in upstate New York because the dam would "deface Storm King Mountain and the Hudson Valley." And a new breed of public-interest lawyer delayed scores of reactors and coal-fired plants until utility executives revised environmental impact statements.

Power company officials initially responded to environmental concerns in superficial terms, adding shrubbery around relay stations, painting towers a sky blue color, and putting power lines underground. Con Ed launched its campaign against air pollution by placing a staff member with binoculars on top of the Empire State Building to monitor the visibility.

Knowing they couldn't advocate increased pollution, most utility executives pleaded for a "balanced approach" that would permit more power plant construction while modest clean-up efforts proceeded. Without expansion, they predicted consumers would face blackouts and brownouts. Potomac Electric Power Company, in fact, asked District of Columbia residents to shut off their air conditioners on the hottest day of the 1969 summer to avoid overloading the utility system. Denied the Storm King facility and faced with technical problems at the giant Big Allis coal plant, Con Ed was forced to buy emergency power from the Tennessee Valley Authority (TVA) in August 1970.

But argue as they might, power company officials faced an array of new regulations and costs that would dramatically change their business practices. According to David Freeman, then director of the White House Office of Science and Technology and later chairman of the TVA, the time had come "in which environmental concerns must be considered as an integral part of the planning process."

THE EMBARGO: KUWAIT, OCTOBER 1973

The Middle East has long suffered political tensions. In the fall of 1973, however, the region flamed with violence and passion. Saudi Arabia's King Faisal hinted to oil company executives that Israel would probably be attacked and that if the United States wanted more Saudi oil at reasonable prices it must "disavow . . . Israeli policies and actions."

Neck-deep in the political mire of Watergate, Richard Nixon's White House believed the king was "calling wolf where no wolf exists except in his imagination." But the wolf pounced on October 6, 1973, when Egyptian troops crossed into Israeli-occupied Suez and closed the canal. Spurred by Arab unity against Israel, Sheik Zaki Yamani, Saudi Arabia's oil minister, convened a meeting of the Organization of Petroleum Exporting Countries (OPEC) by calling for a 100 percent increase in the posted price of oil, then only $3 a barrel.

U.S. oil executives, facing a worldwide shortage of petroleum, panicked. John McCloy, attorney for several oil companies, warned

President Nixon that military aid to Israel "will have a critical and adverse effect on our relations with the moderate Arab producing countries." The foreign ministers of Saudi Arabia and three other Arab states also tried to lobby the White House, but Nixon approved a massive $2.5 billion arms shipment to the Jewish state.

Angered by U.S. actions, the Arab ministers, meeting in Kuwait on October 17, agreed to increase oil prices 70 percent, to $5.12 a barrel, and to cut production 5 percent each month "until the Israel withdrawal is completed . . . and the legal rights of the Palestinian people restored." Within days, Saudi Arabia cut production 20 percent and announced a total embargo on oil to the United States and the Netherlands, Israel's key allies.

Although the Arab cutbacks accounted for less than 10 percent of the world's supply, pandemonium ensued. Within a month, the price of oil on the spot market had increased from approximately $3.00 to $17.00 a barrel. In December, OPEC ministers agreed to a floor price of $11.65 a barrel, a 400 percent rise in two months, an increase that would cost the United States more than the entire war in Vietnam.

Petroleum price hikes severely pained electric companies and their consumers. Although utilities burned only 13 percent of the nation's oil and gas, OPEC's actions led to a rise in the cost of other fuels, including coal, upon which the industry depended.

OPEC, however, was not responsible for triggering higher utility rates. In fact, electricity prices had skyrocketed sometimes as much as 20 percent per year after 1967, the year that new generating equipment could no longer be made more efficient than the machinery it replaced. The peak of efficiency improvements had been passed, largely because the properties of construction materials reached theoretical limits. Rather than lower the average cost of electricity, a new station would increase it. Economies of scale no longer applied to the utility industry; expansion no longer benefited the consumer.

A variety of other factors also contributed to higher rates. The overheated Vietnam-war economy accelerated inflation and interest rates, increasing electric companies' cost of borrowing. And new regulations extended the time and expense of building power plants. When the 1973 oil embargo accelerated the price hikes, Americans were shocked into conserving energy, causing the growth of electric sales to drop in 1974 for the first time since World War II.

But most utility executives, viewing the slowdown as an aberration, maintained their commitments to costly construction projects. In fact, they and many politicians argued that America needed additional electric capacity, particularly nuclear power, to combat OPEC's energy stranglehold. Announcing "Project Independence," Presidents Nixon and Ford declared the United States must reduce reliance on OPEC oil by building 200 nuclear reactors, 150 coal-fired power plants, 30 oil refineries, 20 synthetic fuel plants and digging 250 major coal mines.

THE MISSED DIVIDEND: NEW YORK CITY, APRIL 23, 1974

Warning signs appeared in New York long before the embargo hit. Con Ed's construction expenses more than doubled between 1968 and 1974, in part because underground cables required by new regulations cost 20 times more to install and maintain than unsightly overhead wires. The company's labor costs rose 65 percent, an industry high. And the utility paid almost 3 times more than other power companies in state and local taxes.

The future offered no relief. Con Ed was penned in, unable to expand into prosperous suburban industrial parks. And serving a densely populated urban area, it could build few nuclear or coal-fired power plants because of opposition from environmentalists. Thus, 85 percent dependent upon low-sulfur coal and imported oil, Con Ed sat defenseless against OPEC's price hikes, which soon raised the utility's daily cost of fuel from $720,000 to $2,480,000.

In response to these financial burdens, New York's Public Service Commission granted massive rate increases, raising a New Yorker's average monthly bill in March 1974 to $250, up 85 percent from the previous year. Many outraged consumers refused to pay or delayed payment, further complicating Con Ed's cash crunch.

New York regulators also allowed the use of complex accounting techniques that enabled the company to show continuing profits. Although net earnings for the fourth quarter of 1973 had dropped 21 percent from the previous year, the new formula allowed Con Ed to show sufficient earnings to maintain its regular dividend to shareholders. Financial problems, however, could not be hidden forever. In February 1974, Moody's Investors Service downgraded Con Ed's rating, making it more difficult and expensive for the company to issue bonds and borrow money. In early April, New York City Civil Court judge Bernard Weiss suggested the utility reduce its quarterly dividend to help alleviate its cash plight. And on April 23, Con Ed chairman Charles Luce went beyond Judge Weiss's suggestion and canceled the dividend for the first time in the company's 89-year history.

Skipping the dividend, according to Florida Power & Light's president, Marshall McDonald, "really clobbered all the utilities. They have long been considered the best stocks for widows and orphans, and now we have the largest of them in trouble and passing a dividend. This throws the viability of the entire industry in doubt." Luce's action shocked Wall Street and sparked a selling frenzy that plunged the price of the average utility stock 18 percent. By September, stock prices fell 36 percent, the greatest drop since the Depression. Moreover, Standard and Poor's rating service lowered its evaluations of Con Ed and several other utilities. The drop of Detroit Edison's credit rating from AA to A added

$7,000 in annual interest charges for every $1 million the utility borrowed, or approximately $7 million for a large nuclear plant. Con Ed's rating fell so low that several institutions, including savings and loan associations, were legally forbidden to invest in its bonds.

Desperate for a short-term solution, Luce (who had previously directed the Bonneville Power Administration) asked New York State for help. Politicians, swayed by Con Ed's political clout and the fear of a power company bankruptcy, obligingly approved an $800 million bond to purchase two of the utility's partially completed power stations, a nuclear reactor at Buchanan and an oil-fired generator in Queens. Con Ed's delighted financial manager declared, "When we sell those plants, we will get more money than we normally raise in a year."

The industry's long-term solutions, however, were less clear. Rising construction costs were forcing electric companies to flood the financial markets with requests for money. In 1973 alone, utilities raised a whopping $4.7 billion by issuing new common and preferred stock, almost seven times more than that sold by all manufacturing companies combined. Future financing needs seemed even more enormous, with General Electric's Reginald Jones predicting utilities would require $500 billion by 1985 to cover necessary construction projects.

Despite such prohibitively high capital requirements, most officials within the power industry refused to abandon their historical commitment to growth. American Electric Power's Donald Cook, considered "one of the most thoughtful of utility executives" by *Business Week*, continued to project widespread blackouts if utilities did not build new power plants. The cash crunch forced several utilities, including Carolina Power and Public Service Electric & Gas Company of New Jersey, to sell new common stock below the book value of the company's assets, decreasing stockholder's equity.

Con Ed's problems, however, convinced a few executives and Wall Street analysts to avoid expansion. Detroit Edison, for instance, announced a $650 million cut in its five-year building program. Charles Benore, then with the Mitchell Hutchins investment company, advised his clients against buying stocks and bonds in utilities with large construction programs. These few recognized that the dream of abundant and inexpensive electricity was turning into a financial nightmare.

THE ACCIDENT: THREE MILE ISLAND, MARCH 28, 1979

In early March 1979, Americans were flocking to movie houses to watch Jane Fonda's and Jack Lemmon's thriller about a nuclear accident and a utility's efforts to cover it up. *The China Syndrome* became a box office hit and "meltdown" a household word.

On March 28, fiction became reality. On a thin island in the Susquehanna River, not far from Harrisburg, Pennsylvania, a pressurized-water reactor lost its coolant, and its radioactive fuel overheated. For five days, Americans and the rest of the world flocked to their televisions and newspapers for information about "the worst nuclear power accident in history."

Problems began shortly after 4:00 A.M. when pumps feeding water into the steam generators at Three Mile Island's Unit 2 stopped working. The plant's safety system automatically shut down the steam turbine and the electric generator it powered. Without the release of steam, the reactor's coolant heated up, expanded, and created enormous pressure within the reactor vessel. Operators opened a valve to release the pressure but were unaware it did not close. Believing that cooling water covered the core, they mistakenly shut off the emergency cooling pumps. For 2 hours and 22 minutes, about 32,000 gallons of vital coolant became radioactive and leaked out of the chamber. Without sufficient liquid, part of the intensely hot uranium core melted and produced a hydrogen gas bubble within the reactor. The core continued to overheat.

Although no one knew the extent of the accident, Metropolitan Edison, Three Mile Island's operator, held press conferences to assure the public that everything was under control. It was not. On the third morning after the accident began, a helicopter with monitoring equipment detected a sudden release of radioactivity from the reactor. Volunteers quickly evacuated pregnant women and young children from nearby Middletown, and residents as far as 200 miles away began to worry about the wind bringing deadly radioactivity into their backyards.

Government regulators also provided little assurance. For long hours during the crisis, they ineptly debated the wisdom of evacuating entire communities. Joseph Hendrie, the chairman of the Nuclear Regulatory Commission (NRC), later admitted, "We were operating almost totally in the blind."

Hundreds of reporters descended upon Harrisburg, Middletown and Three Mile Island. For days, the world's media traced technical developments and interviewed frightened residents. Some reporting was clearly sensational or politically motivated. The tabloid New York *Post,* for example, blazoned the headline: "Race With Nuclear Disaster," while the conservative Manchester (New Hampshire) *Union Leader* announced: "No Injuries Reported in Nuke Mishap." Many of the stories, however, accurately investigated the lack of control. The constant news exposure convinced most Americans that utilities and nuclear power were in trouble. A CBS/*New York Times* poll found "only 46 percent of Americans now favor further development of nuclear power, compared with 69 percent who were asked the same question in a July 1977 CBS/*Times* poll."

Utility executives, however, continued to applaud nuclear power's safety record. John Herbein of Metropolitan Edison maintained enough confidence to declare, "We didn't injure anybody with this accident. We didn't seriously contaminate anybody and we certainly didn't kill anybody."

President Jimmy Carter, who had studied nuclear engineering under Admiral Rickover, visited the plant to reassure local residents. He also appointed John Kemmeny, president of Dartmouth College, to head an independent investigation. The so-called Kemmeny Commission reported in October 1979 that "fundamental changes will be necessary in the organization, procedures, and practices—and above all—in the attitudes of the Nuclear Regulatory Commission and, to the extent that the institutions we investigated are typical, of the nuclear industry." The document also declares that Metropolitan Edison was hopelessly unprepared to deal with the accident.

The NRC's own investigation, headed by lawyer Mitchell Rogovin, presented a more frightening picture. The Rogovin account explained that Three Mile Island had been within one hour of a catastrophic meltdown and that the release of substantial radioactivity into the air and water was avoided mainly by dumb luck.

Although Three Mile Island was the most publicized nuclear power accident, it was not the first. In 1952, a technician at Canada's Chalk River experimental reactor mistakenly lifted 4 of the system's 12 control rods out of the fuel core and caused a chain reaction that melted almost all the uranium. For 42 hours in 1957, operators at Britain's plutonium-production reactor did not realize radioactivity was leaking from the plant; although the government never explained the danger, health officials destroyed half-a-million gallons of milk from dairy farms in a 200-square-mile area around the plant.

The first major U.S. accident occurred on January 3, 1961, at a small military power plant in Idaho. Three young servicemen, John Byrnes, Richard McKinley and Richard Legg, were completing a routine operation when the control rods suddenly slipped out of the core. The fuel instantly went "supercritical," creating a steam explosion that scattered debris throughout the reactor. An ejected control-rod plug speared McKinley's body and hurled it into the ceiling. The other two soldiers died of radiation burns. All three bodies remained so radioactive that three weeks would pass before officials could handle them for burial; even then, the military used lead-lined caskets within lead-lined vaults.

In October 1966, the cooling system at the Enrico Fermi plant in southeast Michigan, which an AEC safety committee had found inadequate, malfunctioned, causing part of the fuel core to overheat. Radioactive gases accumulated in the containment structure. Although plant operators celebrated a birthday party for Detroit Edison's chairman during the crisis, police and civil defense authorities say they were asked to prepare for an emergency evacuation of the surrounding countryside. Government investigators later concluded that the accident had stopped just short of a complete meltdown. One official announced, "We almost lost Detroit."

On October 22, 1975, a 20-year-old untrained worker was using a candle to check for air leaks around electrical cable at TVA's Browns Ferry reactor near Decatur, Alabama. Unfortunately, the candle set fire to the polyurethane insulation around the cables. Workmen tried unsuccessfully to douse the fire with extinguishers. Automatic sprinklers had not been installed, and flames destroyed 1,600 cables, including those controlling key safety equipment. After the fire department had finally persuaded the manager to spray the fire, plant operators successfully arranged a makeshift system to cool the reactor's heated fuel. Engineers later admitted privately that a meltdown was avoided "by sheer luck."

By 1976, leading nuclear engineers admitted that safety could not be taken casually. Robert Pollard, a 35-year-old official at the NRC, resigned in February and declared that the federal agency failed to enforce its basic safety regulations. The popular "60 Minutes" television show broadcast Pollard's message to millions of Americans. The following month, three senior engineers left General Electric's nuclear energy division and began working for antinuclear organizations. One of them, Dale Bridenbaugh, said nuclear power had become a "technological monster and it is not clear who, if anyone, is in control."

Many of the technical problems resulted from early competition among nuclear vendors and the government's premature licensing of an immature technology. To gain business, General Electric, Westinghouse and other equipment manufacturers aggressively promoted larger and more powerful reactors, often without waiting for operating experience with existing designs. According to James Deddens of Babcock & Wilcox, "When you get into that kind of competitive situation, you may sell something that hasn't been tested as thoroughly as it would be today."

Utility executives, lacking nuclear expertise, could not adequately evaluate the vendors' claims. Having relied only on promises that bigger reactors would minimize costs and maximize profits, Donald Brand of Pacific Gas & Electric lamented, "We did not anticipate the detail in documentation and independent inspection of workmanship which would be required" to construct a reactor. Expressing the power companies' casual approach to the nuclear gamble, one utility vice-president told author Daniel Ford, "We got into nuclear power because the president of my utility used to play golf with the president of another utility. They bought one, and so we bought one."

After Three Mile Island, the public demanded stricter safety regulations and enforcement. But as power executives tried to restore public confidence in nuclear power's safety, they faced another problem: Reactor cost overruns were sending utilities to the brink of bankruptcy.

THE DEFAULT: PACIFIC NORTHWEST, JULY 25, 1983

Robert Ferguson had a reputation for getting jobs done. For more than 20 years, the engineer and administrator had completed government nuclear projects on time and within budget. In August 1980, Ferguson confronted his greatest challenge—rescuing the overbudget nuclear plants being constructed by the Washington Public Power Supply System (WPPSS, commonly known as "Whoops" for its mangled acronym and its problems).

WPPSS was in chaos when Ferguson arrived. The estimate of what it would cost to build five nuclear plants in the Pacific Northwest had almost tripled since 1975 to $15.9 billion. The NRC had recently fined WPPSS $61,000 for inadequate welds in a shield surrounding a reactor vessel. Workers at three of the plants had been on strike for five months. And more than 45 general contractors at each reactor jockeyed to get their equipment into crowded, poorly managed construction sites.

In a relatively short time, Ferguson greatly improved WPPSS's operation. He replaced the project managers at each plant, decentralized the cumbersome administrative system and centralized the hiring of contractors. He also pushed a bill through the state legislature allowing one prime contractor at each site. According to many in the Northwest, Ferguson had performed a management miracle.

But the hard-headed administrator also took a new look at the WPPSS budget and was shocked at what he found. While previous budgets were nothing more than "annually updated guesstimates," Ferguson began a "bottoms-up" review, systematically calculating the amounts of concrete, pipe, cable and labor needed to finish the job. He checked the numbers several times, but the more he investigated, the higher the cost estimates rose. Rather than $15.9 billion as he was told when he took over as managing director, Ferguson concluded in May 1981 that the true figure was $23.8 billion, a 50 percent increase.

Ferguson also began to doubt that WPPSS could raise the money needed to continue its construction projects. WPPSS had already saturated the U.S. bond market with $6 billion of tax-exempt offerings, including $1.6 billion in 1981. Moreover, bonds for Units 4 and 5 were less attractive and more expensive than those for the first three plants, primarily because they were not backed by the federal Bonneville Power Administration (BPA). And for the first time, the Washington State legislature and several industrialists were suggesting that the last two reactors might not be needed because a lot more energy was being saved by conservation efforts than was previously thought possible.

Ferguson remained committed to building all five units, but the numbers cried out for action. "For the past ten months I spent every waking hour dedicating myself to completing these projects at the earliest possible date and at the lowest possible cost," he explained. "But I didn't in all honesty know how to deal with the problem."

Ferguson called a board meeting on May 29, 1981, and after explaining his budget findings, abruptly recommended a moratorium on Units 4 and 5 for at least six months. Most board members, who were farmers and ranchers committed to bringing more electricity to the Pacific Northwest, were shocked by the public announcement. Although they met a week later to endorse Ferguson's recommendation, they hoped either that the move was only a temporary slowdown or that the BPA would buy the facilities.

Construction stopped on Units 4 and 5, but some carrying and maintenance costs continued. By mid-October, WPPSS ran short of money to pay its bills, and Ferguson desperately tried to gain more financing from his members, investor-owned utilities, aluminum firms and other industrialists. WPPSS officials appealed to a spirit of regional cooperation but also threatened rate shocks if the two reactors were simply allowed to sink. It was a hectic, high-pressure operation that gained the reluctant support of most utilities and businesses.

The Clark County Public Utility District, however, refused to go along, beginning a chain reaction that shattered the region's unity. Clark County had commissioned a report from the accounting firm of Touche Ross & Company which concluded that "the county's objectives may differ from those of WPPSS" and that it "should make no additional financial commitments" for the nuclear projects. By the time the WPPSS board met in January 1982, 15 other utilities, representing 30 percent of the plants' output, accepted the same logic and withdrew from any maintenance effort. And noting WPPSS's growing problems, Wall Street brokers dashed any hopes that additional bonds could be economically sold. There was no way out. Ferguson painfully recommended termination of Units 4 and 5. Not long afterward, the overworked and exhausted manager went to the hospital for quadruple-bypass heart surgery.

Investors in Units 4 and 5 still assumed their bonds were secured by "take or pay" contracts that obligated the 88 participating utilities to take the electricity as soon as it was produced or to pay WPPSS for it even if the power was not delivered. But bondholders failed to anticipate the anger of Northwest ratepayers expected to pay for WPPSS's mistakes. Speaking for consumers about the pending rate shocks, Mark Reis of the Northwest Conservation Act Coalition remarked that the BPA and WPPSS "promised power without cost, and they delivered cost without power." All but two of the 88 utilities bowed to public pressure and decided to withhold payments and keep rates low, arguing that the contracts were invalid because they did not have the authority to sign such agreements. The Chemical Bank, representing bondholders, filed suit against the power companies, but the Washington State Superior

Court ruled in June 1983 that the utilities need not pay WPPSS for the overbudget and unfinished reactors.

On July 25, WPPSS, unable to continue work on Units 4 and 5 or to repay its bondholders, filed a $2.25 billion default, the largest in U.S. history.

How could such a disaster have occurred? To appreciate the rise and fall of the Washington Public Power Supply System, one must understand the almost religious significance of electrical power in the Pacific Northwest. Since the 1930s, when Senator George Norris and other public power advocates created the BPA to supply hydropower from federal dams along the Columbia River, electricity had been a synonym for prosperity. It attracted aluminum companies and defense contractors to cities along the West Coast and pumped water to farmers on the dry, eastern side of the mountains. Woody Guthrie wrote a ballad, "Roll on Columbia," which praises the huge hydroelectric projects and is still sung in elementary schools and at utility picnics throughout the region: *"Roll on, Columbia, roll on! Your power is turning our darkness to dawn, so roll on, Columbia, roll on!"*

WPPSS, a consortium of 23 small public power companies throughout the Pacific Northwest which banded together to tackle projects they couldn't complete on their own, began modestly in 1957 by building a small hydroelectric dam at Packwood Lake in the foothills of Mount Rainier. But board members, a group of well-meaning sheep ranchers, apple farmers and small-business owners with little construction experience, soon began to dream of huge projects on the scale of the Grand Coulee Dam.

Government officials at the BPA encouraged their dreams. As the region's growing economy gradually absorbed the output of Columbia River dams in the early 1960s, Administrator Charles Luce argued for the construction of nuclear and coal-fired plants. Supported by aluminum manufacturers and electricity-intensive industrialists, Luce proposed 50 large power stations by the year 2000. To assure development, BPA offered to buy and distribute all electricity from new facilities, enabling WPPSS to easily gain financing for three reactors. Construction began in 1969, at the very end of the utility industry's golden age.

Within four years, Donald Hodel had become BPA's administrator, and OPEC had transformed energy into a "crisis." Several analysts predicted higher fuel prices would reduce the growth of power demand, but Hodel insisted that the three reactors under construction were an inadequate match for the region's power needs. In 1976, he issued a formal "notice of insufficiency" to BPA's utility customers, warning that after 1983 electricity rationing would begin unless more power plants were completed. "Homes will be cold and dark or factories will close or both because the (power) deficits are no longer manageable," Hodel predicted. WPPSS officials believed him and began building Units 4 and 5.

But Hodel had failed to anticipate the impact of higher prices on the demand for electricity, the cutbacks resulting from an economic recession, or the potential of conservation in a region that used power extravagantly. As energy costs rose throughout the 1970s, individual consumers and industrialists found many ways to use electricity more efficiently, and by Hodel's year of reckoning—1983—the region faced huge surpluses rather than shortages. Unfortunately, Hodel's forecasting mistake became evident to the general public only after billions of dollars had been invested in the unneeded reactors.

Poor management accompanied bad forecasts. To share the bounty among their neighbors, WPPSS's inexperienced directors employed 500 contractors, 20,000 workers and 300 financial institutions. Confusion reigned and costs skyrocketed. Speaking of his fellow WPPSS directors, Carl Halvorson later admitted, "They became captives of the mystique of the nuke. And they had unlimited money. That was the worst of it."

For a time, WPPSS was Wall Street's darling. Because the first three reactors were backed by an agency of the federal government, the credit-rating agencies, Standard & Poor's and Moody's Investors Service, gave the bonds their highest rating, AAA. Underwriters profited handsomely by selling more than $8 billion of the offerings, more tax-exempt bonds than have been issued by any other corporation in American history. But by the time construction began on Units 4 and 5, the rules had changed. The Internal Revenue Service had charged BPA with violating its charter to sell only hydropower, restricted the federal agency from purchasing power from additional nuclear reactors and forced the final two units to be backed by nothing more than the 88 participating utilities.

The ambitious nuclear projects were not without their critics, even at the beginning. Before bonds for the first units were sold, the Seattle City Council conducted an extensive energy study and voted to launch conservation campaigns rather than buying a share of the WPPSS projects. In July 1976, Skidmore, Owings & Merrill, a planning firm in Portland, Oregon, issued a report for BPA showing that conservation could meet energy demand six times more cheaply than new nuclear reactors. (Hodel, who became President Reagan's secretary of energy and later, secretary of the interior, immediately denounced the conclusions and continued to solicit utility sponsors for Units 4 and 5.) And the *Seattle Post-Intelligencer* frequently ran articles describing WPPSS's cost overruns, incomplete records, sloppy accounting procedures and defective work.

However, the region's leading utility executives and industrialists ignored all warnings and continued to equate power growth with prosperity. In April 1981, several months after the Washington State Senate blasted WPPSS for "an absence of any realistic and disciplined budget," WPPSS offered more bonds for sale and, in its 99-page prospectus, listed fewer than a handful of references to the project's growing problems.

"We were duped," moans one bondholder who watched his securities plummet in value to only 12 cents on the dollar; he and 78,000 other investors from across the country can sell bonds with a face value of $5,000 for only $600, and then only to speculators. Robert Kahn of Hollywood, Florida, is another victim. "I felt secure," laments the retired court reporter. "That was the whole point of buying the bonds. I didn't want to make extra money. I just didn't want to lose what I had. I am not a rich man."

The damage from WPPSS, of course, hit the Pacific Northwest hardest. Thanks mainly to overbudget reactors, ratepayers saw their electricity bills rise almost 600 percent in five years. Elderly residents in Grays Harbor County along the Washington coast now spend up to half their income for electricity. Several businesses left the region because of high-energy costs, taking jobs with them. In the communities around one of the reactor sites, employment fell from a high of 15,000 to less than 2,000. Empty storefronts line the city streets, hundreds of apartments lie vacant, and home values are depressed. One worker, speaking of the region's malaise, mourns: "It's the combination of seeing friends laid off and the insecurity of wondering if you'll be next."

The only winners in this sad tale are the lawyers handling the 60 lawsuits in which participants try to blame someone else for the economic mess. The WPPSS utilities, for instance, complain that Donald Hodel and other BPA officials twisted their arms to sign contracts for the unneeded power. In contrast, BPA charges that "the project simply ran away from the Supply System" and its inexperienced managers. Bondholders argue that investment houses provided misleading information about WPPSS's financial condition. But the brokerage firms and rating companies say they couldn't foresee a judge allowing utilities to "walk away from contracts."

The WPPSS fiasco, which shattered many of the utility industry's basic assumptions, marks a turning point in electricity economics. Instead of providing economies of scale, today's large power plants burden electric companies with huge construction costs, high interest charges and pollution-control expenses. Instead of offering a secure investment, some utilities skip dividends and default on loans. And instead of growing regularly, the future demand for electricity is uncertain. Frustrated and frightened, many utility executives are turning to the government for help.

CHAPTER 9

GOVERNMENT'S HELPING HAND

The electricity market is anything but free. Utilities burn subsidized fuels, pay few taxes and enjoy guaranteed profits. Turning to government is not a new gambit for power companies. For many years, both private and public utilities have found a gold mine within state and federal bureaucracies.

Government-owned enterprises such as municipals and cooperatives naturally rely upon taxpayers, receiving low-interest Rural Electrification Act loans and tax-exempt municipal financing that are major benefits during times of high interest rates. They also enjoy preference to low-cost electricity generated by federal power projects, almost a $4 billion subsidy from the Hoover Dam alone over the next decade. Public power systems also pay no property taxes, although many make "payments in lieu of taxes" and provide free services to local governments, which add up to roughly 10 percent of their revenue—about what private utilities pay in state and local levies. And because publics earn no profits for stockholders, they also avoid federal income taxes.

Yet almost a quarter of the investor-owned companies don't pay federal taxes, either. Accountants, lawyers and lobbyists, as important to a private utility's profits as engineers, have established and utilized scores of incentives that annually cost the U.S. Treasury almost $15 billion, about one-third of the power industry's yearly capital spending.

Like other businesses, private utilities receive a 10 percent federal tax credit for investments in new machinery and power plants, saving the industry $1.5 billion in 1981. Utilities also deduct more than half of their long-term financing costs, saving another $5.3 billion. And like other firms, they quickly depreciate new investments, thus further reducing federal tax payments. Conventional power plants, which should operate for 30 or 40 years, can be depreciated in just 15; nuclear reactors get an even larger break, with a tax life of only 10 years. Although these provisions are not unique to power companies, utilities benefit more than other industries because of their huge capital investments.

An additional Internal Revenue Service provision, specifically designed to encourage utility investments, allows power companies to charge ratepayers for federal taxes that they may never pay the U.S. Treasury. Former Federal Power Commission chairman Howard Morgan calls these unpaid charges "phantom taxes"; utilities prefer the term "tax normalization." Whatever the name, the nation's 150 largest investor-owned utilities pocketed more than $5 billion in 1982, raising their total unpaid taxes to $34 billion—the equivalent of more than $400 for every U.S. household. According to the Environmental Action Foundation, 28 utilities actually received tax refunds totaling $248 million in 1982. Sam Insull's old company, Commonwealth Edison, reported the nation's largest tax overcharge and an accumulated $1.6 billion in deferred taxes. Even if the taxes are eventually paid, which utility critics say is unlikely, power companies will have enjoyed a massive interest-free loan from Uncle Sam.

Washington's guiding hand has been strongest in steering nuclear reactors through rough waters. Some economists maintain that the federal government has sustained the nuclear power industry by artificial means—subsidies—for many years. Cornell University professor Duane Chapman, for instance, calculates that taxpayers assume 31 percent of the lifetime costs of a private utility's reactor, almost double the subsidies for fossil-fuel-fired power plants.

David Lilienthal, the Atomic Energy Commission's first chairman, warned in 1952 that he "wouldn't advise anybody who is responsible for private investment under any conditions to put his money or the money of those who rely on him into the development of power plants employing nuclear fission as a source of heat." But Washington, anxious to develop the "peaceful atom," swaddled the infant nuclear power industry in benefits. In one way or another, it took care of the costs of building fuel enrichment facilities, regulating reactor construction, disposing of nuclear wastes, and coping with environmental radiation. By 1979, the last year the Battelle National Laboratory calculated subsidy levels, the federal government had spent more than $21 billion to promote the commercial nuclear power industry. (One expert claims the benefits actually reached a total of $40 billion.)

But most utility executives argue that government participation in the electricity market burdens more than it aids power companies.

Facing regulations that sometimes change and always cost money, they feel bludgeoned by state commissioners and susceptible to the whims of politicians. Subsidies, they say, are counterbalanced by restrictive regulations that increase their costs and limit their profits. The federal government may have provided at least $21 billion in nuclear benefits, but it also doubled the amount of equipment, materials, and labor, and tripled the engineering costs required to license each new reactor.

Conservative utility executives, who rely upon stability, were startled and confused by the turbulent 1960s and 1970s. As if dealing with blackouts and embargoes was not enough, they faced rapidly changing government policies as well. The Clean Air Act of 1970 and other environmental legislation virtually forced many utilities to convert from dirty coal to oil, which was abundant and relatively cheap before the embargo. But after OPEC's price hikes in 1973, politicians, who wanted to conserve oil and get their angry constituents out of gasoline lines, whipsawed utilities back to coal, despite the substantial expense of pollution-control equipment.

Some executives blame Washington for aggressively promoting nuclear reactors and then burdening the technology with extensive safety requirements. Without federal subsidies and insurance coverage, they say utilities would not have taken the nuclear gamble. Financially strapped executives managing expensive reactors now feel the federal government is obligated to rescue the industry.

Power company officials also attack state regulators for approving inadequate returns on utility investments. Unlike corporate executives, state commissioners seldom view their jobs as a career. The political appointees, who are receptive to other job offers and vulnerable to changing administrations, often take the short-term view of electricity planning and concentrate on keeping rates as low as possible during their tenure. By opting for the politically popular path of blocking rate increases, regulators, warns one critic, have "set the nation on a collision course with power shortages and soaring electricity rates."

Whether state regulation is viewed as a benefit or a burden to utilities, it is clear that the role of commissioners has changed dramatically since Sam Insull helped transfer oversight from corrupt urban politicians to professional state analysts. Today's regulators have been overwhelmed by the increasingly complex issues posed by inflation, consumerism and environmentalism, and most lack the resources to adequately monitor huge utilities selling bulk power across state boundaries. It is also becoming clear that while government actions may temporarily improve a utility's balance sheet, increased protection curtails incentives for efficiency and innovation, qualities electric companies need if they are to survive in this era of uncertainty. The decades-old regulatory system may require dramatic change to keep pace with modern needs.

A FEDERAL BAILOUT?

As the utility industry's problems spiral in the mid-1980s, many public and private power companies are increasing their appeals for government help, calling for a bailout many times the size of that given to Chrysler or Continental Illinois Bank. But more and more state commissioners, fearful of a political backlash when rate shocks hit, are rejecting pleas for higher electricity prices, forcing utility investors to pay a larger share of the costs associated with overbudget power plants. In December 1983, for instance, Missouri regulators denied Union Electric permission to charge its customers for any of the $63 million it spent on the abandoned Callaway 2 plant. Virginia's commission allowed Virginia Electric Power Company to recover only $258 million of its $649 million in the North Anna 3 plant. And Montana's Public Service Commission allowed only $4.1 million of a $96.4 million rate increase to help pay for the controversial Colstrip 3 coal-fired plant.

Because local officials are turning against utilities, many executives are turning to the federal government to rescue them from bankruptcy. The Long Island Lighting Company (LILCO) found a friend in Alphonse D'Amato, the Republican senator from New York. D'Amato, claiming "the people of Long Island deserve the benefits of tax-exempt financing," devised a scheme whereby LILCO could refinance its expensive Shoreham reactor with low-interest, government-subsidized industrial development bonds. After the Treasury Department rejected his request to expand the law's definition to include LILCO, D'Amato offered a series of amendments to the Deficit Reduction Act of 1984. And despite Treasury's estimate that the deal would reduce tax payments to the United States a half-billion dollars by 1989, the provision sailed through Congress with virtually no debate. (After acquiring this huge subsidy for his constituents, the conservative senator tried to regain his antigovernment image by denouncing the overall bill for its "total lack of spending curtailment.")

The Reagan administration doesn't know what to do about threatened utility bankruptcies. On the one hand, philosophically it opposes federal rescues for faltering private companies. But the President wholeheartedly supports nuclear power.

The conflict is no more apparent than at the Shoreham reactor, where county and state officials have blocked the issuance of an operating license for the almost-complete reactor by refusing to participate in an emergency evacuation plan. "It's not that we're unwilling to evacuate," says Suffolk County deputy executive Frank Jones. "It's that it simply can't be done. We spent one year and $600,000 studying this. The Long Island Expressway is jammed right this minute. If we had an accident, we'd have 1.5-million people on a five-road network fleeing into New York City. It'd be absolute, total, complete chaos." Donald Hodel,

President Reagan's former energy secretary, doesn't want to attack a local Republican official, but he worries that Jones's argument could "establish a precedent" that poses "a potential threat to the viability of the nuclear power industry." Hodel, feeling the required evacuation plan is only a "technicality," thinks the federal government should finance a drill or exercise police powers in place of local officials in the event of an emergency.

Despite Shoreham's cost overruns, Hodel claims nuclear power is the least expensive energy technology. A group of 450 Long Island businessmen and women disagree. In April 1984, they began running anti-LILCO radio advertisements, warning that electricity rates will skyrocket if Shoreham is licensed and its construction costs are passed on to consumers. "LILCO is at it again, looking for favors from the federal government," a man's voice says disapprovingly in the ad. "Look LILCO, you don't pay for our mistakes. We don't wanna pay for yours."

Such sentiments have tempered the administration's calls for any full-fledged bailout of power companies. Still, President Reagan is quietly providing a package of very expensive benefits to aid the distressed industry. In 1983, for example, he signed legislation adding $3.4 billion to utilities' cash flow—more than twice what the government used to rescue Chrysler from collapse—through a dividend reinvestment plan that defers the collection of taxes payable by investors. (The subsidy allows utility stockholders to use $750 worth of dividends to reinvest in newly issued utility common stock without paying any taxes until the stock is sold.) *Business Week* calls the plan an "unabashed—and unneeded—subsidy." One utility executive privately admits the tax-free provision is the only reason he owns power company stocks. "If Congress overturns the law," he says, "I'm selling my entire portfolio."

An obscure 1983 Internal Revenue Service ruling also allows utilities to use pollution-control bonds to finance as much as a quarter of their nuclear construction projects. Because the interest on these bonds is tax-exempt, utilities can save millions of dollars by attracting investors with just 10 percent interest, rather than the 14 percent they pay on most new certificates. Power companies issued at least $4.8 billion of low-interest bonds in 1984, which will cost the U.S. Treasury more than $6 billion in revenues over the next 30 years.

President Reagan tried to add a few more benefits by requesting a 36 percent increase in the nuclear research budget, authorizing the federal government to collect radioactive wastes, approving reactor sales to China, and regularly sending energy secretary Hodel to argue for rate increases and power plant construction before state regulatory commissions. His administration also set aside $8.4 million for a variety of public relations efforts to promote nuclear power development.

Even more important to utilities, Reagan's Federal Energy Regulatory Commission liberalized accounting rules, allowing wholesale power producers to earn a return on their costs of so-called construction work in progress (CWIP) before their plants are completed. Utilities say CWIP, which allows an immediate return on expenditures, lowers their borrowing costs, eases their financing burdens and cushions rate shocks. Opponents argue that the provision only encourages utilities to make poor investments in unneeded power plants.

More government benefits come from the Rural Electrification Administration (REA), an agency of the Department of Agriculture, which continues to subsidize cooperatives' investments in 17 reactors, including the troubled Seabrook Unit 2 in New Hampshire and Illinois' Clinton Unit 1. The federal agency has $9.75 billion tied up in nuclear projects and expects to contribute more. In May 1984, REA quietly subsidized Public Service Company of New Hampshire by helping to purchase the investor-owned utility's share of an operating Maine reactor; the $57 million payment, made as a loan to the New Hampshire Electric Cooperative, allows Public Service to continue financing its troubled Seabrook nuclear plant.

Nuclear power problems are bringing the REA to "the choking point," admits Jack Van Mark, the agency's deputy administrator. But a majority of the members of Congress want to support the politically popular organization and have signed petitions to forgive the cooperatives' $7.9 billion debt to the U.S. Treasury. This would be more money than the federal government extended to rescue Continental Illinois Bank.

To date, these complex and indirect subsidies have not been carefully scrutinized by the general public. If a power company files for bankruptcy, however, the political climate will change dramatically. Pressure for more massive subsidies will come not only from utilities and their individual investors, but also from banks. U.S. banks have about $6 billion in loans and other credits outstanding to the largest investor-owned utilities, according to Kidder, Peabody & Co. Capital-hungry LILCO owes four New York banks more than $800 million.

The Federal Deposit Insurance Corporation (FDIC) recently saved several banks, including Continental Illinois, the nation's seventh largest, which was burdened with bad debts to oil-exploration companies. In early 1984, FDIC injected $1 billion of capital into the bank and assumed $4.5 billion of its worst loans in exchange for an 80 percent share of the firm. Utility bankruptcies and defaults could seriously injure other banking institutions, already shaky with uncertain loans to Third World nations, and spur additional rescue operations.

Will LILCO, Consumers Power or any of the other faltering utilities file for bankruptcy? The Wall Street analysts and utility executives I have met feel the odds are about even. Will politicians rescue the faltering institutions? No one knows for sure. Pressures for a government bailout will certainly increase, but propping up a dying firm is an expensive and short-term solution that may be less productive than encouraging new enterprises.

STRUGGLES FOR PREFERENCE

For almost a century, public and private power companies have battled each other for government's helping hand. It is ironic, therefore, that the American Public Power Association (APPA) held its 1984 conference a week before private utility executives gathered for the Edison Electric Institute's (EEI) convention—and at the same Boston hotel.

Participants at both events discuss "megawatts," "switch gear," and other esoteric topics. Most are white, middle-aged males. But it's the contrasts between the groups that are most striking. Private utility executives, who usually represent multi-million-dollar businesses, parade about in expensive three-piece suits; public officials, who typically control small operations, don sport coats or short-sleeved shirts. While EEI conventioneers enjoy music from members of the Boston Pops orchestra, members of the APPA listen to the Smith Sisters, two folk singers with guitars. And while conservative columnist Patrick Buchanan tells private executives about the glories of the Reagan administration, liberal economist John Kenneth Galbraith blasts the President's broken promises to public officials; both speakers enjoy hearty applause from their respective audiences.

Public power officials typically service small-town America, the areas initially ignored by investor-owned utilities in favor of the more profitable large cities. Most manage no power generators, but rely on electricity from federal dams or private companies. One of the conference highlights is the announcement of the "Seven Hats Award," given to the manager of a tiny utility system who, in the course of doing his daily job, best assumes roles that range from negotiating power supply contracts to answering the phone.

Because small public utilities rarely build their own power plants, few representatives from Westinghouse, General Electric and other contractors attend the conference. But investment bankers are everywhere, trying to convince public officials to let them market the utilities' tax-exempt bonds. E. F. Hutton, for instance, charters ten buses to transport executives and their wives on an evening tour of Boston and to a catered dinner by the harbor. But as if to maintain the populist mood, the buffet is far less elaborate, the dessert table is about half the size of the one that appeared the following week for the more wealthy private utility executives, and the liquor is offered at a cash rather than an open bar.

Public power officials see themselves as progressive public servants, literally and figuratively bringing power to the people. Their liberalism, however, is founded in sincere patriotism. To open the conference, for instance, all 2,100 voices joined the Smith Sisters as a choir to proudly sing "The Star-Spangled Banner."

Unlike the EEI conventioneers, public power officials readily admit the utility industry faces fundamental problems, acknowledging construction-cost overruns and the reduced demand for electricity. To survive in this era of uncertainties, several officials advocate efficiency and optimistically discuss alternative energy development. Despite these progressive notions, they share the private utilities' continued confidence in the power of the atom. The conferees broke out in spontaneous ovation only once—when one of the speakers expressed his confidence in the safety and economy of nuclear power.

Throughout the 1970s, tensions between public and private utilities temporarily subsided as the two groups formed joint-action agencies to construct nuclear reactors. These partnerships pleased both groups: Public power companies could own more of their own generating capacity while private utilities could use the public firms' special status to raise low-cost capital in the tax-exempt bond market. But like most recent nuclear power managers, the joint-action agencies have run into severe problems, and other issues are rekindling the traditional animosity between investor-owned and government-owned utilities.

Nothing stirs the passions of public and private power advocates more than the struggle for priority access to the nation's waterways and dams. This battle is actually an old one that was initially settled in 1920 when Congress passed the Federal Power Act, granting 50-year licenses for dams on public rivers. Most licenses went initially to private utilities because they had the necessary financing to build dams, although the law clearly states that the government "shall give preference to applications ... by states and municipalities, provided the plans for the same are deemed by the [Federal Energy Regulatory] Commission equally well adapted to conserve and utilize in the public interest the water resources of the region." The Federal Power Act, however, says nothing about relicensing, and as the costs of nuclear and coal-fired plants accelerate, cheap hydropower looks increasingly attractive. Private power executives maintain the nation and its energy needs have changed dramatically since this legislation was adopted in 1920 and that the principle of public preference for hydropower no longer applies. Alex Radin, executive director of the American Public Power Association, disagrees vehemently. The debate is heating up because federal licenses held by private utilities on about 170 dams—worth more than $3 billion annually in saved fuel costs—will be up for renewal within the next decade. By early 1985, public agencies were challenging 11 of those permits.

In the final months of the Carter administration, the Federal Energy Regulatory Commission (FERC) sided with public power companies by granting the Bountiful, Utah, municipal utility's request to take over a small dam on the Weber River, operated by the investor-owned Utah Power & Light Company. Specifically, FERC declared that if the two utilities' plans for managing the river's ecosystem and power generation were equal, the public agency would have preference to take over the dam. The decision, immediately challenged by a group of 37 private utilities, was upheld by a federal appeals court in September 1982 and finally by the U.S. Supreme Court in July 1983.

But the Reagan-appointed FERC, after months of legal wrangling, reversed the 1980 Bountiful decision, leaving an unequivocal proprivate utility stamp on electricity regulation. FERC also rejected challenges from two public firms in Washington State, giving Pacific Power & Light a 30-year renewal on its license to operate the 136-megawatt Merwin dam.

Both sides hope Congress will settle the issue, but legislators seem inclined to avoid the controversy. Fortunately for consumers, the relicensing competition has already produced some healthy results. Consider Pacific Gas & Electric's (PG&E's) renewal application for the Rock Creek-Cresta Project. The private utility initially told FERC there was no basis for spending any money to improve the dam; the existing project, it claimed, "develops the full potential power head of this stretch of the North Fork Feather River and makes full use of all the water available for power production." Public power officials were not convinced. In June 1980, city managers of Santa Clara, Azusa, Banning, Colton and Riverside filed a competing application that proposed to construct two new generating units, upgrading the project's capacity 40 percent. PG&E may have looked silly, but it filed an "amended" license application in May 1981 that incorporated many of its competitors' proposals. Municipals say this type of competition would be lost if Congress eliminates public "preference."

Battles for government aid promise to continue between private and public utilities, with each side boasting that their system provides cheaper and more reliable power. But in the 1980s, new competitors within America's electricity industry are superseding these private-versus-public arguments. The benefits of a pluralistic electric industry, in fact, may be more fully achieved by these independent power producers than it has been by public power advocates. Efficiency, rather than politics, could well determine success in the emerging electricity market.

CHAPTER 10

THE NEW COMPETITORS

The existence of independent power producers is guaranteed by the Public Utility Regulatory Policies Act of 1978 (PURPA), but their rosy prospects stem from the weakening grip of the traditional utility giants. High electric rates are spurring the invention and promotion of an array of electricity-supplying alternatives that are bringing to the energy field the kind of dynamism and excitement that already pervades the computer industry. Today's individual shining examples may not be as dazzling as Samuel Insull's, but there are a lot more of them—and at a time when utilities are canceling a large power plant each month, the new competitors are expanding.

These electric entrepreneurs—who employ cogenerators (machines that simultaneously supply heat and electricity), burn wastes, and harness the sun, wind, falling water and geothermal steam—are ganging together to become one of the nation's fastest-growing industries. In California, where the phenomenon has been most rapid, independents supplied only 100 megawatts of the state's electricity in January 1982. Three years later, in January 1985, they had installed 1,659 megawatts of power plants, about the equivalent of two medium-sized nuclear reactors, and were constructing another 9,229 megawatts, enough to boost the output of independents to 25 percent of California's current electrical capacity. If additional contracts now under active negotiation with utilities are signed and executed, electric entrepreneurs will provide approximately 18,000 megawatts—a whopping 40 percent of the Golden State's capacity.

The enormous growth results from power plants averaging only 12 megawatts in size, 100 times smaller than a large nuclear reactor. Being less complex, these small facilities demand only 1 to 3 years to construct versus the 12 now required for reactors. About 43 percent of the signed contracts come from cogenerators, 30 percent from wind-energy developers, 12 percent from biomass burners, 8 percent from small hydro operators, and the remaining 7 percent divided between geothermal and solar entrepreneurs. The dramatic statistics, however, represent only part of the phenomenon since they include solely independent producers, not those entrepreneurs supplying power through conservation or energy management programs. Still, the contracts already signed by independent producers double the combined potential production of California's six nuclear reactors—only one of which operated at full power in 1984.

Independent power production is not limited to the Golden State; similar, if less spectacular growth is occurring in Maine, southern Texas and other pockets across the country where utility rates are high. In Houston, for example, cogenerators added 1,300 megawatts, more than a large nuclear reactor, between 1982 and 1984; later in the decade, they will supply almost 6,000 megawatts of electricity, more than half the capacity of Houston Lighting & Power, forcing the utility to cancel several of its planned power plants.

The new competitors are an array of large and small businesses that supply alternatives to the utility's electricity, including insulation, efficient appliances and computer-controlled energy management systems, as well as independently produced electricity. Within only a few years, electric entrepreneurs have become a multi-billion-dollar industry.

Some competition, of course, existed in the energy market well before the rise of independent producers. Ever since Thomas Edison established the Pearl Street Station, electric companies have struggled for markets against natural gas and fuel-oil distributors. Even today in regions where the same utility doesn't supply both electricity and gas, an advertising war is being waged between the electric heat pump and the gas condensing furnace for the home heating market. The Gas Company of Kansas, for example, has produced commercials declaring: "The fact is, 41 cents of gas can provide as much heat as $1 worth of electricity." Kansas City Power & Light Company, calling the ads "unjust, unresponsible and detrimental to the public interest," urged the state utility commission to halt the campaign.

Direct competition between a private and a public power company exists in perhaps a dozen U.S. cities, including Cleveland, Ohio. According to one economist, these contests have consistently stimulated lower prices and better service than are provided by regulated monopolies in similar markets. Even without direct competition, public power officials say municipalities and rural cooperatives provide some benefits of competition by creating a yardstick by which private power companies can be judged. But independent power producers in the 1980s are providing a quantum leap in the amount of competition within the electricity market, supplying a rich assortment of alternatives to the utility monopolies' power.

PRODUCING BY SAVING

Bob Williams has been demonstrating that the average American home need not be an energy sieve. Beginning in 1973, Williams and other Princeton University researchers designed and studied a townhouse complex in Twin Rivers, New Jersey. Every unit employs double-glazed windows, caulking and weather stripping. But the "house doctor" went further, prescribing extra-thick insulation for the attic and basement, installing movable window insulation, and blocking "hidden" air leaks around pipes, stairwells, recessed lights and unfinished ceilings. The common-looking homes are uncommonly efficient, using less than a third the energy of similar structures.

Since the 1973 oil embargo, conservation has become a science. Energy auditors use powerful fans to pull air rapidly out of existing homes in order to track down air leaks with a smoke gun. Infrared photography, the newest of the practical arts, can also indicate where a building is losing heat. Although not all homes are as efficient as those monitored by Princeton physicists, today's average new house uses about half the fuel of the 1975 prototype. In 1982 alone, 30 percent of the country's 61.4-million single-family units and mobile homes added some kind of conservation device. The potential for continued improvement remains high; studies show that even in 1984 less than 15 percent of Americans have made most of the cost-effective conservation investments possible.

Today, a few builders tap this potential by designing superinsulated homes that require almost no fuel for space heating. The buildings are so tightly constructed that the heat cast off by occupants, lights and appliances provides adequate warmth. Sufficient shading and natural ventilation virtually eliminate cooling costs, too.

Efficiency improvements are not limited to building designs. Lennox sells a residential gas furnace with an astonishing 95 percent efficiency rating, contrasted to 50 percent from a conventional furnace. Since the 1973 embargo, U.S. steel companies have cut oil use per ton of steel produced by 40 percent. (Japanese steel firms have done even better, reducing oil use 68 percent.) And a recently developed aluminum smelting process consumes about 40 percent less electricity per pound than current technologies.

Home appliances have also become significantly more efficient. Consider the refrigerator. Today's typical cold-box annually devours about 1,200 kilowatt-hours. The most efficient model being mass-produced in the United States, a Kenmore, uses 900 kilowatt-hours, a 25 percent reduction. (But the best Japanese refrigerator, a Toshiba, consumes only 480 kilowatt-hours, having improved almost sixfold in the past decade.) The modern model boasts separate refrigerator and freezer cooling units, extra-thick polyurethane foam insulation, an improved door seal and condenser fan motor. By buying the efficient Kenmore, consumers can annually earn 34 percent on their investment—above inflation and tax-free—from energy savings. Trading in the entire U.S. stockpile for more efficient refrigerators would obviate the need for approximately 12 nuclear reactors, about one-seventh the total now operating in the United States.

Other examples abound. This year's light bulbs are almost twice as efficient as their pre-embargo counterparts. And the recently developed Philips "SL" light bulb, which screws into a standard socket, provides excellent color and does not flicker, uses only one-quarter the electricity and lasts ten times longer than existing bulbs.

The U.S. appliance industry—dominated by General Electric, Whirlpool, Westinghouse, Lennox, Magic Chef and Carrier—annually sells $13 billion of refrigerators, washing machines, furnaces, air conditioners and other domestic electrical machines. More efficient designs, which are promoted in an unregulated environment, essentially compete with utility power plants to satisfy the needs of consumers for food preservation, clean clothes and heat. Replacing all current appliances with the most efficient models on the market, however, is unlikely. Landlords and homebuilders, who purchase most appliances, care more about their up-front costs than about users' long-term energy bills. And consumers wanting to make their own conservation improvements often lack the necessary financing and engineering expertise.

An array of new businesses—known as energy service companies—are solving many of these problems by managing electricity use for industrialists and owners of big apartment and commercial buildings. A nonexistent industry only a few years ago, more than 100 firms now invest what are often large amounts of money to install conservation measures in buildings and then share the savings on energy bills with their customers. The new companies, which signed $1 billion of contracts in 1984, offer modern computers that cut the temperature in unused rooms, stop exhaust fans at night, minimize unnecessary lighting and reduce electricity usage during expensive peak hours. One of these energy service firms is run by a scion of America's best-known political family.

When oil prices were soaring in 1978, Joseph P. Kennedy II spent weeks in his basement office learning how crude oil is produced, processed, shipped, stored and delivered to homes. Schooled in public service, the eldest son of Ethel and the late Robert F. Kennedy wanted to provide the public with the cheapest energy possible. After months of negotiations, including meetings with Sheik Zaki Yamani, Saudi Arabia's oil minister, Kennedy launched the Citizens Energy Corporation, a nonprofit company purchasing crude oil on the open market.

Citizens remains a unique petroleum company. Its contracts with Venezuela, Nigeria and other countries are on the same standard terms and conditions as other large purchasers, but it returns about one-quarter of its revenues to the people of the producing nation in the form of alternative energy programs. Saying he wants "to improve under-standing and cooperation among nations," the 33-year-old Kennedy supports large solar hot water systems at public hospitals in Jamaica and Venezuela, as well as a waste-burning energy project in Costa Rica. Moreover, Kennedy uses the revenues earned from the sale of petroleum products refined from Citizens' crude to reduce fuel-oil costs for more than 200,000 low-income families in Massachusetts. By 1984, Citizens had delivered 25-million gallons of heating oil at 30 to 40 percent below market rates.

In the early 1980s, the six-foot-tall, husky Kennedy expanded from fuel oil into the energy efficiency business, promising to reduce the fuel bills of schools and hospitals by installing computer controls, insulation and more-efficient lights and boilers. In May 1984, he inaugu-rated a "shared savings project" at the 99-bed J. B. Thomas Hospital in Peabody, Massachusetts, which is guaranteed to save the institution $354,000 in energy costs over the next decade. (If for some reason Kennedy's projected 30 percent energy savings doesn't materialize, Citizens will pay the difference. Any greater savings will be split between the hospital and the corporation.) After ten years, the hospital will own the conservation equipment free and clear.

A similar effort focuses on landlords who own multi-family buildings occupied by low- and moderate-income tenants. Kennedy pays for improvements of up to $2,000 per apartment, solicits competitive bids from contractors and supervises construction of the conservation retrofit. Businesses and landlords, therefore, receive guaranteed savings without having to pay for capital improvements; their monthly payments, slightly less than previous energy bills, cover actual fuel costs after conservation and amortize the investment in energy-saving improvements. By 1984 Citizens had weatherized 500 units in 30 separate buildings, reducing energy use approximately 35 percent.

Competing to bring efficient technologies to America's commer-cial buildings and factories are some of the nation's largest companies, including Honeywell, Shell Oil, IBM, ITT, United Technologies and Johnson Controls. The latter firm, maker of DieHard batteries, intro-duced millions to the world of computerized building automation systems with a series of television advertisements during the 1984 Summer Olympics. The list of buildings employing Johnson Controls' computers to reduce fuel bills is long and nationwide, including New York's Rockefeller Center, the U.S. Naval Academy in Annapolis, the Library of Congress in Washington, D.C., Coca Cola's headquarters complex in Atlanta, New Orleans' Superdome, Wisconsin's state capitol complex, Detroit's Metropolitan Airport, St. Louis' Convention Center, Rice University in Houston, the MGM Grand Hotel in Las Vegas, Brigham Young University in Utah and Honolulu's Royal Hawaiian Plaza. Time Energy Systems, a Houston-based firm and a leader with energy service contracts, monitors 900 buildings across the country with one central computer.

Total U.S. spending for energy efficiency—including sales by energy service companies and insulation contractors—rose from less than $2 billion in 1978 to $8.7 billion in 1980. *Business Week* estimated that outlays would reach $30 billion in 1985 and $50 billion in 1990.

Conservation advocates believe the government should do more to promote these efficient products and to reform practices that encourage consumption. California has taken the lead in this area. Rather than rely on the marketplace to promote new technologies, the state sets minimum efficiency levels and prohibits the sale of "energy guzzling" appliances. California officials also require urban developers to take solar orientation into account in laying out streets and siting buildings. San Diego County goes a step further, requiring all new buildings to feature solar water heaters. Although President Reagan eliminated most national conservation initiatives, the Federal Trade Commission still requires appliance manufacturers to display efficiency labels on refrigerators, freezers, water heaters, dishwashers, clothes dryers and room air conditioners.

Even without policy changes, the new technologies "produce" electricity for less than a few cents per kilowatt-hour, motivating cost-conscious and informed consumers to purchase *efficiency* rather than *electricity*. A new breed of energy managers and appliance manufacturers, therefore, is supplying alternatives to electricity and competing with utility companies.

INDUSTRY'S BONANZA

The hottest item in industrial energy right now is the cogenerator. This ingenious machine produces both heat and electricity and can mean huge savings for businesses that might otherwise vent most of their energy to the great outdoors. The benefit of cogeneration is efficiency—the hybrid machines more than double the useful energy obtained for each dollar invested. A power plant producing only electricity is approximately 32 percent efficient; a cogenerator using the same amount of fuel can be 80 percent efficient.

Thomas Edison built some of the first cogenerators almost a century ago, including a unit installed in 1888 at the Hotel del Coronado near San Diego, where it operated without a hitch for 50 years. Before the rise of dependable electric companies, in fact, more than half of all American factories operated their own power equipment, but they slowly abandoned cogenerators as the utilities' fuel and construction costs fell.

With utility rates soaring in the 1980s, cogeneration is enjoying a renaissance among petroleum refiners, wood and food processors, steel and chemical producers, cement mixers and other companies that need both heat and electric power. "There is more business out there than you can possibly imagine," gloats one cogeneration developer. Even the Hotel del Coronado installed a new system that now saves the resort almost $6,000 each month in energy costs. By late 1984, cogeneration provided over 15,000 megawatts of power in the United States; another 200 projects with a total capacity of 6,000 megawatts were under construction. By the century's end, analysts expect cogeneration to be a $63 billion industry, supplying 15 percent of the nation's total electricity, more than is now produced by nuclear reactors. Achieving this enormous potential, however, requires complex negotiations among entrepreneurs, utility executives and government regulators.

The cogeneration industry already includes an array of companies, both large and small. Some employ the hybrid machines as a means to reduce their own energy costs; although they sell their excess electricity to the local utility, they typically do not view themselves to be in the power business. Others are developers—ranging from one-room companies to General Electric—which try to sell cogeneration equipment or independently produced electricity to consumers.

In a typical cogeneration system, fuel (often natural gas, although wood, plant wastes, coal, residual oil and even peach pits are used) is burned in a boiler to produce steam. The steam spins an electric generator and then is captured for heating, refrigerating or manufacturing processes, rather than being discarded to the air. Large businesses needing both heat and electricity usually purchase custom-designed systems, using the steam for their own operations and selling excess electric power to the local utility. Commercial establishments—such as hospitals, restaurants and dairy farms—demand smaller, packaged units. Cogeneration systems usually cost between $500 and $1,000 per kilowatt of electric capacity—less than half the price of new coal or nuclear plants.

Cogenerators come in all shapes and sizes. The S&W Cannery burns peach pits and other wastes to generate the heat and electricity required by its Modesto, California, factory, a facility that supplies half the nation's canned peaches. "We're reducing our trash, saving energy, and earning revenue from sales of excess electricity to Pacific Gas & Electric," brags Allan Christie, S&W's plant engineer.

Georgia Pacific views its machines as a hedge against higher electric rates. The giant lumber-products company spent $100 million to install a 140-megawatt system at its Plaquemine, Louisiana, chlorine production plant. Getty Oil has even bigger plans. By early 1986, a giant, 300-megawatt cogenerator will flood Getty's oil wells near Bakersfield with steam to enhance recovery of thick oil deposits; the gas-powered unit will also sell Southern California Edison enough electricity to power 150,000 homes.

Rosedale Village, an apartment complex constructed over New York City's old Jamaica Racetrack, generates all its own electricity and heat. Towers housing more than 35,000 families—approximately the size of Charlottesville, Virginia—have totally disconnected from Consolidated Edison's grid.

James Dunlop, vice-president of Brooklyn Union Gas, says his firm's natural gas powers more than 100 megawatts of independent electric generators in the New York metropolitan area. Brooklyn Union is one of several gas companies that view cogeneration as a lucrative way to capture some of the electric industry's market. Gas sales to a large cogeneration project near Houston, for instance, will total more than $1 billion over the next decade. According to *Oil & Gas Journal*, "the burgeoning U.S. cogeneration industry holds the best promise of triggering a significant increase in demand for natural gas."

Although cogeneration is extremely efficient, it is not problem free. While cleaner burning than most utility power plants, gas-powered cogenerators emit some nitrogen oxides that must be scrubbed by pollution-control equipment. As long as efficient cogenerators substitute for dirty power stations owned by a utility, the environment benefits; but additional pollution occurs if cogenerators displace cleaner alternatives.

Cogeneration is also not for everyone. Consumers must need both heat and electricity on a fairly continuous basis to capitalize on the hybrid machine's efficiency; if they use heat only a few hours each day, a cogenerator would emit wasted heat the same way a conventional power plant does. And many industrialists, worried about investing in technologies foreign to their main business activity, do not want to manage their own power plants. A new wave of entrepreneurs, however, is eliminating these concerns by building and operating cogenerators for businesses.

Roger Sant has advocated energy alternatives as a bureaucrat, an academician and an entrepreneur. After a brief stint as President Ford's top official for energy conservation, Sant directed the Mellon Institute's energy research center, publishing provocative books about efficiency. By 1981, this graduate of Harvard's School of Business Administration, tired of writing and lecturing, decided to put his theories into practice and form Applied Energy Services (AES), a privately held corporation that builds, owns and operates cogeneration facilities. "I've never had so much fun," exclaims Sant.

His stockholders are also pleased. AES's first project, to be completed in 1986, will sell up to 135 megawatts of electricity—enough to meet the power needs of 67,500 homes—to Houston Lighting & Power, and 600,000 pounds of steam an hour to Atlantic Richfield for its refining processes. To arrange the $275 million deal, Sant assembled a "Who's Who" of American business: Morgan Guaranty (considered the "bastion of banking conservatism") organized a financing consortium to provide the construction loan while the Bechtel Group (builder of dams and nuclear power plants) served as the prime contractor. But AES's Deepwater Power Plant is unconventional, in part because it burns petroleum, coke or refinery waste instead of high-cost oil or natural gas. Its major distinction, however, is that Sant the entrepreneur—rather than the electric utility monopoly—owns and operates the power plant. "We are the pioneers of an unregulated electricity business," the AES president declares.

If Sant enjoyed controversy as a bureaucrat and academician, he relishes competition as a businessman. Bankers expect Sant and other small developers will be run out of the unregulated electricity business by giant engineering firms, utilities and electrical-equipment manufacturers. But Sant confidently asserts that the history of American business shows that "the big boys have never developed new markets." Utility executives, he claims, lack the management skills needed to successfully compete, and equipment vendors remain locked into their own technologies. That leaves the market open to new entities that can quickly produce low-cost and efficient generating equipment.

Sant doesn't overestimate AES's importance, admitting "we're nothing but a little pimple in the total electricity market at this point." But the young company will soon put $1 billion of assets to work generating electricity, and Sant believes independent power producers "will generate a big hunk of future electricity expansion." Within a quarter century, he predicts they will be the rule, rather than the exception.

Dick Nelson's face conveys experience; his voice delivers confidence. He learned how to cut deals as President Lyndon Johnson's personal assistant for eight years (LBJ's pictures still line his office walls). Before working in the White House, the short, dark-haired Nelson established assembly lines for Continental Can and earlier ran an investment banking operation. With experience in politics, manufacturing and finance, he feels perfectly prepared to manage a cogeneration company.

While Roger Sant designs site-specific machines for large industries, Nelson targets small businesses, offering packaged cogeneration systems for hotels, hospitals, office buildings, waste-water treatment centers, prisons or light manufacturing plants that demand both heat and electricity. The president of Cogenic Energy Systems knows that most U.S. businesses want the benefits of lower electricity prices but not the bother of managing complex power equipment. Nelson illustrates this point by describing his first meeting with a New York dairy farmer who could save lots of money with a cogenerator. "It took me 40 years to learn how to make cottage cheese," the farmer said, "and I don't want to start learning how to make electricity." Like most consumers, the dairyman enjoys flipping switches and assuming the lights will go on. While he doesn't appreciate the high rates he pays to his utility company, he doesn't want to buy and operate an electric generator.

To the farmer and hundreds of other small firms, Nelson says, "I'll take all the risks of installing and operating a cogenerator. Without making any up-front investment, you get to cap your energy costs and add half the system's energy savings to your bottom line." Nelson pockets the other half. This "shared savings" approach presents an offer few cost-conscious businesses refuse. It also maximizes Cogenic's profits. "If I simply sell a cogenerator," admits Nelson, "I make a profit of 40 cents on each dollar I invest, period. But if I continue to own and operate the system, my share of the energy savings equals 20 cents each year. After two years, my profit margin continues to rise."

Holiday Inn is one of Nelson's best clients. After years of testing alternative energy systems, the national hotel chain concluded that "cogeneration is the best approach for us because it gives a good source of steady power." In late 1983, the company installed a Cogenic system at its hotel near New York's La Guardia Airport. If the demonstration annually saves $63,000 in fuel costs as Nelson projects, Holiday Inn plans to place cogenerators at its other 230 hotels and to encourage its 1,800 franchises to follow the example. McDonald's is also testing cogeneration for its thousands of fast-food outlets. But packaged cogenerators are not yet sufficiently inexpensive or maintenance-free to be placed in home-owners' basements.

Unlike many independent power producers, Nelson usually avoids tough negotiations with power companies because his small systems qualify for standardized contracts approved by state regulators. He sees Cogenic as a "partner with the utility, not as an alternative," whereby the cogenerator reduces the power company's need to build expensive power stations, while the utility sells "back-up" electricity to meet the commercial building's peak demand.

Despite this talk of cooperation, Nelson becomes agitated and angry when he discusses Consolidated Edison (Con Ed) of New York. "Con Ed has truculently opposed independent cogenerators since the beginning," he declares. The giant utility often refuses to provide back-up power, forcing Cogenic to install extra machines and to uncouple from the grid. And even when Con Ed offers supplementary service, it charges "obscene" rates, says Nelson, 15 times more than some other utilities.

What really irks Nelson is Con Ed's claim that cogenerators pollute the environment. "As if utilities are putting Arpege into the atmosphere," decries the executive sarcastically. While both the power company and the cogenerator burn fossil fuels, Nelson claims Con Ed spews nitric oxides from its old, inefficient oil-burning boilers. "If cogenerators efficiently burn clean natural gas for the same purpose," he concludes, "we are not polluters."

When Nelson founded Cogenic Energy Systems in January 1981, he became the first manufacturer of packaged cogeneration systems. He now faces a dozen competitors. Industry sales have jumped from fewer than 5 throughout the nation in 1981 to more than 200 in 1984. Consultants predict 80,000 small units will operate by the century's end, providing the equivalent of 12 large nuclear reactors. "Small-scale cogeneration will soon be a multi-billion-dollar industry," predicts a confident Nelson, "and we'll be glad to take half the market."

The pain of the utilities' power plant cancellations quickly trickles down to equipment manufacturers, engineering firms and building contractors. Bechtel Group, the giant construction company, laid off almost 4,000 employees in 1984 due to delays and cancellations of nuclear power projects. Manufacturers of generators, switch gear and transformers operate at only 40 percent of capacity. "The utility market is tight, and will remain tight," laments John Hopkins of the National Electrical Manufacturers Association, adding that he has sent his résumé out in search of new job opportunities.

As the utility market flounders, these industrialists enviously eye cogeneration. "Right now, it's about the only business out there of any consequence in power equipment," says Frank DiNoto, corporate business development manager for Hawker Siddeley Power Engineering of Houston. To assemble Cogenic's packaged system, for instance, Richard Nelson buys scores of engines from Caterpillar and 700 other components from 200 vendors.

Helping entrepreneurs who compete with utilities troubles many of these engineers, including Paul Carroll of Fischbach and Moore. Even today, the giant electrical contractor receives 27 percent of its income from maintenance and repair contracts with power companies. "Utilities are very upset that we develop cogenerators," admits Carroll, "but they have nothing to offer. It's an issue of staying alive for us."

Thomas Edison's old company has entered the emerging cogeneration market in a big way. "General Electric has been building cogenerators ever since its birth," comments Dave Wallace, manager of market development for General Electric's cogeneration division, "but PURPA is creating a whole new market opportunity for us." It's an exciting business for the executive. It's also a profitable business for an electrical-equipment manufacturer that has laid off almost 3,000 workers in its nuclear operations because of the utility industry's construction slowdown.

General Electric sees itself as a "full service" cogeneration company that will perform detailed engineering designs, manufacture the major turbine equipment, provide financing through the General Electric Credit Corporation, install and even operate the facility. Its largest project is the Bayou Cogeneration Plant, a joint venture with Big Three Industries in Bayport, Texas. General Electric will design, construct, operate and maintain the facility, which utilizes four of General Electric's heavy-duty gas turbines. Big Three plans to use most of the steam for its production of oxygen, nitrogen and argon, and to distribute the excess by pipeline to five neighboring chemical plants. By March 1985, the project will also sell 300 megawatts of electricity—enough to power 150,000 homes—to Houston Lighting & Power.

Wallace acknowledges that sales to independent power producers seem to conflict with General Electric's traditional marketing of turbines to electric companies. "In this new and exciting market," he claims, "we are simply responding to industrialists who must cut their energy costs and increase their productivity in order to compete on the world market." The reborn technology, he predicts, holds promise for utilities, too, if they cooperate in joint ventures. Still, he admits, "We're looking at a major change in the method of producing electricity and steam in this country—driven by the demand for efficiency."

MODERN-DAY QUIXOTES

Windmills may have gotten the better of Cervantes's hero, but a new generation of dreamers is using sophisticated wind-energy machines to challenge utility giants. By early 1985, small, innovative firms had installed 8,469 turbines throughout California, producing enough electricity for 70,000 modern homes. The California Energy Commission expects wind machines to supply at least 8 percent of the state's electric power by the century's end, enough electricity to run all the homes in the city of Los Angeles.

Fifty miles to the southeast of San Francisco, scores of new businesses have already turned Altamont Pass into a "Silicon Valley" for wind-energy development. Five years ago, the barren, rolling hills supported only a few herd of cattle. In early 1985, ranchers shared their land with more than 2,500 turbines that convert the constant breezes into electricity and profits.

Well-designed machines placed at windy sites generate electric power for less than ten cents per kilowatt-hour; researchers believe more sophisticated and mass-produced turbines can reduce that cost to approximately four cents per kilowatt-hour, making it cheaper than power from new coal or nuclear plants. In fact, developers cut per-kilowatt costs in half between 1981 and 1984, and they continue experimenting with a variety of designs, including vertical-axis machines that look like inverted eggbeaters. Some wind companies promise turbines costing only slightly more than $1,000 per kilowatt of capacity by mid-1985, almost a third the cost of power from nuclear reactors.

During the energy panic in the 1970s, the federal government paid several large aerospace companies to produce giant five-megawatt machines with blades as long as a jumbo jet's wing. Eight huge turbines still operate in the United States, but several of the complex systems suffered engineering breakdowns. The huge windmill in Boone, North Carolina, for instance, cost the federal government $30 million to design and build; four years later, it was scrapped and sold for only $51,600. Boeing and Bendix, however, claim their new designs for large windmills compete economically with conventional power plants.

The real boom is with "wind farms," clusters of smaller turbines connected to an electric grid. The first such commercial enterprise began generating power in New Hampshire in 1981, but California boasts the most progress with thousands of wind-energy machines lining the ridges of Altamont, San Gorgonio and Tehachapi passes. Prompted by the state government's generous tax credits, Golden State entrepreneurs have signed 10- or 20-year contracts with utilities to sell 2,200 megawatts of wind-generated electricity. Smaller wind farms have been developed in Vermont, Hawaii, Oregon, New York and Montana; industry analysts expect activity soon in the Rocky Mountain states and Texas.

U.S. Windpower Corporation, the largest wind-energy firm, discovered that prospective clients, who associate wind-energy machines more with Don Quixote than with profits, worry about purchasing unconventional technologies. Rather than buck the impression, the San Francisco-based company decided to sell electricity rather than windmills. In the early 1980s, U.S. Windpower began offering long-term contracts for low-cost electricity. Taking advantage of tax incentives, the firm assumes all the risks, attracts its own investors, and leases land on which to construct the machines. By late 1984, U.S. Windpower employed 300 workers and sold 80 megawatts of power to Pacific Gas & Electric; by 1988, it expects to sell an additional 440 megawatts to California utilities.

Wind availability, of course, varies by region. Relatively few sites possess the necessary average wind speeds of at least 15 miles per hour to produce electricity economically; mountain passes and coastlines appear most promising. Technical problems also temper optimism. On the windy day in May 1984 when I drove over California's Altamont Pass from the Central Valley to San José, only about half the turbines were spinning. U.S. manufacturers privately admit their machines frequently break down, because the designers failed to appreciate the enormous stress on the equipment caused by rapidly shifting winds; but they also claim performance is improving as the young industry gains experience. Danish turbines, in contrast, outperform their American counterparts, largely because Europeans concentrate on durability and reliability rather than sophisticated technology.

As with all decentralized power systems, wind-energy companies must develop the organizational structure to ensure that technically competent personnel constantly maintain their machines. In contrast to the rosy pictures of trouble-free windmills painted by early renewable-energy advocates, an experienced engineer put the business of independent power production into perspective: "Unless you've walked into a totally dark generator room with a flashlight in one hand and a toolbox in the other, you haven't had a firsthand experience with on-site power." Not unlike dispersed pumps for oil fields or water irrigation, decentralized power plants benefit by being of standard design and sufficiently close together for regular monitoring and maintenance.

In addition to having performance problems, a few wind-energy firms and energy service companies have been criticized for exploiting tax benefits rather than supplying energy. Some have exaggerated the value of their equipment as much as 20-fold in order to take exorbitant tax credits and depreciation allowances. The Internal Revenue Service and trade associations have begun to police these abuses, but several politicians have used the examples to argue against extending the renewable-energy tax credits beyond 1985. Termination of the credits will certainly drive several wind-energy companies under. Still, Ed Blum, a vice-president of Merrill Lynch Capital Markets, predicts lean, aggressive entrepreneurs in windy sections of the country will continue to generate electricity economically and make substantial profits.

Marcellus Jacobs has been tapping wind energy since the 1920s, when he devised a machine that supplied electricity to his remote Montana ranch. A decade later he moved to Minneapolis to manufacture his device, selling thousands throughout the world. The Jacobs windmills became a familiar sight on American farms, providing electrical and pumping power before rural electric co-ops extended the utility grid.

Jacobs's most famous machine powered Admiral Richard Byrd's

base camp near the South Pole in the mid-1930s. Operating under extreme weather conditions, the system delivered electricity for the expedition's lights and radio. Byrd returned 22 years later to find the snow had built up to within ten feet of the tower's top but that the blades were "still turning in the breeze."

The market for wind-energy machines died in the 1950s when utilities extended abundant and inexpensive electricity to remote regions of the United States. Jacobs and his son, Paul, closed their Minnesota factory and moved to Florida, where they continued experimenting with blade designs. The 1973 oil embargo revived interest in their research, and in 1980 they began collaborating with the giant Control Data Corporation to produce a new generation of Jacobs wind-energy plants.

"Today's market is much larger than my dad first thought," says Paul Jacobs, now a vice-president with the company. In the 1930s, Marcellus sold stand-alone units to farmers far from the utility grid. Today, Paul uses microprocessors to connect the machines into transmission lines, allowing customers to use the wind-generated electricity for themselves or to sell it to the local utility.

RESURGENCE OF AN ANCIENT FUEL

For Bernard Bartos, a Dow Corning executive, the choice lay between building his own wood-fired cogenerator or buying expensive nuclear electricity and steam from Consumers Power, Michigan's largest utility. A decision to become an independent power producer would mean energy independence for Dow Corning but financial headaches for Consumers.

The story begins in 1968 when Dow Chemical, which jointly owns Bartos's firm with Corning Glass Works and also operates a separate plant across the street, agreed to purchase most of the electricity and steam from the proposed Midland reactors. Consumers Power projected the two-unit nuclear plant would cost $267 million and open by 1975. But a series of construction and safety problems mired these plans. The facility, for instance, began to sink because of faulty soil preparation, forcing the utility to conduct an expensive tunneling and shoring-up operation. Consumers Power eventually admitted the Midland plant would raise rates at least 68 percent by 1990, a financial shock for Dow Corning, a big user of electricity and steam in its chemical manufacturing processes. Bartos believed he could generate less expensive power.

In July 1983, Dow Chemical sued Consumers Power to break its Midland contract, declaring "fraudulent misrepresentation" of construction deficiencies that delayed the reactor's completion. Bartos added another blow six months later when he inaugurated Dow Corning's cogeneration system, fueled largely with wood wastes from sawmills, pulp mills and lumbering operations within a 75-mile radius of Midland. In mid-1984, Consumers was forced to abandon the Midland project, declaring that the $4 billion reactor—costing 15 times the original estimate—lacked an adequate market for its expensive power. As a result, Consumers' stock plunged in value.

"Dow really left us in the lurch," laments the utility's Tom Holliday. The troubles wracked the entire city of Jackson, Michigan, leaving numerous department stores along Michigan Avenue vacant, including those across the street from Consumers Power's headquarters. Utility lawyers have sued Dow to receive a $460 million penalty for the chemical company's withdrawal from the Midland project, but Dow has filed its own countersuit.

Meanwhile, Dow Corning's 11-story, $35 million facility generates 22 megawatts of electricity and 275,000 pounds of steam per hour. Although much smaller than the proposed Midland reactors, the cogenerator supplies electric power and heat at 25 percent below the price offered by Consumers Power. And ironically, because of PURPA, Dow Corning sells its excess electricity to Consumers at a lower rate than the utility could gain elsewhere.

Bernard Bartos doesn't think a lot about Consumers' problems. He enjoys boasting of his project, especially since the National Society of Professional Engineers identified Dow Corning's wood-fired power plant as one of the ten outstanding U.S. engineering achievements of 1983. But the system's most important contributions, claims Bartos, are the energy savings and self-reliance it provides the company. "I can see the reactor from my window," admits Dow Corning's cogeneration director. "But we're pretty much independent of it and OPEC oil."

New technologies for gathering forest wastes make wood-fired boilers attractive for other industries, too. Instead of high-quality logs, businesses can burn the branches, bark and diseased trees left in the wake of timber and pulp operations. Since the 1973 OPEC embargo, industrialists have added more than 2,000 large wood-fired boilers and many thousands more small facilities, accounting for 10 percent of all U.S. boiler sales. Cost savings can be dramatic, as a Massachusetts firm discovered when its annual fuel bill fell from $720,000 for oil to $270,000 for wood.

Paper and lumber companies have always been pioneers in the burning of wood, partly because they own so much fuel and partly because utilities initially refused to run transmission lines to remote mills. Today the forest products industry receives more than half its energy needs from wood wastes. Weyerhaeuser, the industry's largest firm, generates two-thirds of its energy from wood and plans to gain total energy self-reliance by 1990.

Other industrial examples abound. The Scott Paper Company in Westbrook, Maine, uses its bark, pulping wastes and wood chips to generate 30 megawatts of power. After satisfying its own needs, Scott sells its excess electricity to the local utility. In 1983, Procter and Gamble spent $30 million to convert its large Staten Island, New York, detergent and food factories from oil to wood, and now annually saves $3 million in energy costs.

While more and more Fortune 500 firms produce their own power, new engineering and construction companies are beginning to generate electricity exclusively for sale to the utilities. Ultrasystems, a $77 million company located in Irvine, California, began with defense and space contracts in 1969, but as oil prices rose, the company put its forces to work building alternative energy plants. Ultrasystems' three 11-megawatt generators in the California cities of Westwood, Burney and Chinese Station will begin distributing electricity to the grid in 1985. The fast-growing firm, which views itself as one of the nation's largest unregulated power companies, plans to build 20 similar plants over the next five years.

After a century-long decline in demand, humanity's oldest fuel is enjoying a renaissance. It already supplies twice the power—including both heat and electricity—of all U.S. nuclear reactors combined. And the resource's popularity is not limited to industrialists. Residential wood stoves, for example, have become common features in American homes, particularly throughout New England where lumber is plentiful and fuel oil expensive.

The statistical rise is impressive: From the 1973 embargo to the decade's end, annual sales of residential wood stoves increased ninefold. Americans purchased two-million units in 1981 alone. Almost 29 percent of U.S. homes burn wood; 4.6 million employ wood stoves as their primary source of heat. This resurgence of wood use results from higher conventional energy costs and from recent improvements in stove designs. Airtight Scandinavian stoves, which cost between $600 and $2,000, burn wood more efficiently and slow down the escape of hot gases so the stoves radiate more heat.

Rate shocks are spurring interest in a variety of other fuels derived from plants, a form of energy known as "biomass." In Hawaii, bagasse, a fibrous residue from sugarcane, is the second-largest energy source, surpassed only by petroleum. On Kauai, an improved bagasse boiler produces more than half the island's electricity. Sugar-plantation owners also burn field wastes and hay, as well as convert a small portion of their 320,000 tons of sugarcane molasses into alcohol fuels.

Several city public works departments anaerobically digest a mixture of organic garbage and sewage to produce methane (which they feed into existing natural gas pipelines) and a rich residue they use as fertilizer. An innovative system developed by Biogas of Colorado converts the manure from 40,000 head of cattle at a huge feedlot in Lamar into enough methane to provide half the fuel for a 50-megawatt power plant.

San Diego believes it's got an energy gold mine within its urban wastes. When completed in 1987, an independent power plant will extract noncombustibles and ferrous metals from 1,500 tons of trash each day before burning the coarsely shredded refuse in a $100 million waste-to-energy power facility. The facility, which will sell approximately 30 megawatts of electricity to San Diego Gas & Electric, increases local tax revenues and reduces the need for landfill space.

Biomass burners, of course, face the same environmental constraints as other power generators. The state of Oregon and several towns in Montana and Colorado regulate wood-burning stoves in order to reduce the organic emissions that can shroud mountain valleys. Some communities require catalytic converters be added to wood stoves to decrease pollutants; the equipment recoups part of its $100 cost by increasing the unit's efficiency. For industries, electrostatic precipitators remove virtually all particulates. Dow Corning's pollution-control equipment raised construction costs 15 percent, still significantly less than adding precipitators to coal-fired plants. The San Diego trash-burning facility includes an extra $10 million of equipment to meet California's strict environmental requirements.

Gaining a long-term, wood-supply contract—which bankers require for loans—presents another problem for entrepreneurs. The U.S. Forest Service, the largest owner of woodlands, rebids slash contracts every few years in order to assure competitive prices for public resources. Lumber companies, the other major source of wood, are not reliable suppliers either, because their operations fluctuate with the housing market; during the 1982 recession, only two mills operated in Oregon.

Still, entrepreneurs are profitably burning wood, other biomass fuels and wastes to generate electricity. An energy gold mine, they say, remains to be tapped in America's forests and landfills.

RIVERS OF ENERGY

David Goodman could finally smile when he helped cut the ribbon on a 750-kilowatt generator, powered by the water of the Fishkill River falling 34 feet over a century-old granite dam near Beacon, New York. It had taken the young entrepreneur four years to secure $1.7 million of financing and a dozen permits from federal and state agencies. Goodman, the president of United American Hydropower Corporation, will sell enough electricity to Central Hudson Electric & Gas to power about 375 homes and to give himself a 25 to 30 percent return on his investment. But he feels the venture also provides a public service: "It's not nuclear, it doesn't burn coal which creates acid rain, and it doesn't burn oil which we are trying to get away from."

Shortly after the passage of PURPA, interest in small-scale hydroelectric projects rose dramatically. The U.S. Army Corps of Engineers fanned the enthusiasm by estimating that the potential output from small dams totaled a staggering 24,000 megawatts—enough electricity to run all the homes in the New York, Los Angeles and Chicago metropolitan areas. Renovating larger flood-control and irrigation dams could provide another 44,000 megawatts. With congressional passage of generous tax credits and utility buy-back requirements, permit applications to tap this enormous potential rose from 101 in 1979 to a "record-setting" 1,282 in 1983, according to the Federal Energy Regulatory Commission.

The dreams of a "hydro gold rush," however, were greatly exaggerated. "The fuel—falling water—is free, but building a small hydro dam is more complex and expensive than anyone first imagined," admits Leslie Eden of Hydro Consultants, a research and publishing firm located in Boston. Of the initial estimate of 24,000 megawatts, Eden predicts only 2,400 megawatts can be economically developed.

For one thing, negotiating with electric companies frustrates many hydro entrepreneurs. A small hydro project is contingent on a long-term contract with the utility, but power companies often refuse to sign agreements because they don't know the future price of energy alternatives and because dams can't provide reliable supplies during droughts.

Hydro developers also say stacks of rules and permits send their engineering costs through the roof. "I never thought I'd sympathize with nuclear reactor builders," protests one developer, "but my hydro project is being strangled by regulations." A European manufacturer of water turbines examined the U.S. market, expressed regret that Americans do not practice free enterprise, and returned home.

Finally, hydropower, although a "renewable" or "safe" energy source, often provokes the ire of environmentalists. Dams, they say, flood prime farmland, destroy wilderness preserves and damage fish and plant habitats. Although environmentalists have praised the addition of turbines and fish ladders to a few existing dams, they vehemently oppose the construction of new structures. Working with the tourist industry, they successfully lobbied for the Wild and Scenic Rivers Act to protect parts of 36 rivers—with a combined capacity equaling 12 large nuclear reactors—from further development. Given the choice, environmentalists prefer efficiency initiatives—such as load management or appliance standards—to any form of energy development. They have drawn battle lines in the Pacific Northwest where more than 1,400 hydropower permit applications await approval.

Despite setbacks to the initial euphoria, small hydro developers believe they offer an economic and relatively gentle alternative to centralized power plants, particularly when they are adding turbines to existing dams. Enough "rich sites," for instance, are scattered throughout New York State to match the Shoreham reactor's output at only half the cost. Concludes Leslie Eden: "Clearly, hydropower presents long-term benefits or serious businessmen wouldn't be involved."

THE ELECTRIC INFERNO

Unlike wind, water or solar power, geothermal energy percolates constantly, providing predictable, round-the-clock power. While most people only relate the earth's heat to Yellowstone's geysers and occasional hot springs, there are those who dream of tapping the large amount of water boiling below ground to generate electricity.

Pacific Gas & Electric has proven that such technology works. At the Geysers, the world's largest geothermal power complex, 200 wells provide 1,000 megawatts of power more cheaply and more reliably than could a similar-size nuclear reactor. In 1983, the San Francisco-based utility started another unit at the north-central California facility.

Hawaiians are also trying to tap the enormous power of Madame Pele, the locally revered goddess of fire and volcanoes. When I approached the "Big Island" of Hawaii in January 1983, strong winds swept Mount Kilauea's billowing clouds far out to sea. At night, the volcano's red glow brightened the sky. While no one advocates harnessing an erupting volcano, the region's unstable geology provides the world's hottest geothermal wells, feeding 675-degree-Fahrenheit steam into a three-megawatt generator to supply about 1,500 homes with electricity. The potential for additional wells is vast, claims John Shupe, director of the Hawaii Natural Energy Institute. Shupe estimates geothermal plants could provide more than 900 megawatts of electricity by the century's end, more than ten times the Big Island's current demand.

Geothermal sites offer many opportunities for independent businesses, which must borrow the skills and equipment of the petroleum industry to tap the earth's power. Because survey and drilling techniques are also similar, McCullough and a few other mid-sized oil companies have entered the geothermal market and will probably dominate the emerging industry.

The resource, of course, can be economically tapped only where molten rock lies close to the earth's surface, although scientists are trying to find ways to use more abundant, lower-temperature water or steam for electricity generation. Harnessing a potential site, moreover, requires overcoming the corrosion and pollution problems associated with the mineral-laden geothermal water. Still, geothermal use has expanded more than 10 percent each year since the mid-1970s.

TAPPING THE SUN

Shortly after the 1973 oil embargo, Americans became fascinated with schemes to harness the sun's inexhaustible power. Technophiles predicted that satellites the size of the island of Manhattan would orbit outside the earth's shadow and beam microwaves back to receiving stations on earth. Others foresaw the world's deserts covered with mirrors that would concentrate sunlight on "power towers," which would convert the white-hot reflections into electricity. Some futurists predicted rectangular solar collectors would transform every rooftop into a hot-water heater.

The most grandiose solar dreams, of course, have not been realized. Orbiting power stations were abandoned because the $60 billion price tag was too high, the microwaves were considered harmful, and the satellite would have been difficult to protect from sabotage or enemy attack. One "power tower" operates in California's Mojave Desert, but Southern California Edison has been reluctant to order a larger unit. And only 650,000 American homes—about 1 percent of the total housing stock—heat a portion of their water with solar collectors.

Much of the disappointment in the residential market results from American solar-collector manufacturers having concentrated on reliability instead of economics, emphasizing cold-weather protection above low prices. A typical U.S. solar hot-water system costs more than $4,000, compared to Israel's $500 thermosiphon collector used by 65 percent of that nation's homes. Kevin Finneran of the Solar Energy Industries Association, a trade group in Washington, D.C., admits high-priced devices cannot compete against conservation measures or efficient gas heaters, especially if the solar tax credits are not renewed beyond 1985. Peter Barnes feels solar businesses' "salad days are over until the next energy crisis." San Francisco's worker-owned Solar Center, with which Barnes is associated, still pushes solar equipment, but is diversifying into small-scale cogenerators.

Still, solar panels on rooftops are a common source of domestic hot water in California, Arizona, Colorado, New Mexico and Florida. President Carter installed the "First Collector" on the White House in 1979. Throughout the Tennessee valley, commercial and residential solar applications displace the equivalent of 40 megawatts of electric power; by 1990, this contribution will increase to 500 megawatts, about half the output of a large nuclear reactor.

Throughout the 1980s, solar designers have slowly shifted their focus from these "active" collectors to "passive" techniques that do not require fans or pumps to move heat. Building "with the sun" is actually an ancient idea revived by high-energy costs; over 2,000 years ago, Socrates observed that "in houses that look toward the south, the sun penetrates the portico in winter, while in summer the path of the sun is right over our heads and above the roof so there is shade." Today's U.S.

solar architects concentrate windows on a house's south side (which receives the most sunlight in the Northern Hemisphere) and install a thick masonry floor, topped with brick or tile, to absorb sunshine and gradually release heat hours later. They often use sophisticated computer programs to determine a building's optimum amount of window area and heat storage for different climates. A typical, low-cost passive addition is an attached greenhouse or solarium; the glassed-in space collects heat as well as provides a pleasant living area.

Technical and architectural improvements capture and store the winter's sun and block the summer heat in 150,000 passive solar houses built since 1978. What once was considered avant-garde today accounts for about 10 percent of all houses built. While few structures are 100 percent solar, design factors alone can lop 30 to 90 percent off energy bills.

A few private companies (as well as a few utilities) are trying to concentrate the sun's heat in parabolic troughs or dishes in order to produce high-temperature steam that can operate electric generators. Luz Engineering, for instance, has completed the first phase of a 43-megawatt system that will feed power into Southern California Edison's utility grid. And in 1984, the La Jet Company constructed 700 dishes that deliver 4.4 megawatts of power to San Diego Gas and Electric. But the cost of such plants must decline dramatically before the technologies can achieve more widespread use.

One solar dream remains strong. Converting sunlight into electricity may sound like modern alchemy, but in 1954, researchers at Bell Laboratories fashioned silicon crystals into palm-sized power plants that require little maintenance, have no moving parts and produce no pollution. The dream, however, has a catch: economics. Initial solar or "photovoltaic" cells cost $600 a peak watt, several hundred times more than conventional energy sources.

Were it not for the U.S. space program, photovoltaics might have been abandoned long ago. But the light, durable wafers proved to be the most efficient means of powering communication satellites that maintained constant exposure to the sun. Then, skyrocketing electricity prices in the early 1970s brought interest in solar cells down to earth, where scientists quickly lowered costs to approximately $50.00 a peak watt. By late 1984, the bulk price had fallen to $5.00, much closer to the $1.50 now considered necessary to compete with conventionally generated electricity. Even at today's price, installing solar cells is less expensive than extending the utility grid to many remote sites, including isolated communications stations and water pumping stations. Although experts argue about the timing, all agree larger manufacturing plants and more advanced processes will continue to lower photovoltaic costs. According to Paul Gray, the president of the Massachusetts Institute of Technology (MIT): "As one who was weaned on vacuum tubes, grew up with transistors, and watched the phenomenal increase in performance/price ratios associated with large-scale integrated circuits, I can assure you that it takes a very brave person—or a fool—to assert that photovoltaics will not become competitive in cost."

A variety of firms in Japan, Europe and the United States are trying to lower prices by experimenting with several materials, including amorphous rolls, single-crystal silicon wafers, polycrystalline silicon, cadmium sulfide and gallium arsenide. U.S. photovoltaic sales topped $200 million in 1984, a 4-fold rise in two years. If costs continue to drop, production should expand at least 50-fold, making photovoltaics a multi-billion-dollar business by the early 1990s.

If solar cells do compete economically with utility-generated power, how should they be used? The Electric Power Research Institute, the utility industry's study center, argues that a concentrated PV station that minimizes marketing costs could be attractive in sunny areas heavily dependent on expensive oil, such as California and New England. Before 1983, the largest arrays provided 225 kilowatts of electricity for the Sky Harbor Airport near Phoenix, Arizona, and 350 kilowatts for three Saudi Arabian villages. As solar-cell prices dropped and electricity costs soared, entrepreneurs launched larger projects. In February 1983, Arco Solar (a large power producer independent of any utility and a subsidiary of the Atlantic Richfield oil company) took advantage of state tax credits and completed a photovoltaic power plant that sells one megawatt of electricity to Southern California Edison. Not to be outdone, Pacific Gas & Electric contracted with Arco Solar for an 8-megawatt facility, while the Sacramento Municipal Utility District began work on a 100-megawatt, $250 million photovoltaic power station scheduled for completion by 1994.

Other photovoltaic advocates, pointing out that the cells are modular by nature, argue that little is gained through centralization. Better, they say, to apply solar cells in a decentralized fashion—perhaps incorporated in the roofs of buildings—to minimize the problems associated with electricity transmission and storage. General Electric and MIT are separately developing photovoltaic shingles that can protect houses from nature's elements and convert one of those elements—sunlight—into electricity. If photovoltaic prices continue to drop and the shingles or other applications prove durable, the market for solar cells will expand dramatically, greatly reducing the need for centralized power plants or a utility monopoly.

Stan Ovshinsky is a leading photovoltaics entrepreneur, sometimes compared to Thomas Edison because he is launching a technological revolution. Skeptics, however, say Ovshinsky is nothing more than a talented hustler.

What the modern inventor hustles are amorphous materials found in neither naturally occurring substances nor plastics. Twenty years ago, when researchers concentrated on transistors and crystals, he "spoke a new language" of replacing ordered crystals (which must be very pure) with disordered synthetic materials fashioned from infinite combinations of alloys. Most scientists scoffed at the machinist who had no college education. But Ovshinsky possesses a strong will and believes in his ideas. With his wife, Iris, he formed Energy Conversion Devices (ECD) in Troy, Michigan.

In 1975, Sir Nelvin Mott, an ECD consultant, won a Nobel Prize for his work on amorphous materials. Suddenly, says Ovshinsky, researchers began to reexamine ECD's efforts, and financiers became interested in new wear-resistant substances that could be fashioned into automobile and appliance coatings.

It is in the energy field, however, that Ovshinsky has gained the most attention. According to the inventor/promoter, amorphous solar cells will dramatically slash the costs of generating electricity from sunlight. To prove the point, ECD recently fashioned the first machine to mass-produce thousand-foot-long rolls of flexible photovoltaic cells. His shop, in Detroit's northwestern suburbs, displays solar cells on window shades, tote bags and car tops, which generate electricity when exposed to the sun. Ovshinsky dreams of the day when amorphous solar cells provide homes and businesses with their own electric power.

Not unlike Thomas Edison at the turn of the century, entrepreneurs in the 1980s must integrate engineering, business and political skills if they are to prosper. Sophisticated technologies and dreams alone are not sufficient to overcome the numerous frustrations these electric pioneers face trying to challenge an existing structure of energy suppliers. Entrepreneurs are advancing over uncharted territory by developing new resources and testing old regulations. Their risks and rewards loom large.

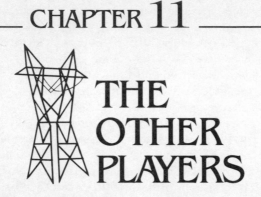

CHAPTER 11

THE OTHER PLAYERS

Although unregulated, the new electricity competitors depend upon and are vulnerable to political decisions. It was Congress that created a market for independents by passing the Public Utility Regulatory Policies Act of 1978 (PURPA). It was President Carter who signed tax incentives to promote alternative energy development. It was the Supreme Court that beat back legal challenges from the nation's utilities. And it was a few state regulatory commissions that set favorable buy-back rates and contract provisions. Changing political winds could destroy these provisions and seriously damage the emerging industry.

Today's laws may help entrepreneurs compete, but they don't guarantee success. Negotiations with utilities remain difficult, even with those power companies that want electric capacity, and bargaining with recalcitrant utilities is next to impossible. Also needed is construction financing from investors who demand sophisticated business plans, proven technologies and limited risks. Like Thomas Edison in the 1890s, today's independent power producers rely upon other players, especially bankers and politicians. In short, electric entrepreneurs can't go it alone.

THE FINANCIERS

"Independent power producers are the only game in town," declares Del Ferris, a vice-president of First Interstate Bank in Los Angeles. No wide-eyed solar energy advocate, Ferris displays all the trappings of a conservative banker. For the past eight years, he loaned money to utilities, and he continues to support nuclear power development. Still, Ferris is part of a growing group of bankers and investors who understand that utilities are out of the building business and that alternative energy projects are developing rapidly. He wants part of the action.

PruCapital is also bullish on independent power producers. From her large office overlooking the San Francisco Bay, vice-president Susan Morse declares that her support for electric entrepreneurs produces multiple benefits: Independents receive financing at fixed rates; Pru-Capital, a subsidiary of Prudential Insurance Company, earns steady income; and the nation acquires safer and more reliable electricity.

Although Ferris and Morse share the same goal, they have different styles. Ferris, for instance, focuses on strict economic criteria while Morse demonstrates a little of the personal side to banking. Having maintained an interest in environmental protection since college, she is enthusiastic about waste-to-energy projects that might eliminate the garbage problem while providing a source of safe energy. While Ferris won't lend money to wind or solar ventures until the technologies have "sufficient track records to prove their reliability and profitability," Morse is partial to wind farms and small hydro projects.

Both want to select the least risky projects. "Any banker can make loans," says Ferris. "Getting paid back is the real problem." Morse and Ferris want 40 to 60 percent of a project's costs to be financed by the company's stockholders; the more speculative the project, the less the loan. They want experienced developers, a long-term, power-purchase contract from the electric utility, a stable regulatory environment and high-quality equipment. In short, the financiers want security. "I like to sleep at night," admits Ferris. "I don't want to stay awake calling the project manager for wind reports."

Ferris and Morse agree that the young industry is growing very rapidly and that they will adjust their loan criteria as alternative technologies are tested. Morse recently returned from a three-month maternity leave to discover PruCapital "had given birth to a cogeneration and wind-energy project" while she was gone. Such ventures continue to comprise small portions of the total portfolios for PruCapital or First Interstate, but the financiers are convinced money is to be made with independent energy producers.

A few bankers are troubled by the rise of electric entrepreneurs. "Selling utility stocks and bonds paid for my house on Long Island and put my kids through school," admits one Wall Street analyst. "But I make money by selling stocks and bonds, and today's only action is with independent energy producers." How, he asks, "can I stab my utility friends in the back by promoting their competitors"?

Bankers and fund managers, of course, will not totally abandon utility monopolies. According to banking critics, financiers are as beholden to utilities as they are to Latin American countries with huge debts. Rather than allow the troubled companies or nations to default, banks continue to offer cash, further increasing their vulnerability. They are living the proverb: Loan someone a little money and he is indebted to you; loan him a lot, and you are indebted to him.

For too long, Wall Street analysts cared more about next quarter's earnings than about the utility industry's long-term prospects. They failed, for instance, to acknowledge the significance of nuclear cost overruns and were surprised every time a nuclear-exposed utility began to suffer. Only in the mid-1980s, at least five years too late, are brokers pushing utilities to minimize their capital investments.

Today's smart money is moving away from centralized power plants and toward entrepreneurs developing new technologies and markets. Merrill Lynch, for instance, has established a mutual fund that buys alternative energy equipment and then leases the machines to businesses trying to reduce their electric bills. In late 1984, Kidder Peabody launched an Alternate Energy Investment Management Program that the brokerage firm hopes will invest $500 million in cogeneration and waste-to-energy projects.

As independent power suppliers expand, they increasingly challenge the utility industry's structure and Wall Street's habits. Leonard Hyman, a vice-president of Merrill Lynch and a leading utility analyst, concedes, "The concept of a regulated natural monopoly, if not already obsolete, may soon be."

Money managers have happily provided cash to large companies launching large energy projects, such as nuclear reactors and oil wells, but getting a small loan for a home improvement has traditionally been an uphill battle. For bankers, the paperwork is greater, the glamour less.

When the cost of energy and the cost of money began rising in tandem in the late 1970s, things began to change. Perhaps more than any other factor, the rise in mortgage defaults woke bankers up. Slowly, loan officers figured out that borrowers are a lot less likely to miss mortgage payments if they don't have high energy bills to contend with, too.

This awakening hit the West Coast first. As early as 1977, Home Federal Savings and Loan of San Diego was offering a preferred-rate, home-improvement loan for energy-conservation retrofits. The more of a home-improvement loan used for energy efficiency, the larger the interest-rate reduction.

Then it spread. In 1979, the Charlestown Savings Bank of Boston earmarked $2.5 million for energy-improvement loans. Homeowners borrowing from Charlestown get a rebate for the cost of an energy audit and a whole percentage point off the going loan rate. They can also finance up to $5,000 in energy-related improvements as part of their mortgage. Similar arrangements are available in Minneapolis, Richmond, Des Moines and a few other cities.

Alternative financing also attracts government agencies. The state of Montana, for example, socks away part of its coal-severance tax in a fund that supports "post–fossil-fuel" energy experiments, including cogenerators, efficient alcohol stills and solar greenhouses. Maybe you have to mine coal to develop the political courage needed to spend $700,000 a year preparing for the day when it will be gone, as Montana does, but a few other states are taking out similar insurance policies.

North Carolina's Public Utility Commission began suffering chest pains in the late 1970s when it realized rising electricity demand was forcing state utilities to build centralized power stations that North Carolinian ratepayers wouldn't want to pay for. At the same time, other agencies decided it was time to do something about the state's $72 million annual electricity bill. Raising capital through a small charge on consumers' bills, the state now pumps $2.3 million a year into an Alternative Energy Corporation (AEC). In turn, AEC works with private investors to put solar and conservation technologies in prisons, hospitals, colleges, elementary schools and dog pounds—places where, until recently, accountants and building supervisors didn't have much to say to each other.

Twenty-four states offer tax credits to investors in alternative energy equipment. But the largest tax breaks come from Washington, D.C., where just four months after Sun Day in 1978, Congress approved incentives for individuals and businesses to install solar, wind and geothermal systems. As amended, the tax credits allow consumers to reduce their taxes by 40 percent of the first $10,000 they spend on a renewable-energy system. Thus, the provision reduces the cost of a $4,000 solar water heater $1,600. Businesses using renewable-energy equipment benefit from a 15 percent energy tax credit, in addition to the existing 10 percent credit for all capital investments.

Some alternative energy promoters package these credits with other tax provisions to create a third-party financing arrangement, whereby a group of investors buys equipment and leases it to businesses. Similar leases have been employed for years by oil companies, airlines and other industries using expensive equipment; in fact, almost all domestic passenger planes are owned by New York banks, which lease them to the airlines and gain the appropriate tax benefits. In practice within the electricity market, a group of investors might form a limited partnership to purchase cogeneration equipment from a vendor. When the partners (known as the third party) lease the system to a hospital or any other business, they reap the energy tax credits and the regular investment credit. If they qualify under complicated Internal Revenue Service rulings, they can also rapidly depreciate the system's cost over five years. Because arranging tax benefits is complex, independent power producers, not unlike utilities, often rely on lawyers and accountants, as much as engineers, to maximize their profits. With a successful third-party financing, investors reduce tax payments and earn monthly rental fees; the client cuts his energy costs without paying for the alternative energy equipment; and the vendor makes a sale.

THE POLITICIANS

What politicians give, they can also take away. In late 1984, the Treasury Department proposed sweeping reforms to simplify the tax code by eliminating many credits and deductions. The controversial proposals, if enacted, would hurt independent power producers who have relied on tax benefits to gain initial financing for new technologies that bankers are reluctant to support. Specifically, the Treasury Department plan would terminate solar and conservation tax credits, eliminate the 10 percent investment tax credit, and lower the depreciation allowances.

If federal officials cut incentives for small power production, ask independents, shouldn't they also curtail other energy credits? Handouts from Washington, D.C., currently bewilder and distort the energy market. Depletion allowances for oil, subsidized loans for synthetic fuel, price controls for natural gas, federal insurance coverage for nuclear power, and tax credits for solar energy are only a few of the many federal "adjustments" to free enterprise. According to the Battelle Memorial Institute, market tinkering on behalf of the oil, coal and electric industries cost taxpayers more than $249 billion by 1978. (And this doesn't include fuel bills!) In 1978 alone, almost $32 billion—ten times the federal government's total budget for energy research and development—made its way from the public coffers to the energy industry through direct grants or tax write-offs.

To free the market of distortions working against emerging technologies and innovative enterprises, the federal government faces two options. The first is to eliminate all government subsidies, from nuclear insurance policies to solar tax credits. Without benefits, our energy economy would more closely approximate a free market, which is a goal of the Treasury Department's plan. Despite its philosophical appeal, this proposal is politically unrealistic and inappropriately assumes that Washington doesn't have an important role to play in helping to solve the nation's energy problems. Continued reliance by the United States and its allies on imported oil poses military and diplomatic perils that government can reduce only by protecting shipping lanes or accelerating the development of energy alternatives. Iran's attacks on oil ships passing through the Strait of Hormuz throughout 1984 and 1985 illustrate that these problems are becoming more pressing.

The government's second and preferable option is to develop a balanced energy program that curtails market barriers to efficient new enterprises. A low-cost approach would redirect government support away from centralized power stations controlled by utility monopolies, and toward efficient and dispersed technologies operated by innovative enterprises in a competitive market. But if electric entrepreneurs are to achieve such a balanced government program, they must develop political muscle.

In California, Jan Hamrin helped launch the Independent Energy Producers (IEP) in May 1982 to represent electric entrepreneurs before the state's legislature and utility commission. By early 1985, the trade association had 125 member companies, including many of California's largest firms.

No novice political idealist, Hamrin knows altering the basic structure of a huge industry will be neither quick nor easy. Efficient technologies, PURPA and a few sympathetic politicians are not sufficient to guarantee competition within the heavily regulated electricity market. Utilities have enormous political influence, largely because they have long dominated energy debates through their research, campaign contributions and constituency of shareholders and employees. "When you have had the whole game to yourself," Hamrin explains, "you certainly are reluctant to let other players in."

IEP is rapidly gaining strong political allies. Louisiana Pacific, for instance, was, until recently, only concerned with timber policy, but the huge paper- and wood-products company now sells cogenerated electricity to utilities and has a self-interest in electricity buy-back rates. Unlike the backyard tinkerers and long-haired "hippies" who pioneered some alternative technologies in the 1970s, a giant lumber company or other industrialists can often match an electric utility in political might and legal sophistication.

IEP's members, who personally conduct much of the lobbying, range from individual solar-energy advocates to giant corporations. When I visited Hamrin in May 1984, she interrupted our talk for a complex negotiating session with Southern California Edison officials. She was assisted by three businessmen, one wearing jeans, another in a polyester suit, and the third in a classic three-piecer. At first glance, these independent power producers seemed to have nothing in common. The challenge for Hamrin, one of the few women in the electricity industry, is to organize them and the interests they represent to "march in one direction."

Hamrin knows the young industry's meteoric growth in California will slow down. When the Supreme Court upheld PURPA in 1983, hundreds of anxious developers surged into the electricity business. But avoided costs (the price utilities would pay per kilowatt-hour to build their own power plant) will drop when sufficient electricity is available, discouraging new entrepreneurs from building generators until demand picks up again or existing power plants are retired. Hamrin's goal is to create a stable, independent power production industry that can adjust to market fluctuations more efficiently than can utilities that depend upon centralized power plants. To gain secure buy-back contracts, Hamrin helped negotiate a series of four "standard offers" between independents and utilities, including one agreement that provides long-term pricing stability. She also works with bankers and legislators to assure the young industry's orderly transition from tax-credit–based financing to conventional loans from banks and other investors.

With her Sacramento office only three blocks from the capitol, Hamrin concentrates on California legislation and regulation. Acknowledging that the state possesses a unique combination of abundant resources and sympathetic regulators, she nevertheless sees the market for independent power producers quickly spreading throughout the West and into pockets across the country. She regularly receives calls from developers in other states who want to establish their own trade associations; even regulators request information. One Texas commissioner, frustrated by his utilities' "rate shocks," expressed hope that his state will learn from IEP's work.

Entrepreneurial expansion is rapidly reforming the electricity market, eliminating the need for central power stations. If it continues, the utility monopoly's primary remaining function will be to transmit and distribute competitively produced electricity. Thus, a regulated utility will continue to service individual customers, but it will be buying electricity from competitive suppliers rather than producing its own power. In her moderate manner, Hamrin compares the link between a utility's distribution and generation divisions to an old marriage—"the couple may no longer have a lot of reasons for staying together, but they may have so much community property that they can't find a way to split it reasonably." Creative thinking and patience, Hamrin concludes, are required to change the complex electricity industry. But change is inevitable.

THE UTILITIES

Even if independent power producers receive a fair shake from the government, they must still deal with electric utilities, which for many decades have monopolized the generation and distribution of electric power. Although PURPA theoretically allowed entrepreneurs to participate in the electricity market, many utilities, after failing to lobby against the legislation's passage, fought diligently to block PURPA's implementation. Mississippi Power & Light Company, for example, convinced federal judge Harold Cox to rule that PURPA is a "direct intrusion" of the federal government into the affairs of the "sovereign state of Mississippi." Electric companies in Georgia, Louisiana, Mississippi, the District of Columbia and several New England states immediately canceled contracts to purchase independently produced power. In June 1982, the U.S. Supreme Court overturned the Mississippi judge's ruling.

Utility attorneys, however, continued fighting. American Electric Power, Consolidated Edison and Colorado-Ute Electric Association challenged PURPA before the U.S. Court of Appeals, arguing that utilities should not be required to interconnect with or pay full avoided costs to independent power producers. The Appeals Court agreed, although the Supreme Court put the matter on hold until it again reviewed the law. Finally, in May 1983, the High Court unanimously upheld PURPA's regulations, ruling it important to "provide a significant incentive to the development of cogeneration and small power production, and that ratepayers and the nation as a whole would benefit from the decreased reliance on scarce fossil fuels and the more efficient use of energy." Independent power producers sighed with relief although they knew many utilities would still oppose signing the long-term contracts entrepreneurs need to gain financing.

After the Supreme Court ruling, states issued a variety of different regulations, making the progress of independent power producers dependent, to a large degree, upon the strength of those regulations and the willingness of local regulators to prod unenthusiastic utilities. The advance of electric entrepreneurs in California results in part from former governor Jerry Brown's promotion of environmentally sound alternatives to oil and natural gas, upon which the state depends for much of its power. Brown's appointees on the Energy Commission blocked unnecessary power plant construction; those on the Public Utilities Commission established a series of standard contracts between independent power producers and utilities; and the governor personally supported state tax credits for solar, wind and biomass development. While taking a slightly different approach, George Deukmejian, the present California governor, continues to endorse competition within the electricity market. Many of the state's largest industries, which use cogeneration equipment and contribute generously to the Republican Party, have convinced Deukmejian to support the emerging industry.

A growing number of state commissions are intervening to assist electric entrepreneurs. In September 1984, for instance, Iowa regulators, anxious to develop the state's abundant wind and biomass resources, increased fourfold the rate utilities must pay for electricity generated by independent producers. Several weeks later, the New York State Court of Appeals upheld the regulatory commission's order placing a floor of six cents per kilowatt-hour on the price utilities must pay for electric power from independents.

To understand negotiations among entrepreneurs, utilities and state regulators, consider PURPA's requirements. To avoid the costs of being regulated as utilities, small power producers using solar, wind, geothermal or biomass resources can employ systems no larger than 80 megawatts, and at least 75 percent of the fuel must come from biomass, wastes, renewable resources or geothermal steam. Qualifying cogenerators, which can be of any size and burn any fuel, must provide both heat and electricity. In return for developing alternative energy resources, independents are to receive reasonable rates for interconnections with the utility and for back-up power.

At PURPA's core is the requirement that utilities purchase electricity from qualifying facilities (called QFs within the industry) at a price—reviewed by state regulators—based on the power companies' avoided costs. Calculating the exact figure for these avoided costs stirs heated debate between entrepreneurs and power companies. Avoided prices in 1984 vary from approximately 1.2 cents per kilowatt-hour in Nebraska, to 6.5 cents in California, to more than 8 cents in Vermont. For a homeowner building a 4-kilowatt wind machine in the backyard, annual revenue from sales to the utility would range from $100 to $700.

This buy-back rate is composed of two factors. *Energy costs,* the easiest to figure, include the utilities' fuel and some operating and maintenance expenses associated with running generators or purchasing electricity from other power companies. *Capacity costs* measure the savings to utilities if they don't need to build a large generator. For example, when power companies plan to build new power plants, capacity costs will rise dramatically. The rate, of course, will vary according to the reliability of the entrepreneur's power; a cogenerator running almost constantly is more valuable and receives a higher payment than an intermittent wind-energy machine.

Federal regulators say ratepayers should feel no economic difference between a utility producing its own power or buying electricity from independents. Thus, entrepreneurs receive the highest payments for their electricity in regions where utilities rely on expensive fuel, as in oil-dependent California and New England, or where utilities need new power plants to meet a rising demand for electricity or to replace retired facilities.

Negotiations are always tough because utilities and independents, quite obviously, have different needs. Power companies want to purchase electricity at the lowest possible price, while entrepreneurs desire to sell it at the highest. Utilities demand reliable and steady supplies of electricity, while independents want assurance the future buy-back rate will not fall dramatically. Power companies argue that paying the full avoided costs for independents' power is unnecessary since many entrepreneurs earn a higher profit than utilities are allowed by state regulators; but the Federal Energy Regulatory Commission (FERC) rejects these protests, saying successful entrepreneurs should be rewarded for their enormous risks with new technologies and new legal requirements.

The conflict is perhaps most bitter in Idaho, where James Bruce leads the charge against PURPA and independent generators. The Idaho Power Company chairman provides the nation's lowest electric rates, largely because he relies on cheap hydropower, and he abandoned his nuclear projects early. "If I had my way, I'd stop the 250-megawatt coal plant we are building with Sierra Pacific," says Bruce. "We don't need any power and the facility will raise rates 15 percent." The lawyer, who spent 35 years working his way up the corporate ladder, knows "you don't make friends by raising rates."

Bruce, however, didn't make friends with independent power producers and state regulators when he called for a cogeneration moratorium. The animated executive says PURPA creates a "gold-rush enterprise flooding utilities with unneeded power at inflated rates." Although federal regulations prohibit buy-back rates above the utility's avoided costs, Bruce maintains Idaho Power Company must unnecessarily pay more than $73 million to independent producers by 1988, rather than buy less expensive hydropower from the Bonneville Power Administration.

Bruce, who runs an aggressive lobbying campaign, labels government policies hypocritical. For instance, while FERC recently denied Idaho Power's application to build a small hydro dam at Wiley, calling additional power unnecessary, the regulators continue to license entrepreneurs selling hydroelectricity to the utility. To gain political allies, the chairman encourages environmentalists to join his fight, although he admits they have an ingrained suspicion of utilities. In 1983, Bruce convinced the National Wildlife Federation, of which he is a member, to oppose licenses for independent dam projects disturbing fish runs on Salmon River tributaries.

In trying to avoid signing contracts, Bruce describes entrepreneurs as unreliable hustlers wanting "only tax breaks and fast bucks." He says some small power producers build with inexpensive cinder blocks rather than durable concrete, and that their water canals wash out because of poor construction. Bruce asks: "How can I supply electricity to 265,000 customers when I don't know how many entrepreneurs will be operating next year?" The burly westerner displays many of his region's antigovernment sentiments, including the perception that Washington is cramming PURPA down utilities' throats. Bruce doesn't object to the law's goal of reducing oil consumption, "but when I'm required to buy power from someone else, I can no longer plan for the future."

The Idaho Public Utility Commission has a different perspective and calls Bruce "an outlaw" for refusing to sign contracts with independent power producers. Citing the Supreme Court's decision upholding PURPA, the regulators claim entrepreneurs can supply abundant, inexpensive and reliable electricity.

Even public power officials, who seem to embrace alternative energy development more enthusiastically than their investor-owned colleagues, virtually dismiss independent producers. Don Von Raesfeld, Santa Clara's city manager who operates 20 small hydro, wind and geothermal projects, feels "small power producers will never make the kind of contribution PURPA envisioned. People not in the utility business are simply not prepared to build and operate power plants."

Many municipalities flatly refuse to negotiate with entrepreneurs, and, because public power systems are usually not regulated by state commissions, independents have little power to enforce PURPA unless they pay expensive legal fees to challenge public systems in court or at FERC. On the West Coast, for example, investor-owned Southern California Edison has signed more than 223 contracts with small power producers, but its public power neighbor, the Los Angeles Department of Water & Power (DWP), has negotiated only a handful. The giant DWP claims independents may provide unreliable power, but critics argue that the municipality simply wants to maintain its monopoly. Smaller public power systems are usually no more cooperative, rejecting independently produced power in favor of subsidized electricity from federal hydroelectric projects.

Municipals also stifle independent development of small hydro facilities by employing their federally mandated "preference" for dam licenses. When independent developers or speculators file license applications with FERC for attractive river sites, municipals follow, sometimes copying the entrepreneurs' engineering studies. And when two applications are similar, FERC awards the license to the government-owned entity. "Public power companies have not developed their own resources," grumbles one entrepreneur. "They sought permits only to block competition from independents."

Except for a few exceptions, utility executives claim electric entrepreneurs and alternative energy technologies have very limited potential. Speakers at the Edison Electric Institute's (EEI's) convention, for instance, failed even to mention the multi-billion-dollar phenomenon of independent power generation. *Electrical World,* an industry magazine, publishes detailed statistics on utilities' generating capacity, but lists no cogeneration or renewable-energy projects before 1984; even the publication's 1984 numbers represent less than one-sixth the actual total for California alone.

Glenn Lovin, who knows the utility industry inside and out, is frustrated by his colleagues' reluctance to accept change. The engineer began his career building power plants in Utah, worked for 13 years at the EEI, and still knows most regional utility executives by their first names. With an engineer's desire for efficiency, Lovin turned to cogeneration in the mid-1970s and now directs the International Cogeneration Society, a nonprofit research group located in a small office within the same downtown Washington, D.C., building as EEI. He maintains industrialists must employ efficient cogenerators if the United States is to compete in the world market. America's businesses have only two options, warns Lovin: "Either they find alternatives to expensive power from the local utility or they abandon factories and jobs. Cogeneration simply makes economic sense."

Why do utility executives resist alternative technologies? Lovin thinks their stubbornness results from the industry's Competitive Service Committees, designed in the 1950s to block gas companies, self-generators and all other competitors. Although utilities officially abandoned the committees several years ago, today's top executives learned a set of legal and economic tactics that they still use to protect their monopolies.

The morning I met with Lovin, he had ridden the office elevator with Doug Bauer, EEI's executive vice-president. Bauer, considered one of the industry's more thoughtful and progressive executives, asked his former colleague about cogenerators, saying he hadn't seen or heard of any developments. Lovin remained angry about the encounter when we talked, declaring that "cogeneration is the fastest-growing electricity source," and asking "how long can utility executives ignore it?"

A utility's willingness to embrace independent suppliers depends, in large part, on its need for capacity. Companies desiring additional power often find purchasing electricity from independents more economical than building their own central power stations. It makes more sense, a few utility executives admit, for entrepreneurs to risk their capital than for the power company to finance expensive facilities. Several utilities, including New England Electric System, also encourage alternative energy development to avoid burning costly oil.

But capacity-rich companies, such as Consolidated Edison of New York, vehemently oppose entrepreneurs who threaten to further idle their own power plants. Often, recalcitrant utilities impose double standards to block competition. One power company, to justify a rate increase, argued before state regulators that the next hydroelectric dam it was to build would provide electricity at 15 cents per kilowatt-hour. Several months later, the same utility, this time trying to justify paying low rates to independent producers, stated that new capacity was only worth 4 cents per kilowatt-hour.

Houston Lighting & Power is particularly unhappy about its interactions with Dow Chemical, the largest operator of cogeneration plants in this country. Dow has become such a huge electricity producer that it jeopardizes Houston Lighting's plans to build a giant lignite-fueled power plant later this decade and may threaten Texas Utilities' half-completed Comanche Peak nuclear plant. Dow, which has been supplying 600 megawatts of power to Houston Lighting since 1982, believes the utility and its consumers would save more money by paying the chemical company for cogenerated power than by the utility building expensive power plants. The utility, however, claims it doesn't need Dow's power and wouldn't pay the price Dow is demanding even if it did. The dispute was temporarily settled in July 1984 when the Texas Public Utility Commission ruled that utilities must refrain from building new power plants if buying cogenerated power—even if it must be wheeled across the state—would prove cheaper. The controversial order also requires utilities to regard new construction as their avoided cost, thus raising the rates paid to independent producers. Houston Lighting, however, anticipates dragging the battle into court.

Even those utilities considered aggressive alternative energy promoters receive significant criticism from independent producers. Consider Southern California Edison (SCE). After lobbying against certain PURPA provisions, SCE chairman William Gould declared in October 1980 his commitment to derive 30 percent of the utility's new capacity— approximately 2,150 megawatts of electricity—from alternative sources, a major shift from the industry's traditional reliance on coal and nuclear facilities. In a heavily publicized letter to employees, SCE's 37-year veteran said the utility's policy is "to devote our corporate resources to the accelerated development of a wide variety of future electrical power sources which are renewable rather than finite." Most of SCE's renewable energy, he maintained, would be purchased from independent power producers.

It can't be denied that the giant utility has signed many power purchase contracts with entrepreneurs. But in January 1983, the California Public Utility Commission penalized SCE a large $8.1 million for avoiding negotiations with entrepreneurs. The commission also charged that SCE had greatly underestimated the potential of cogeneration and had fallen significantly behind its proposed schedule for introducing alternative energy sources.

Pacific Gas & Electric (PG&E) has a similar story. Prodded by California regulators, the San Francisco-based utility adopted an aggressive campaign to promote energy alternatives and signed many contracts with independent producers. But wind-power advocates claim PG&E often stifles ranchers, homeowners and small businesses trying to sell excess power to the utility, most recently by requiring at least $5 million of insurance for each project, at policy costs reaching $7,000 a year. The California Wind Energy Association argues that "small power producers just cannot obtain insurance in the amounts now being required. The premiums cost more than the amount small outfits make selling their power to the utilities." The association accuses PG&E of constructing another roadblock to small-scale power production. The utility denies this, insisting risks must be covered.

Executives at SCE and PG&E admit they may have provoked the wrath of state commissioners. But they argue the rapid rise of independent power production presents an array of complex issues for the traditionally slow-moving utility industry. "It's clearly in our long-term interest to adapt to a competitive marketplace," concedes one executive, "but the rules are changing quickly and we are being forced to learn as we progress."

CHAPTER 12

STRENGTH THROUGH DIVERSITY

"Nothing endures but change," declared Heraclitus, the ancient Greek philosopher who could have been talking about 20th-century technologies. Within the past three generations, the telephone destroyed the telegraph's dominance. The automobile put most trolley lines out of business. Pocket calculators replaced room-size computers. The electric light bulb displaced the kerosene lamp.

Companies also rise and fall. Fifty years ago, 4 of the 10 largest U.S. corporations were railroads—Pennsylvania, Southern Pacific, New York Central and the Baltimore & Ohio. Changing economic conditions, the introduction of alternative technologies and poor management eliminated these 4 from today's top firms. For more evidence, look also at *Fortune*'s list of the largest industrial companies. Since 1955, when the survey began, 8 of the original top 20 firms—including Bethlehem Steel, Swift, National Dairy Products and Boeing—have dropped significantly in the rankings or disappeared, while a few high-tech companies like International Business Machines have advanced.

As a society, we are still in motion, and the broad changes are having a profound impact on the electricity market. In his best-selling book, *Megatrends,* John Naisbitt describes America's transition from an industrially oriented economy to one based on the creation and distribution of information. For electric companies, the trend means customers are changing: Users of computers and telecommunications equipment are demanding more reliable supplies of power, while industrialists, once the nation's largest energy consumers, have decreased in size and reduced their energy use.

181

In the search for new jobs, Americans are moving from the old industrial cities of the North to growing metropolitan areas in the South and West. These shifts encourage electricity suppliers to reduce rates in the North to stem the economic drain, and to provide modularly built power stations to meet changing energy needs in the burgeoning regions.

Naisbitt also notices that "centralized structures are crumbling all across America" while citizens rebuild this nation "from the bottom up into a stronger, more balanced, more diverse society." Nowhere is this "megatrend" more apparent than in the electricity industry.

Change has been the energy market's enduring characteristic, despite the conservative nature of today's utility executives. My grandparents, for example, welcomed the rapid introduction of electric appliances, which reduced the drudgery of their lives. My parents could choose among several power suppliers before utility monopolies gained control of the electricity market. I was born when nuclear power promised abundance rather than bankruptcy. And only since the Supreme Court upheld the Public Utility Regulatory Policies Act (PURPA) in 1983 have independent energy producers expanded rapidly.

What does the future hold for the electricity industry? Specific projections, of course, cannot be made with certainty because unforeseen factors will alter the best considered plans; 50 years ago, for example, few experts predicted the prospects of nuclear power or the wealth of desert kingdoms in the Middle East. Still, an analysis of broad trends suggests that this much is clear: Consumers and businesses are substituting energy-efficient technologies and independent generators for the commodity once exclusively provided by utilities. Moreover, a new generation of utility executives, struggling to survive in this era of uncertainties, is expanding into nonregulated businesses and preparing for increased competition. The electricity market is becoming more diverse.

A NEW GENERATION OF EXECUTIVES

Utility critics suggest that the only way power companies can survive is if the "old guard" executives, who traditionally came from the bottom third of their engineering class and were protected from competition by regulatory bureaucracies, are given pink slips and sent into retirement. *Fortune* criticizes utility officials as "generally unimaginative men, grown complacent on private monopoly and regulated profits." Can industry leaders shed their "clumsy" and "sluggish" ways? Can a younger generation of managers take the bold actions necessary to survive today's uncertainties?

Arthur Hailey presented a flattering image of utility executives in his best-selling novel, *Overload,* published in 1979. Nim Goldman, the vice-president for planning at the fictional Golden State Power & Light, which is described as a "General Motors among utilities," is a swashbuckling, public-spirited hero who rescues workers from dangerous accidents, shows compassion toward an iron-lung patient dependent upon electric power, makes passionate love to almost every woman in the book (including the quadriplegic), and battles bomb-throwing environmentalists and thick-headed regulators. Goldman rallies his colleagues by delivering fiery speeches about the need to bring more power to the people. "Any fool can see what's coming," he predicts, if utilities don't build new generating stations: "Three years from now, blackouts every time it's hot; and in six years, blackouts every summer day."

Goldman and most real-life utility executives who sympathized with his predictions were proven wrong. In 1985, six years after Hailey's book was published, Pacific Gas & Electric (PG&E), the northern California utility upon which the novel was based, bears the burden of huge excess capacity, including an unneeded and expensive nuclear reactor, rather than shortages. As a result of their mistakes, the "grow and build" executives, symbolized by Nim Goldman, are beginning to change or be replaced by managers trained to minimize the uncertainties faced by today's utilities. Arthur Hailey's son, in fact, works in PG&E's conservation division to ensure that the giant utility doesn't again waste its investments building unnecessary power plants.

Without question some senior executives of the older generation have made daring moves to adapt to changing economic conditions. Guy Nichols, for instance, successfully launched diversification and conservation campaigns that improved New England Electric's finances and kept rates in check, while William Gould at Southern California Edison instituted an array of alternative energy technologies. But the utility fraternity normally abhors change.

John Bryson, one of the bright young managers schooled in innovation, symbolizes the emerging generation of utility leaders. Bryson has explored all sides of electric companies as critic, regulator and executive. In 1969, fresh out of Yale University's law school, he cofounded the Natural Resources Defense Council (NRDC), a respected group of environmentalists that forced utilities to cut emissions of sulfur oxides and to stop building the Clinch River Breeder Reactor in Tennessee.

After establishing NRDC's California office, Bryson was asked by California governor Jerry Brown to direct the state's Water Resources Board. After three years of hostile water politics, Bryson was nominated to manage the state's Public Utilities Commission (PUC) just as the Iranian revolution sent oil prices skyward. Remembering Bryson's environmental advocacy, energy companies vehemently opposed his nomination, delaying the confirmation a full year with four legislative hearings.

During his term as PUC president, Bryson believes he forged an "independent and tough commission" that prodded and pushed the state's utilities to cancel most power plants under construction and to devote substantial funds for energy conservation and renewable energy development. In 1981, the regulator coauthored a controversial article on deregulation that concluded "changes in the underlying economic structure of the industry have made competition more plausible than it was previously." Bryson's actions and ideas were not popular on Wall Street, where investment analysts gave the California commission poor ratings for not automatically approving rate increases. State utility executives also attacked Bryson, predicting California's lights would go out unless they built more central power stations. Today, they privately admit he saved them from foolhardy investments.

Bryson's appointment as the senior vice-president of Southern California Edison (SCE) in early 1984 shocked both friends and opponents. He considers himself the oddball liberal within the utility industry, but feels a senior position at one of the largest power companies allows him to practice what he espoused in state government.

Bryson, although clearly among a minority of utility executives, is not alone. Several of his colleagues are beginning to examine an array of alternatives to building conventional coal and nuclear facilities. A few, for instance, hope to keep power plants in service past their retirement dates by upgrading burners and generators. Known as repowering, these efforts will double the average age of fossil-fuel plants by the end of this decade, saving enormous building costs although adding maintenance expenses.

Researchers are also trying to make the direct burning of coal more efficient and cleaner by igniting the fossil fuel in a bed of granular particles suspended in an airstream. Although several technical problems remain, government studies suggest such fluidized beds offer significant potential for reducing emissions of sulfur oxides and for saving money.

Another new approach to utilizing America's huge coal reserves is gasification, or the conversion of solid coal into a gas before it is burned in an electric power plant. In late 1984, SCE's $294 million Cool Water gasification station in the Mojave Desert began producing 100 megawatts of electricity. If the experiment proves successful, this technology could reduce pollutants and allow utilities to add capacity in relatively small increments with little sacrifice to the cost of power.

A space-age option is the fuel cell, which powers the space shuttles and offers quiet operation, quick installation, high efficiency and little pollution. Like batteries, it relies on an electrochemical process to transform the energy of a fuel (such as natural gas, naphtha or hydrogen) and oxygen continuously into electricity. Unlike batteries, it doesn't run down and require recharging, but will operate as long as both fuel and oxidant are supplied to the electrodes. Once touted as a solution to the energy crisis, fuel cells have so far failed to meet expectations; corrosion problems and faulty instruments have delayed most projects and kept costs high. In summer 1984, Consolidated Edison of New York abandoned construction of the utility industry's major demonstration project, although SCE agreed to purchase a $25 million experimental facility.

SCE also boasts the world's largest solar thermal station near its Cool Water generating facility in the Mojave Desert. Completed in April 1982, Solar One consists of 1,818 giant mirrors (called heliostats) that focus sunlight on a boiler atop a 300-foot concrete tower. By early morning, the column's tip glows white-hot like a Coleman lantern. The computer-controlled mirrors track the sun across the sky to constantly reflect sunlight back to the boiler. The federal government financed most of the $141 million "power tower," McDonnell-Douglas built it, and Edison sells its electricity to 5,000 homes.

Some utility executives are putting their emphasis on better management of the demand for what electricity they have rather than on the generation of new power. Taking advantage of new telecommunications technologies, these companies can shut off noncritical appliances during times of peak demand, thus reducing the need to build more power plants. In 1983, U.S. utilities controlled more than 600,000 water heaters and 500,000 air conditioners through signals carried over the transmission lines, by a radio signal, or through a cable-television link. Customers receive rebates or lower rates for the interruptible service.

In 1983, Arizona Public Service tested a more high-tech approach to load management on 1,000 homes in its service area, using tiny computers similar to the automatic timers that operate home-security lights. The microprocessors ensure that water heaters, dishwashers and washing machines operate only during off-peak hours when rates are low. They can be programmed to rearrange electricity usage so that monthly bills do not exceed limits placed by consumers. In other words, the communications revolution allows homeowners and industrialists to determine their electric bill at the beginning of the month, rather than be surprised at the end.

A few utilities are experimenting on a grander scale. In northern California, for instance, PG&E plans to spend more than $1 billion on energy conservation and load management programs in the coming ten years. It already offers zero-interest loans to consumers installing conservation equipment in their homes and rebates for the installation of energy-saving lighting systems. "We're mining energy out of houses, businesses and industrial operations just as you mine coal out of the ground," boasts a PG&E vice-president. The giant utility expects the efficiency programs to cut its need for new capacity over the next decade by 38 percent.

In southern and eastern Florida, Florida Power & Light Company plans to reduce its generating capacity 16 percent through a variety of efficiency measures. By 1984, the utility had performed energy audits on 300,000 homes and provided cash rebates for the replacement of 50,000 inefficient central air conditioners and heating systems. By 1992, the utility expects such energy management efforts will reduce the area's peak demand for power by 2,100 megawatts, eliminating the need to build two large nuclear reactors.

Despite these examples, most electric companies experiment reluctantly, spending less than 1 percent of their annual revenues on research, and most of this meager amount focuses on short-term needs rather than problems looming in the coming decades. And despite the economic advantages of conservation, most rank efficiency as a low priority. According to the U.S. General Accounting Office, "power companies do not factor conservation into their forecasts because they assume it will have a marginal impact on ultimate demand." One traditional utility executive speaks more bluntly: "My people spent their careers building large generating plants, and that's what they want to do."

Still, a new generation of utility executives is trying to adopt new technologies. Recognizing that the age of centralized coal and nuclear plants is waning, John Bryson and a few other young leaders are challenging the old guard of engineers who fondly remember the industry's golden age and ignore lessons from the oil embargo, the Three Mile Island accident and the Washington Public Power Supply System's default. In contrast to their elders, the new generation wants to minimize financial uncertainties by scaling back expenditures and building up energy alternatives. They are providing vitality and new ideas to this traditionally staid industry. But will enough of the old guard retire in time for utilities to successfully adapt to the new age of competition?

RECONSIDERING ELECTRICITY

Frustrated with low electricity earnings, a few power executives are trying to sell anything from cattle to parking lots. "We are in a critical financial condition," declares one utility executive, "and we must not hesitate to make major surgical changes in order to manage our way out."

Pacific Power & Light has led the industry's diversification efforts. The coal and telephone subsidiaries of the Portland, Oregon, utility provide about half the company's total operating income. "The nice thing about the phone business," says Chairman Don C. Frisbee, "is that it has changed from an increasing-cost to a decreasing-cost business, while electric power has been going the other way."

Minnesota Power, Wisconsin Power & Light and the Southern Company are also enamored with telecommunications, while another dozen utilities soon plan to enter the field with electronic mail, telephone, video and cable-television services. AT&T's breakup and the development of cost-effective fiber optics create an historic opportunity for electric companies to reap a "trillion-dollar dividend," predicts one promoter. Utilities are well-prepared for telecommunications ventures, because they already possess franchises to lay underground cables as well as billing relations with virtually every customer.

Most utilities interested in diversifying invest in conventional-fuel subsidiaries, such as coal or uranium mines, which are closely related to their main line of business. Montana Power Company, for example, drills oil, leases Canadian natural gas properties, and mines coal in Montana, Wyoming and Texas; about half its earnings come from these nonelectric activities. Several utility subsidiaries market conservation and alternative energy services, "induced, in part, by the fear that market share is being lost to others who supply the new technologies," states James Akers of the Edison Electric Institute.

Diversification is quickly gaining adherents. The Reagan administration and New York senator Alphonse D'Amato think the industry's economic "problems will continue and perhaps worsen" unless Congress allows utilities to branch out. They want to repeal the Public Utility Holding Company Act (PUHCA), the 1935 law advocated by George Norris and President Franklin Roosevelt to break up the giant holding companies that controlled most of the nation's electric generation. "The days of the great utility conglomerates and the great profits are over," D'Amato declares. "The utilities of today are in deep trouble."

Some utilities—such as Long Island Lighting and Public Service Company of Indiana—are too burdened with cost overruns to consider expanding into other businesses. But several firms without expensive construction programs enjoy a "cash glut," and they would rather diversify than risk their funds on centralized power plants. By spreading investments over several ventures, the cash-rich utility can theoretically increase its security and possibly its earnings, an important consideration if electric sales stabilize or fall. By investing in fuel subsidiaries, they can also benefit (rather than only lose) if energy prices rise. And by providing more avenues for growth, the generally conservative utility industry can attract high-quality personnel interested in advancement. Such advantages have encouraged Wall Street to reward diversified companies with significantly higher values than the industry average.

Executives of diversified utilities, however, complain they are often bludgeoned by state commissioners who require that high earnings from nonregulated ventures be used to reduce rate increases. "Every time we try to innovate," laments one senior official, "we can't win. Regulators force us to pay for our failures, but they take away the fruits of our successes." The Edison Electric Institute blasts these diversions of earnings as "profit grabs." Central Louisiana Energy went a step further by spinning off its electric utility subsidiary after regulators used profits from the holding company's natural gas wells to justify electric rate reductions.

Some utility officials also grumble that PURPA's rules restrict them from owning more than 50 percent of a nonregulated project. Other regulations disqualify utilities from using renewable-energy tax credits and limit their use of the gas and oil that is available to cogenerators. "We are very much in favor of cogeneration, but the utility industry believes there must be a sharing of the benefits of cogeneration with utility ratepayers," says David Owens of the Edison Electric Institute. Industry critics, however, laugh at the utilities' cry of discrimination, noting that power companies receive enormous subsidies from Washington and guaranteed profits from state regulators.

Most power companies, of course, still sell nothing but electricity. They believe extraterritorial ventures are too controversial and risky, especially considering how badly most oil companies were burned when they tried to branch out in the 1970s. Many consumers and regulators, hoping the industry will continue to avoid nonelectric ventures, have blocked Senator D'Amato's efforts to repeal PUHCA. To some stockholders, diversification means utility executives won't pay full attention to their primary business of supplying electricity. To consumer advocates, the problem is that ratepayers may be held "captive," as utilities subsidize their new ventures with ratepayer funds. Regulators have another complaint: Expansion promises more difficult monitoring of transactions between subsidiaries and the power company.

Many independent power producers also worry that subsidiaries diversifying into conservation or small power production will possess unfair marketing advantages if the parent company remains a regulated monopoly assured of financing and profits. Peter Barnes of San Francisco's Solar Center, for instance, fears electric companies will monopolize and retard the development of any resource they touch. The soft-spoken Barnes points to New Jersey Public Service Electric & Gas's 1979 solar marketing program in which the utility approved only 1 of the area's 25 solar contractors to provide services. The mere announcement of the campaign dried up solar sales across New Jersey for almost a year as customers waited for the program to begin. To avoid stifling innovation and concentrating the market among a few utility-approved (and often utility-owned) contractors, Barnes says electric companies should be excluded from selling conservation and alternative-energy equipment.

Chris Burke has another perspective, drawn from his unique position of having been an entrepreneur controlled by a regulated monopoly. The fast-talking, energetic executive reports that utility officials are totally inept at managing innovative firms and couldn't control new energy technologies even if they tried. He further suggests that if entrepreneurs oppose diversification, they face the awkward contradiction of advocating free enterprise for themselves but restricting utilities from new business opportunities.

Burke, a former small business advocate with the federal Small Business Administration, directed Trident Energy Systems, a solar-energy company located in Davis, California, and a subsidiary of CP National, a diversified utility providing telephone, natural gas and electric service to 150,000 customers throughout the western states. Squeezed by the reduced demand for energy in the late 1970s, CP National decided to diversify into unregulated and more profitable businesses, buying companies manufacturing air-traffic-control equipment, telephone terminals, cogenerators and solar-energy collectors. CP acquired Trident, which produces a sophisticated solar system that supplies a home's total heating and hot water needs, for $1 million.

Burke complains his small firm is burdened by the "emotional baggage" CP managers bring from their regulated utility business. Used to a guaranteed market, the parent company doesn't employ basic marketing techniques, such as lower prices, to stimulate increased sales. Anxious for quarterly profits, CP fails to invest in long-term research. And other CP units, such as the natural gas subsidiary, refuse to publicize Trident's solar systems in its mailings to customers.

In late August 1984, Burke called it quits, resigning because he felt the regulated utility offered only a dead end for entrepreneurs. Stepping back from his daily frustrations, he declares: "I am appalled at a power company's inept and short-sighted management. Today's utility executives must shed their monopoly mind-set, hustle and innovate if they are to prosper in a competitive marketplace."

A growing number of utilities, realizing that their electricity business is challenged by entrepreneurs supplying efficiency and independent power services, are trying to change their stodgy habits and diversify. Such firms appear most likely to weather the changes ahead since they will be able to turn a profit if the utility market remains limp.

ADVANCING COMPETITION

In the early 20th century, Samuel Insull cut a deal with government officials whereby power companies promised to provide all the electricity demanded by all the people at all times, if regulators protected these firms from competition and assured them financial health. Utilities would have an "obligation to serve," while regulators would allow profits comparable to those earned by enterprises with similar risks. In the 1980s, both utilities and regulators are reconsidering Insull's bargain.

Electric companies, for instance, are slowly shedding their obligation to deliver unlimited power by asking consumers to pay for the type of service they want: the less reliable the service, the less expensive. Many residential consumers can save money by accepting interruptible power and reducing the utility's need to build expensive power plants. Almost 200,000 Detroit residents, for instance, receive a 35 percent discount for allowing Detroit Edison to automatically shut off their water heaters when the utility needs to reduce usage. Consumers may soon gain similar "load management" discounts for air conditioners and space heaters, too.

At the same time, computers and new communication technologies can breed competition in the electricity industry by instantaneously balancing consumers' demands and producers' supplies to calculate a "spot price." Rather than relying on imprecise rate schedules periodically approved by state regulators, a spot market would accurately track the varying cost of electricity throughout the day. At night when demand is low, the spot price would fall, and only those generating units with low operating costs (i.e., nuclear, wind or hydro plants) could afford to stay on-line. As demand rose in the morning, so would the spot price. Managers of less efficient units, like oil-fired generators, would begin operating when the rising spot price covered their costs. As demand continued to rise, consumers requiring continuous power would pay the higher spot price; others would reschedule their electric operations until the spot price fell, thus increasing their savings.

Widespread use of this new computation technology, predicts Richard Tabors of the Massachusetts Institute of Technology, will "loosen" the utility industry's structure. "The distinctiveness of a utility will become less clear," he maintains, "and who generates power will become less obvious." When prices, rather than monopoly control, determine what power plants function, entrepreneurs will operate when the spot price rises to the point where an acceptable profit is possible. At the same time, accurate current prices will allow consumers to decide when to buy power. Almost all U.S. industries employ spot prices and operate by the interaction of competitive producers and decentralized consumers. "There is no clear-cut reason why the electricity marketplace needs to be treated any differently," concludes Tabors.

Spurring competition at the generating level would theoretically force power producers (today's utilities *and* entrepreneurs) to plan for and build only the most efficient plants possible and keep operating costs low. (If they didn't, consumers would buy power from cheaper suppliers.) Without a guaranteed market, energy producers would be a lot less likely to build unneeded plants, too—especially expensive nuclear reactors. Moreover, competition would encourage investors to promote innovative businesses that sell power—including conservation and renewable energy—at competitive rates.

Unlike today's system, where the central utility makes all forecasting decisions, many independent generators would participate in a competitive market. While a few generating companies may go bankrupt because of forecasting errors, diversity would provide more overall security than today's centralization, where a single utility's mistake can harm all the customers in a given region.

In the early 1980s, Tabors's ideas gained a forum when the Reagan administration, interested in reducing government oversight of business activities, sponsored numerous conferences and research reports on utility deregulation. The academic studies predicted that a large number of existing firms would compete against each other if state regulation were reduced or eliminated, that current antitrust laws can effectively bar operating companies from cooperating with each other or owning too many units in one area, and that today's environmental regulations would continue to protect public health and safety.

However, a proposal for immediate deregulation would not face smooth sailing. While most utilities want to relax regulations and set their own rates, they adamantly oppose opening the industry to competitors. Public power companies fear deregulation would foster only "phantom competition," leaving a consortium of private firms free to make unspoken agreements that monopolize large regions of the country. Investor-owned firms, in contrast, believe deregulation is a "back door to nationalization" because tax-exempt public systems would have an unfair advantage in a competitive market. "It is not in the public interest," argue American Electric Power officials, "to set about breaking up the most capital-intensive industry in the nation, and placing in jeopardy hundreds of billions of dollars of investment savings, solely upon the basis of a few random and undemonstrated economic theories or notions."

Predictably, many regulators also oppose deregulation, in part because they would lose much of their jurisdiction. Former Federal Energy Regulatory Commission (FERC) commissioner Matthew Holden, Jr., feels the topic is nothing more than a "diversionary intellectual fad." Paul F. Levy, director of the Massachusetts commission, worries that an unregulated industry would be "characterized by relatively few qualified suppliers of power, a large cost-of-entry into the field, and the potential for less than arm's length financial arrangements between the generating consortiums and the retail electric companies."

Certain regions of the country would oppose deregulation if prices immediately moved from average toward marginal costs. The Pacific Northwest, which now enjoys low-cost hydropower, might see large price hikes as local generators sell their electricity at higher market rates to consumers outside the region. Public power customers, who relish cheap federal power, would be especially hard hit if the market priced federal hydropower. (Deregulation supporters argue that efficiency gains sparked by competition will eventually provide the lowest possible price for all regions.)

Immediate deregulation, in which a utility must quickly shed its monopoly assets, would also present financing problems, not the least of which is the bondholders' legal right to these facilities as collateral for their bonds. Even if the generating plants were simply auctioned to the highest bidder, the price paid would vary significantly from the utility's original costs. Uneconomic oil-fired plants in areas with substantial excess capacity, for instance, would command low prices, while efficient hydro or coal-fired facilities would fetch huge capital gains. Who should receive such windfall losses or gains? The auction would pit utility stockholders against ratepayers.

These concerns by powerful interest groups will probably block immediate deregulation. But they need not delay the acceleration of competition. Retarding competition for too long will only make the utility industry's current problems worse.

PURPA, which guarantees independent producers a market for their electricity and freedom from regulation, offers a first step toward competition in the electricity industry. But the law has its shortcomings, especially its reliance on bureaucratically defined prices rather than the spot market. Moreover, PURPA accepts the utility monopoly as the sole purchaser of independently produced electricity, allowing utilities, which naturally prefer buying power from their own generators, to suppress competitors.

The benefits of competition will result only if several deals can be cut and if the market includes more sellers and buyers of bulk electricity. In exchange for the chance to earn higher unregulated profits, for instance, utilities can agree to wheel power at reasonable rates for other producers and consumers. FERC recently arranged such an exchange for bulk-power sales in the Southwest. The deregulation experiment allows participating utilities to charge whatever the market will bear (within broad limits) if they wheel power for other utility participants. Power companies needing electricity can shop around for the least-cost power; generators sell to the highest bidder. FERC is finding that even limited competition provides lower rates and more efficient transactions than offered by regulated monopolies. But to gain a more complete test, Congress could allow independent power producers to participate in these wholesale trades, too.

A separate experiment in Florida also challenges the cozy cooperation that has traditionally existed among utility monopolies. In fact, it encourages power companies to compete with each other for electricity and customers. The Florida "power broker," a sophisticated computer, hourly negotiates bids between sellers and buyers of bulk power. Ten minutes before the hour, each utility within the state informs the computer of how much electricity it wants to buy or sell and at what price. The broker automatically matches the bids and splits the savings from any necessary compromise. Andrew Hines, Florida Power's chairman, admits the brokerage introduces some competition among utilities, but he judges the experiment's success by the millions of dollars his company saves.

To further expand competition, consumers—probably large users at first—may be allowed to shop for the cheapest electricity available. In exchange for the chance to pay lower prices, users would relieve utilities of the obligation to serve them by taking responsibility for the reliability of their own supplies.

In essence, additional competition will require a new social contract between electricity producers and consumers. The one designed by Sam Insull more than six decades ago simply does not apply to modern conditions. New power plants now increase rather than lower rates; larger generators no longer benefit from economies of scale; and alternative technologies can be supplied by an array of businesses. Developing a social contract based on competition will not be easy, but continuing to force the outmoded regulatory system on today's electricity market will only further retard the innovation and efficiency needed by the U.S. economy.

Promoting competition in the electric utility industry probably won't occur in a single dramatic shift, as it did for telecommunications when Judge Harold Greene approved AT&T's breakup. Rapid change would disrupt too many powerful interest groups. But competition is evolving. A decade ago, only academicians in their ivory towers discussed the concept. Four years ago, government officials and utility executives joined the debate. Today, Roger Sant and other entrepreneurs, bored with talking, are financing, building and operating competitive projects.

Most competition advocates admit a monopoly will probably maintain control of the systems that distribute electricity, even if power generation is deregulated. Although scientists may someday discover alternative ways to wheel power, building duplicative electric lines still does not make economic sense. Thus, while electricity generators compete, the transmission and distribution system will probably remain regulated or publicly controlled.

Beyond this, no one knows the exact structure of a competitive electricity market. Even its advocates disagree about specific deregulation plans. But the old admonition warns that if every question must be answered before anything new is tried, no progress will ever occur. In 1978, Congress opened the electric industry to limited competition, and continuing experiments with deregulation promise further innovation. The driving force, as always, is economics, particularly the rising cost of utility power plants and the declining cost of energy alternatives. The concept of a natural monopoly is dying slowly, but die it will.

OPENING THE GRID

As entrepreneurs advance, most utilities will jealously guard their most precious resource—the grid, or the transmission and distribution lines carrying electricity from generators to ultimate users. Controlling a distribution system represents enormous power, as giant oil companies demonstrated throughout the 1960s and early 1970s when their ships and pipelines regulated international petroleum production and prices even after many foreign governments nationalized their oil fields. Charles Ross, a former federal power commissioner, told the Senate Commerce Committee in 1965 that "it is the parties who control the transmission lines, the arteries of the industry, that control the destiny of the millions of ratepayers of this nation."

America's power grid is a technological wonder, with almost 600,000 circuit-miles of high-voltage lines crisscrossing the country, covering an area the size of New Jersey. Sophisticated and mammoth, the system is also sensitive. Electricity supply must be instantaneously matched with demand because this unique commodity cannot be economically stored. Lack of coordination among producers and consumers can cause power outages and huge economic losses.

Utilities, which increasingly prefer buying electricity from other power companies to building their own generators, are upgrading their transmission lines. New England Electric, for instance, is coordinating construction of a $120 million transmission link between Canada's Hydro-Quebec and utilities in New England. The Southern Company, which operates electric companies in Mississippi, Georgia and Alabama, wants to improve the grid in order to sell its surplus electricity to utilities in Texas and Florida. And western utilities hope to share the costs of a $500 million intertie that will wheel inexpensive hydropower from the Pacific Northwest to California.

Deregulation experiments in the Southwest and Florida are opening this expanding grid slightly to interutility competition. William States Lee, the self-assured chairman of Duke Power, is one of the few executives asking for an even less restricted marketplace. The Carolinian favors giving electricity distribution lines the same "common-carrier" status as telephone lines and allowing electric utilities to vigorously compete against one another for power sales across the country. The idea could benefit Duke and other power companies with excess capacity and a good record of constructing inexpensive generating stations. "If we can build plants and operate them more cheaply (than other utilities)," asks Lee, "why shouldn't we be the ones to sell electricity to Memphis or Alabama?" Although Lee's arguments may be logical, they remain unpopular among utility monopolies.

The struggle for access to the transmission network will be fierce and will include more advocates than a few self-assured utility executives.

Power lines, in fact, promise to be the next decade's battleground among investor-owned utilities, public companies and independent producers.

Public utilities, particularly those dependent upon electricity purchases rather than their own generators, have long wanted a more flexible distribution system. The wheeling battle for them is actually an old struggle, beginning in 1920, when the public utilities proposed making the private utilities' lines common carriers, available for a fee to independent producers and consumers. But the private companies amended the Federal Power Act to prevent wheeling if it would hamper power reliability or injure relations among utilities, giant loopholes that essentially prohibited an open grid. In 1924, Senator George Norris of Nebraska proposed that the government build a separate electricity grid to connect existing municipally owned firms with hydroelectric projects controlled by public agencies, thus circumventing the investor-owned utilities' transmission lines. But the bill languished beneath strong lobbying by private utilities.

The Kennedy administration reconstructed the national grid proposal in the early 1960s. On several occasions, the President argued for a cross-country, high-voltage transmission system available to all generators and consumers. Despite the Edison Electric Institute's protests, the administration authorized a piecemeal federal system by pushing government power lines first in Idaho and later along the West Coast. Government officials went so far as to block some investor-owned companies from building transmission lines across national forests or other federal lands. They also ordered those private utilities with existing lines over federal lands to sell access to the grid so that public firms could acquire surplus electricity.

In the late 1960s, the battle shifted to the courts. Four small cities in Minnesota, South Dakota and North Dakota sued the investor-owned Otter Tail Power Company for refusing to wheel low-cost electricity from a federal reclamation project. The Federal Power Commission sided with Otter Tail, saying the private company had no obligation to make its equipment available to another supplier. But in 1972 the Supreme Court disagreed, ruling that Otter Tail's distribution monopoly gave it "effective control over potential competition from municipal ownership. By its refusal to sell or wheel power [Otter Tail] prevents that competition from surfacing." The Court's decision, however, was a close one and battles for access continue.

"Dealing with private utility monopolies is a constant struggle," complains Don Von Raesfeld, city manager of Santa Clara, California. Consider Santa Clara's contract to purchase coal-generated power from Tucson Electric Power Company. The deal would have benefited both parties: Tucson had excess capacity and Santa Cruz needed more electricity. But PG&E, which encircles Santa Clara, refused to wheel the

Arizona power. The private power company also blocked Santa Clara's bid to purchase hydropower from the Pacific Northwest, arguing that its lines were full and could carry no additional electricity. Several months later, PG&E turned around and purchased the same power for its own use.

If Von Raesfeld and other public utility managers had their way, they would build their own transmission lines. But construction costs are enormous, and available corridors are often restricted by wilderness areas, urban developments and military reservations, or they are controlled by private companies. Proposals for new high-voltage power lines also spark hostile reactions from residents concerned about unsightly towers and electromagnetic radiation.

Restricting access is a practice not limited to investor-owned utilities. The few large municipalities that own transmission lines—such as the Los Angeles Department of Water and Power (DWP)—also oppose an open grid. At the American Public Power Association's 1984 convention, Norm Nichols, DWP's manager, declared that opening transmission lines would be an "unconscionable misappropriation of our assets." Arguing that his ratepayers paid for the transmission lines, Nichols doesn't want to share existing facilities, even if the lines are not overloaded or if other power companies pay a distribution fee for access.

Power line combatants in the 1980s are no longer limited to public and private utilities. Consumers—including some of America's most powerful corporations—have joined the fight to challenge a utility's transmission monopoly. The Electricity Consumers Resource Council (ELCON), which represents 20 of the nation's largest energy users, including Dow Chemical, Diamond Shamrock, General Motors and U.S. Steel, is particularly outspoken in favor of competition among electricity suppliers and the lower prices that would likely follow. Several of ELCON's members, hurt by rising utility rates, are also employing their own cogenerators and want to sell excess electricity to other industrialists that might pay more than the local utility.

When the Lukens Steel Company could no longer afford Philadelphia Electric's high rates to pay for the overbudget Limerick reactors in the early 1980s, it tried to break the utility's monopoly. The troubled steelmaker didn't want to leave the area or invest in its own generating equipment, so it tried to buy less expensive power from Pennsylvania Power & Light, a separate investor-owned utility several miles from Lukens's plant. Philadelphia Electric, fearing the loss of its fourth-largest customer, bitterly fought the steel company's plans to build its own transmission line to the other utility's region. To generate public support, Philadelphia Electric threatened residential customers with skyrocketing electric rates if Lukens cut its purchases. A Pennsylvania administrative law judge rejected the Philadelphia utility's logic and shook the industry's very foundations by concluding: "I do not believe that the traditional monopoly model should be accepted as an absolute, immutable principle of utility regulation, even for electric utilities." The judge declared that a new principle is needed: "Competition, even a certain degree of electric utility retail competition, is in the public interest." Philadelphia Electric, however, won a reversal on appeal, and now offers massive rate discounts to keep Lukens and other industrialists as customers.

Other electric users have been better able to punch holes in the utilities' regulatory shield. The Stauffer Chemical factory in St. Gabriel, Louisiana, for example, switched from the investor-owned Gulf States Utilities to the less expensive rates offered by the city of Plaquemine. Grumman Corporation, arguing that hundreds of employees would be laid off to compensate for Long Island Lighting's rate increases, convinced the New York State Legislature to allow large industrialists to buy cheaper power from upstate utilities. But individual homeowners, at least under the current regulatory system, do not enjoy the same political clout and cannot shop around for cheaper power.

In addition to buying power from different utilities, some industrialists want to pay a regulated distribution company to wheel their independently produced electricity to a variety of consumers. But most utility executives maintain that unconstrained wheeling is technically impossible. Some, repeating arguments used against public power companies, claim their lines are full. Others assert that the sophisticated distribution system is designed to serve only interconnected utilities rather than numerous independents.

Utilities do argue legitimately that their interconnections with independents must protect the safety of the transmission system and the quality of customer service. Safety equipment, for example, must be installed (and paid for by the independent power producers) to ensure that linemen will not be accidently jolted while working on the grid. Moreover, the quality of electricity from all producers must meet certain standards or computers and other sensitive appliances throughout the utility system will break down. Engineers claim that these protections can be achieved and point to the open wheeling arrangements adopted by utilities in the Southwest and Florida. "Wheeling is not an unsolvable technical problem," explains one independent producer. "The real barrier is the utility industry's passionate defense of its distribution monopoly."

Hawaii has become a focus for the transmission controversy between utilities and electric entrepreneurs. On the Big Island of Hawaii, scientists estimate that wind, biomass and geothermal resources could provide a whopping 16,000 megawatts of electric power, far more than the 80 megawatts now used by the rugged island's small population. The investor-owned Hawaiian Electric Company, declaring that it doesn't need power from independents, sets its avoided costs very low. Because the utility's retail rate to consumers is very high, entrepreneurs want to use existing transmission lines, or build new ones, if necessary, to directly service consumers without selling their power to Hawaiian Electric at the utility's low avoided rates.

The Waikoloa Water Company provided the first test case when it sought to purchase Michael Lofker's wind-generated electricity. "It's been a constant struggle to overcome Hawaiian Electric's legal and regulatory roadblocks," complains Lofker, a former executive with Northeast Utilities in Connecticut and now president of Renewable Energy Ventures of California. In late 1982, Lofker proposed building up to 45 wind machines in partnership with Hawaiian Electric, but the utility refused. The patient entrepreneur then reached an informal agreement with utility engineers on technical specifications for the wind project to interconnect with the power company's grid. A few months later, Hawaiian Electric's senior executives ignored the agreement and formally challenged the project before the state Public Utilities Commission, arguing that Lofker should be regulated, a complex procedure that would bankrupt his small business.

Months of public hearings followed, accompanied by charges and countercharges. Dudley Pratt, Hawaiian Electric's chairman, feels businesses selling electricity directly to consumers must be regulated to assure reliable supplies and reasonable rates. But Lofker suggests Hawaiian Electric simply detests losing customers, and that rather than compete in the small generator market the utility remains committed to outmoded central power stations. The commission eventually sided with Lofker, ruling that PURPA's regulatory exemption applied because the wind-energy machines would sell power to only one customer rather than to the general public. The utility appealed twice and lost on both occasions. Lofker finally began erecting his wind machines on the Big Island and expects that by late 1985 Waikoloa Water Company, which supplies water to hotels and houses along the Kona Coast, will be buying about 700 kilowatts from an independent producer rather than from the utility.

Most independent power producers have not been as fortunate as Lofker. Rather than fruitlessly negotiate with recalcitrant utilities, some are appealing to lawmakers for new legislation, particularly in regions where independents can sell their electricity at a higher price to the retail market than to a utility with a low avoided cost.

An important but overlooked bill that passed the California legislature in mid-1984 allows independent producers to sell electricity directly to consumers other than the utility. In effect, the legislation permits a cogenerator to sell power to businesses around the block, within the same industrial park or across the state; the entrepreneur would simply pay the utility a reasonable transmission fee for wheeling the electricity.

Consumers, having a choice between the utility and entrepreneurs, would gain lower prices and better service.

Bash Nola of Southern California Edison complains the law will allow entrepreneurs to "confiscate" the utility's transmission lines, "stealing facilities from the companies that paid for them." But Jan Hamrin of Independent Energy Producers argues the law is a logical supplement to PURPA, allowing consumers, who actually paid for the transmission lines through their electric bills, to benefit from the competition that will result from increased access.

In May 1984, the Florida legislature, endorsing Hamrin's arguments, ordered state utilities to expand the "power broker" experiment to allow independents to wheel their electricity to whichever power company offers the best spot price. Utilities quickly appealed to FERC, arguing that the arrangement is illegal because it reduces the reliability of electricity supplies. FERC officials admit they face a conflict between PURPA's order to promote alternative energy development and the Federal Power Act's restrictions on wheeling.

The conflict may need to be resolved by Congress. Some entrepreneurs favor national legislation that would convert the nation's transmission grid into a regulated distribution monopoly that wheels power from competitive firms to consumers. But utility companies, explains one congressman, will "scream bloody murder because they have a religious opposition to wheeling other people's power." Investor-owned utilities, in fact, are gearing up for a bitter congressional contest beginning in 1985 over electricity transmission, fearful that a combination of independent power producers, large industrialists and public utilities will jointly demand more open wheeling. While the outcome of these struggles remains unclear, the pressures for access to the nation's power lines will certainly continue to build.

UNRESOLVED ISSUES

Theoretically, competition lowers costs, increases innovation, spurs employment and fosters economic development. But instilling competition in the electricity industry does not guarantee utopia. In fact, several problems will arise.

Stripped of regulatory protection, power generating companies (whether today's utilities or new firms) would confront the possibility of failure far more squarely than they do today. Poor business decisions could no longer be ameliorated by state commissioners; rather, they would add to a company's costs and benefit its rivals. Although one firm's failure in a competitive market would have less drastic consequences than the bankruptcy of a region's single monopoly, the freedom to earn unregulated profits always carries with it the risk of insolvency.

The recent insertion of competition into previously regulated businesses demonstrates the hazards. The financial crisis at Financial Corporation of America, for example, illuminates the dark side of deregulating the thrift industry. Freed of significant government oversight, the nation's largest savings and loan association took enormous risks—including aggressive lending and questionable accounting procedures—with the hope of earning higher profits. In the first six months of 1984, Financial Corporation increased its paper assets 44 percent. But the Securities and Exchange Commission, which maintains some oversight of corporate reports, objected to such high-flying accounting practices and forced the company to restate its $31.3 million second-quarter profit as a $107.5 million loss. In July 1984, Financial Corporation lost another $582 million as large investors moved their money to less controversial institutions, forcing the company to borrow heavily from the federal government to replace deposit outflows. Some banking analysts, who believe Financial Corporation's problems have weakened investor confidence in all savings and loans, are renewing calls for closer regulatory supervision to prevent similar crises at other institutions. But other experts argue that one company's excesses don't require eliminating the consumer options supplied by competition.

No company's transformation has been analyzed more than that of AT&T. After years of litigation, Federal Judge Harold Greene ordered AT&T to divest itself by January 1984 of its regulated regional telephone divisions if it wanted to compete in the growing computer and telecommunications industries. The results could hardly have been more profound, affecting workers, users, dozens of related industries, hundreds of competing companies and nearly every American in one way or another. AT&T engineers, eager for increased freedom to explore exciting areas of research, welcomed the change. But 43,000 factory workers at AT&T's manufacturing plants lost their jobs in 1984, and more layoffs are expected. "You are talking about the starkness of people with considerable service out on the street after they've given their careers to work for this company," complains Dina Beaumont of the Communication Workers of America, which represents about 90,000 members of AT&T's work force. "There are thousands of people on tenterhooks."

Although angry employees blame the federal judge and divestiture for their financial problems, the complex causes are actually based on technologies in flux. As AT&T markets more plug-in telephones and computers, for example, the company's big service force becomes increasingly unnecessary. And as other firms manufacture telephone sets, AT&T's plants must trim overhead and employee costs to survive. (Of course, employment is up at many AT&T competitor firms.) Competitive pressures promise to accelerate, and as company vice-chairman James Olson admits, "There will never be a return to business as usual." The lesson is clear: While opening new opportunities, technological and business innovations can destroy an industry's traditional stability, and almost inevitably cause pain to many investors and workers.

Some utilities and consumer groups worry that independent power producers could steal the utility industry's most lucrative industrial customers and force residential consumers to pick up a bigger share of the power system's costs. Put another way, large electricity users taking advantage of cogeneration and other alternative technologies may increase electricity costs for those individuals and families who must continue to rely on the utility company. This issue of "cream skimming" presents tough policy and equity issues.

Entrepreneurs readily say they try to service the best-paying electricity consumers in order to gain the highest profit. "I am the ultimate cream skimmer," boasts Tom Casten of Cogeneration Development Corporation. The strong-willed developer says competition requires redefining the market and doing better than existing companies in certain segments. "When Peoples Express entered the airlines business, it didn't seek the rights to fly to some small town like Warren, Michigan," he explains. "No, it struggled to compete on the well-traveled and profitable New York-to-Los Angeles route by lowering its prices." So, too, do small power producers initially target large consumers who face high utility costs. "Cogenerators, who use half the fuel of a power company, can provide a real service for industrial customers, but our machines aren't designed for John Doe in Warren," Casten explains. As to the charge that independents steal the power companies' best customers, Casten responds, "If utilities possess cream to be skimmed, someone is being milked."

Roger Sant of Applied Energy Services admits some residential customers may initially face higher rates as a result of decreased regulation. But continuing utility monopolies, he argues, will only discourage efficiency and eventually raise rates higher than they would have been in a competitive market. Sant maintains that it's the government's responsibility through welfare, not the power companies' through rate structures, to assure poor people have enough affordable electricity to meet their basic needs.

Several utilities are responding to the competition from independents by fighting back. Taking a lesson from Sam Insull, they are lowering rates in order to maintain industrial customers and to increase their sales and earnings. Pacific Power & Light's "on-site generation displacement rate" cuts electric charges by two-thirds for big businesses that abandon their own generators. Crown Zellerbach, Weyerhaeuser and Willamette accepted the offer, and now buy 11 megawatts of power from the Oregon utility rather than produce it themselves. Similar industrial discounts have been launched by scores of utilities, including Guy Nichols's New England Electric in Rhode Island, Detroit Edison and

Public Service Company of New Mexico. "We can't afford to lose customers," admits Charles Harnach of Cleveland Electric Illuminating. "The energy market has become more competitive."

While Wall Street analysts celebrate the conservative utility industry's willingness to compete, consumer groups attack these incentives for large consumers, arguing that if industrial rates go down, homeowner charges must go up. But utility executives, using logic first developed by Sam Insull, explain that if industrialists use more of the utility's electricity, all ratepayers benefit because the system's costs are spread more widely. Independent power producers take a third position, maintaining that if any consumer employs alternatives to the utility's electricity, the power company will need to spend less money on new power plants and can abandon inefficient facilities, thus lowering costs for everyone.

A competitive marketplace effectively promotes efficiency, but it has several shortcomings. Worst, the market is blind to the plight of poor families who spend up to one-quarter of their income on energy. More than 1.5-million American homes shivered through the winter of 1981-82 without heat, and scores of older people died from hypothermia, largely because they could not afford fuel. Some 12-million American families need energy assistance just to stay reasonably comfortable during heat waves and cold spells. But rather than help low-income people reduce their energy needs, the federal government annually provides $1.9 billion in emergency assistance to pay for current bills. Since this money goes to energy companies, utilities lose nothing. But taxpayers wind up paying the ever-rising electricity bills of those who can't afford the efficiency improvements that would reduce monthly fuel bills.

The market also ignores most institutional barriers to alternative energy development. Consider, for example, that about one-third of all Americans live in rental housing, where neither tenants nor landlords have an incentive to make conservation improvements. While the federal weatherization program at least acknowledges the problem, something more than the budgeted $190 million is needed to help tenants overcome their natural reluctance to pay for improvements in the landlord's building, and a landlord's temptation to simply pass through fuel costs in the rent.

And, of course, the market doesn't address the nation's noneconomic needs. To reduce reliance on foreign oil, for instance, the government invests billions of dollars in armaments to protect fragile oil-supply lines. But on its own, the market will neither internalize these costs in energy prices (instead, they show up as higher taxes), nor encourage a wiser approach to national security. From the point of view of national defense, investments in alternative power production may be every bit as effective as money spent on airplanes, submarines or troops.

Competition doesn't take into account environmental quality or public safety, either. The damage of altering the climate from burning fossil fuels or the threat of weapons proliferation from nuclear power don't become economic risks until they are irreversible. Forcing the marketplace to factor in these real but unaccounted costs may require government intervention.

The promotion of alternative energy development around Sun Day in 1978 was initially spurred by a progressive coalition, including environmentalists seeking to curtail pollution, antinuclear activists hoping for an alternative to reactors, and social reformers trying to advance local self-reliance. But as the independent power industry grows, it has gained support from conservatives and large corporations, and this is causing concern among some members of the early coalition.

Some environmentalists, for example, fear entrepreneurs wishing to construct small power facilities will promote production over efficiency, just as most utility executives have done. While acknowledging that renewable-energy technologies are safer than coal plants or nuclear reactors, Ralph Cavanaugh of the Natural Resources Defense Council wants to block the construction of small hydro dams in the Pacific Northwest, because they may undermine the region's comprehensive conservation plan that Cavanaugh maintains is even more environmentally sound. But Jan Hamrin of Independent Energy Producers argues that no inherent conflict should exist between conservationists and entrepreneurs. "Conservation is clearly the least expensive option and consumers must first make sure they are using energy efficiently," she declares. "Still, as long as there is a need for electricity and utilities must replace old plants, there will be room for independent power producers."

Ironically, some solar-energy advocates argue that "the vision of an alternative technological and social future powered by the sun has faded." They criticize the involvement of large corporations in technologies that they had hoped would encourage a more active citizenry and a more democratic society. But they fail to acknowledge the revolutionary changes within America's largest industry, where utility monopolies are being shattered, where safer and cleaner fuels are being introduced, and where energy consumers have more options to satisfy their basic energy needs.

The radical critics, however, do correctly question whether small developers can compete with "the big boys" in the emerging electricity market. Will Americans, they ask, merely substitute Louisiana Pacific and Dow Chemical for Houston Lighting & Power and Consumers Power as the suppliers of electricity? Opinions vary. Several financiers, including Richard Baker of the Bank of America, believe individual entrepreneurs will be gradually replaced by oil companies (like Atlantic Richfield), major engineering firms (like Bechtel), electrical-equipment manufacturers (like General Electric) and "smart utilities," which have the financial wherewithal to launch aggressive projects. But Roy Alpur, president of Independent Power Producers in Oakland, California, disagrees. He maintains that large companies are burdened by large bureaucracies and high overhead, while entrepreneurs can hustle to package the necessary financing, legal and engineering expertise.

The threat of giant corporations monopolizing the unregulated electricity market may be first tested in California, where General Electric hopes to develop a huge 2,300-megawatt, oil-burning cogeneration system near San Bernardino. The project, located in the Kern River oil fields, would sell electricity to PG&E and pump the steam into wells to enhance the recovery of thick oil deposits that fuel the cogenerator. Critics maintain that the system, if completed, could monopolize all of the state's open transmission capacity as well as lower the avoided cost rates available to other independent producers. Others argue that if market forces are allowed to operate, small developers able to provide less expensive electricity than General Electric or any other huge firm will continue to find success. Both sides agree that efficiency and innovation will be best achieved by competition among enough firms—both big and small—so that no single company can control the electricity market.

Can competition flourish in this heavily regulated industry? Changing economic conditions within the electricity market initially encouraged alternative energy development, while PURPA provided independents an outlet for their commodity and relief from regulation. But from now on, market forces, which vary from region to region, will primarily determine an entrepreneur's success.

The most promising economic trend for independent producers would be an increasing demand for electricity. Utilities would consider building new centralized power plants and their avoided cost of power would rise, encouraging scores of efficient entrepreneurs, who can make a profit selling electricity to utilities at high buy-back rates, to build cogenerators or small power plants.

But consider another scenario. When a utility finishes constructing a large power plant, it generally possesses excess capacity. Its avoided costs fall because the utility needs no more power, but retail rates rise because ratepayers must pay for the new generators. Rather than sell power to the utility, entrepreneurs can prosper by supplying less expensive electricity directly to consumers. Energy service companies, for example, would increasingly manage the electricity use of commercial and apartment buildings, while cogenerators would sell power to factories.

In those regions, however, where the demand for electric power does not rise and retail rates remain low (perhaps because the utility relies on inexpensive hydroelectricity or on coal plants that have not yet been forced to install new pollution-control equipment to curb acid rain), independent power producers will have a much more difficult economic climate in which to function.

The declining price of oil between 1981 and 1984 reduced buy-back rates, demonstrating the risky nature and inherent uncertainty of independent power production. The Federal Energy Regulatory Commission believes avoided costs will probably drop even further if more and more small power projects replace the utilities' most expensive plants, allowing less costly facilities to carry the peak loads. Clearly, the progress of independent power producers, assuming government doesn't restrict opportunities, depends upon the market.

A NEW AGE DAWNING

Traditionally when a utility needed more electricity, it built a new coal plant or nuclear reactor. For many years, this system provided reliable, reasonably priced power to consumers across the country. In time, electric companies resembled towering skyscrapers that got new floors slapped on every now and then.

By the early 1980s, critics began to call these electric "skyscrapers" unstable. Economists said they cost too much to maintain. Environmentalists argued they couldn't be kept clean. Military analysts feared they were becoming indefensible. In fact, some critics suggested the economy would prosper if the teetering giants were replaced with dispersed structures.

Even utility executives who manage these skyscrapers now admit their industry's very foundations are being shaken. The addition of overbudget new facilities threatens to bankrupt their entire operation, and engineers can no longer add new units that are more efficient and economical than existing facilities. Executives can no longer argue, therefore, that lower costs result from the expansion of a utility monopoly's system; rather, efficiency is to be achieved as it is in other industries—through competition among numerous companies.

The past decade's 12-fold increase in the price of petroleum also undermined the utilities' dependence on low-cost fuels, jacked up expenses, and stimulated customers to consider a variety of energy alternatives. In fact, a growing number of consumers are relying on an array of entrepreneurs operating lean and innovative facilities rather than on the additional capacity of utility skyscrapers.

These threats to the utility industry's structure have certainly not caused Americans to abandon electricity. Although the uses of power have become more efficient, individual consumers and businesses continue to demand reliable supplies. The changes, however, are transforming the businesses that provide electricity, creating a new social contract—based on market forces—between the power producers and consumers.

For almost a century, the major struggle within the electricity market pitted public against private utility monopolies; the confrontations waged by George Norris and Sam Insull continue today. But a more significant contest has emerged: a battle between competitors and monopolists, where entrepreneurs promoting an open market face stiff opposition from both public and private utilities. The issue is no longer whether the public interest is better served by profit-seeking monopolies or by government-owned monopolies. Today's consumers and politicians must decide whether regulation or competition promises lower costs and more reliable electrical service.

No one expects today's utility companies to abandon operations or expire, even though the days of huge power stations are waning. Just as General Electric and other large engineering firms are shifting their efforts from centralized plants to cogenerators, so will power companies try to adjust and prosper in a competitive market. Those that continue to rely on outmoded practices will suffer.

Independent power suppliers, however, hold enormous promise, and they enjoy growing support. Wall Street investors, for example, prefer innovative businesses to utilities that continue building large power plants in this era of uncertainty. A mixture of efficiency and dispersed generators also pleases environmentalists who have been doing their best to convince us that acid rain and nuclear wastes are unacceptable. And the diversity of growing companies promises workers more jobs than would similar investments in large power plants. Put another way, more sensible than today's monopolies is a pluralistic electricity market regulated by competition.

Such diversity is beginning to flourish. Today's utility monopolies are exploring new business ventures. Power producers and energy service companies are expanding. And pressures are rising to open the electric grid to more sellers and buyers of electric power. Despite several unresolved issues, the advent of competition promises to foster innovation and efficiency within the electricity market.

Restructuring an industry—particularly a giant and critical one— takes time. Electricity remains the most politicized fuel, and many utility executives will certainly exercise their substantial political muscle to oppose independent power suppliers and to demand a return to more centralized control. But market forces have quickly converted efficient and dispersed technologies into multi-billion dollar businesses. Today's utilities are losing their monopolies to a new generation of electric entrepreneurs.

EPILOGUE

WHAT'S IN IT FOR ME?

How will the transformation of America's electricity industry affect individual consumers? Will electric rates rise? If so, by how much? Will investments in electric utilities be sound? Which power companies show the most promise? How can an investor evaluate the new electric entrepreneurs?

This book has traced the major trends—competition, efficiency and innovation—that are evolving in America's biggest business. Translating these themes into predictions about specific companies can never be precise, but rough estimates of future rates and investment opportunities may help consumers and businesses adjust.

RATE SHOCKS

Average electric rates may have already tripled since the 1973 oil embargo, but about one-third of all Americans—more than 35-million households—will soon confront even higher prices because of expensive nuclear power plants. Although utilities canceled more than 180 generating stations over the past decade, 49 reactors remained in some stage of construction in early 1985. Most of these nuclear projects were well over budget, and power companies hoped to soon pass on these construction expenses to consumers as higher charges for electric power.

If you live in an area shaded on the map shown on page 102, you will soon experience rate shock. To discover how high your electric bills will rise, find your electric company on the following chart. The first column shows the additional costs that the average household will be charged during a reactor's first year of operation, compared to what rates would have been if the power plant had not been built. The second column gives the percentage increase over current rates.

The numbers, derived from utility reports and the work of respected economists, represent the best estimates as of late 1984, but they fluctuate frequently and are the subject of cantankerous debates among utility executives, consumers and regulators. Rates will rise even higher, for instance, if power companies remain unable to control construction costs. They could decline if regulators charge investors, rather than consumers, for most of the cost overruns, if state commissioners try to temper rate hikes by spreading the impact over several years, or if utilities abandon the projects before spending the huge sums needed to complete construction.

Not all consumers face rate shocks. As long as fuel costs don't rise dramatically, electricity prices in regions where utilities aren't building power plants should remain relatively stable and track the Consumer Price Index.

(A few notes on the numbers: First, electricity bills in those areas with already high rates, such as New York's Long Island, will rise dramatically when an overbudget reactor comes on-line, but the percentage increase may be smaller than that experienced by consumers now enjoying relatively low rates. Second, a nuclear utility expecting low rate increases either owns only a small share of a construction project or has already incorporated some construction costs into electricity prices. Third, public power companies are not included in this chart, but customers of the Washington Public Power Supply System (WPPSS), the Tennessee Valley Authority (TVA) and the many municipalities or co-ops building reactors can also expect rate shocks. Finally, overbudget reactors may be the major cause of skyrocketing rates, but they are not the only factor; rates may rise even further because of other construction and fuel expenses.)

Projected Rate Shocks for Residential Customers

Utility	Additional Annual Cost per Customer ($)	Rate Shock (%)
Public Service Co. of New Hampshire	1,084	182
Public Service Co. of Indiana	1,010	167
Toledo Edison (Ohio)	664	104
Long Island Lighting (N.Y.)	624	85
United Illuminating (Conn.)	578	92
Kansas Gas & Electric	481	83
El Paso Electric (Tex. & N. Mex.)	480	93
Arizona Public Service	459	59
Philadelphia Electric	425	74
Louisiana Power & Light	419	55

[*continued*]

Projected Rate Shocks for Residential Customers—*Continued*

Utility	Additional Annual Cost per Customer ($)	Rate Shock (%)
Illinois Power	404	82
Maine Public Service	399	91
Ohio Edison	387	67
Mississippi Power & Light	387	57
Consumers Power (Mich.)	375	95
Kansas City Power & Light (Kans. & Mo.)	328	83
Arkansas Power & Light	328	53
Cleveland Electric Illuminating (Ohio)	327	60
Union Electric (Mo.)	321	67
Gulf States Utilities (La. & Tex.)	318	40
New Orleans Public Service (La.)	312	52
Central Power & Light (Tex.)	260	36
Connecticut Light & Power	252	39
Carolina Power & Light (N.C. & S.C.)	246	34
Pennsylvania Power Co.	219	40
Western Massachusetts Electric Co.	218	36
Bangor Hydro-Electric (Maine)	203	44
Duquesne Light Co. (Ohio)	191	40
Commonwealth Edison (Ill.)	185	37
Georgia Power Co.	173	30
Texas Utilities	172	28
Rochester Gas & Electric (N.Y.)	170	35
Pennsylvania Power & Light	169	30
Public Service Co. of New Mexico	157	34
Central Hudson Gas and Electric (N.Y.)	147	24
Public Service Electric & Gas (N.J.)	143	27
Central Vermont Public Service	142	28
Central Maine Power	130	27
Detroit Edison	115	28
Houston Lighting & Power	111	11
Niagara Mohawk Power Corp.	97	22
Pacific Gas & Electric (Calif.)	97	21
Washington Water Power (Wash., Idaho & Mont.)	96	25
Portland General Electric (Oreg.)	91	20
Pacific Power & Light (Calif. & Northwest)	63	15
Duke Power (N.C. & S.C.)	62	10
Puget Sound Power & Light (Wash.)	51	11
Atlantic City Electric (N.J.)	51	8
New York State Electric & Gas	48	9
Southern California Edison	24	6

An estimated 4-million small businesses and 200,000 industries will also soon be forced to pay for overbudget reactors. Because rate structures differ from state to state, business bills may rise disproportionately to residential customers. For those businesses in which electricity is a major expense, higher rates may raise total production costs to uncompetitive levels, forcing factories to close and jobs to be lost—unless efficient alternatives to the utility's power can be found.

The following charts list those utilities soon to charge the largest rate increases to their commercial and industrial customers during the first year of a nuclear plant's operation. Also tabulated are the percentage increases over recent electricity bills.

Projected Rate Shocks for Commercial Customers

Utility	Additional Annual Cost per Customer ($)	Rate Shock (%)
United Illuminating (Conn.)	5,645	91
El Paso Electric (Tex. & N. Mex.)	4,615	92
Public Service Co. of Indiana	4,487	157
Toledo Edison (Ohio)	4,006	93
Public Service Co. of New Hampshire	3,425	186
Kansas Gas & Electric	3,214	78
New Orleans Public Service (La.)	3,127	52
Arizona Public Service	3,088	58
Cleveland Electric Illuminating (Ohio)	2,959	60
Kansas City Power & Light (Kans. & Mo.)	2,853	56

Projected Rate Shocks for Industrial Customers

Utility	Additional Annual Cost per Customer ($)	Rate Shock (%)
El Paso Electric (Tex. & N. Mex.)	886,952	98
Illinois Power	503,744	73
Commonwealth Edison (Ill.)	329,892	32
Maine Public Service	272,434	92
Ohio Edison	243,492	72
Pennsylvania Power Co.	227,273	40
United Illuminating (Conn.)	220,344	91
Public Service Co. of New Hampshire	216,540	187
Pacific Gas & Electric (Calif.)	216,039	20
Public Service Co. of Indiana	141,895	163

INVESTING IN UTILITIES

The stocks of electric utilities have been purchased by more than 8.5-million Americans, including many senior citizens who were confident the industry's regular dividends would help finance their retire-- ments. In fact, individuals own 78 percent of all publicly traded utility shares, primarily because power executives since Sam Insull have tried to convert their ratepayers into investors and because financial institutions have been slowly abandoning utility shares since electricity sales fell and construction costs soared in the 1970s.

Foretelling the stock market performance of specific companies is always tricky; the task is particularly difficult for utilities in transition. Hundreds of very well-paid analysts spend a great deal of their time trying to make such predictions—and many of them have not been very successful. Over the past several years, Wall Streeters have been surprised by construction-cost overruns, fuel price hikes and changing regulations. Many of the utility stocks they follow have taken a beating.

But despite all the bad news about electric companies, the Dow Jones Utility Average hit an 18-year high in October 1984. Reasons for the climb in value are varied, although falling interest rates probably had the major impact, since utilities are such large borrowers of money. Investors also began to realize that the stock prices of power companies without construction projects were temporarily undervalued because they had been beaten down by all the bad news about nuclear utilities. And speculators, hoping federal lawmakers and state regulators will provide enough subsidies and rate increases to allow the companies to avoid bankruptcy, have slightly raised the low prices of troubled utilities.

Security analysts disagree markedly about the future of electric utilities. Some, expecting a rise in demand for electricity, predict stock values will improve dramatically. Others, citing pending rate shocks and competition from independent energy suppliers, foresee more troubles. The only consensus along Wall Street seems to be that utility stocks can no longer be viewed as a homogeneous group and that those firms with large construction projects may be sucked dry by ever-rising costs.

The chart on page 212 is an alphabetical listing of the private utilities still building nuclear reactors in late 1984. It explains what shares each utility owns and how far overbudget the construction project has become. (Note: Not every plant is 100 percent accounted for because public power companies, including Washington Public Power Supply System (WPPSS) and the Tennessee Valley Authority (TVA) are not listed, since they do not issue securities.)

While most Wall Street analysts suggest avoiding power companies that own a large share of an overbudget nuclear plant, they disagree about which utilities will successfully evolve in the emerging era of competition. The key ingredients for success seem to be an ability to innovate and a commitment to efficiency. Southern California Edison is one utility that is testing a variety of energy alternatives and signing contracts with an array of entrepreneurs. New England Electric has also diversified into other ventures and reduced its reliance on imported oil.

Utilities with Nuclear Power Plants under Construction

Utility	Reactor	Share (%)	First Cost Estimate	Current Cost Estimate
Arizona Public Service	Palo Verde 1 Palo Verde 2 Palo Verde 3	29 29 29	$2.8 billion for 3	$9.3 billion for 3
Arkansas Power & Light	Grand Gulf 1 Grand Gulf 2	32 32	$400 million for 1	$3.4 billion for 1; Unit 2 on hold
Atlantic City Electric (N.J.)	Hope Creek 1	5	$600 million for 2 units	$3.79 billion for only 1
Bangor Hydro-Electric (Maine)	Seabrook 1 Seabrook 2	2 2	$900 million for both	$9 billion for both
Carolina Power & Light (N.C. & S.C.)	Harris 1	84	$1 billion for 4 units	$3 billion for only 1
Central Hudson Gas & Electric (N.Y.)	Nine Mile 2	9	$382 million	$5.1 billion
Central Maine Power	Millstone 3 Seabrook 1 Seabrook 2	2 6 6	$400 million $900 million for both	$3.8 billion $9 billion for both
Central Power & Light (Tex.)	South TX 1 South TX 2	25 25	$1 billion for both	$7.5 billion for both
Central Vermont Public Service	Millstone 3 Seabrook 1 Seabrook 2	2 2 2	$400 million $900 million for both	$3.8 billion $9 billion for both

Utility	Reactor	Share (%)	First Cost Estimate	Current Cost Estimate
Cleveland Electric Illuminating (Ohio)	Perry 1	31	$632 million for both	$6.4 billion for both
	Perry 2	31		
	Beaver Valley	24	$321 million	$3.5 billion
Commonwealth Edison (Ill.)	Braidwood 1	100	$934 million for both	$4.1 billion for both
	Braidwood 2	100		
	Byron 1	100	$909 million for both	$4.2 billion for both
	Byron 2	100		operating licenses denied for safety reasons
Connecticut Light & Power	Millstone 3	53	$400 million	$3.8 billion
	Seabrook 1	4	$900 million for both	$9 billion for both
	Seabrook 2	4		
Consumers Power (Mich.)	Midland 1	100	$267 million	abandoned after spending $4 billion; up from
	Midland 2	100		
Detroit Edison (Mich.)	Fermi 2	80	$229 million	$3.4 billion
Duke Power (N.C. & S.C.)	Catawba 1	25	$320 million	$1.8 billion
Duquesne Light Co. (Ohio)	Beaver Valley	13	$321 million	$3.5 billion
	Perry 1	14	$632 million for both	$6.4 billion for both
	Perry 2	14		
El Paso Electric (Tex. & N. Mex.)	Palo Verde 1	16	$2.8 billion for 3	$9.3 billion for 3
	Palo Verde 2	16		
	Palo Verde 3	16		
Georgia Power Co.	Vogtle 1	46	$2.5 billion for both	$7.2 billion for both
	Vogtle 2	46		
	Vogtle 2	46		

[*continued*]

Utilities with Nuclear Power Plants under Construction—*Continued*

Utility	Reactor	Share (%)	First Cost Estimate	Current Cost Estimate
Gulf States Utilities (La. & Tex.)	River Bend 1	70	$350 million	$3.6 billion
Houston Lighting & Power (Tex.)	South TX 1 South TX 2	31 31	$1 billion for both	$7.5 billion for both
Illinois Power	Clinton 1	80	$430 million	$3.1 billion
Kansas City Power & Light (Kans. & Mo.)	Wolf Creek	47	$783 million	$2.9 billion
Kansas Gas & Electric	Wolf Creek	47	$783 million	$2.9 billion
Long Island Lighting (N.Y.)	Nine Mile Pt. Shoreham	18 100	$382 million $261 million	$5.1 billion $4.2 billion
Louisiana Power & Light	Grand Gulf 1 Grand Gulf 2 Waterford 3	13 13 100	$400 million for 1 $230 million	$3.4 billion for 1; Unit 2 on hold $2.7 billion
Maine Public Service	Seabrook 1 Seabrook 2	2 2	$900 million for both	$9 billion for both
Mississippi Power & Light	Grand Gulf 1 Grand Gulf 2	13 13	$400 million for 1	$3.4 billion for 1; Unit 2 on hold
New England Electric	Millstone 3 Seabrook 1 Seabrook 2	10 10 10	$400 million $900 million for both	$3.8 billion $9 billion for both
New Orleans Public Service	Grand Gulf 1 Grand Gulf 2	15 15	$400 million for 1	$3.4 billion for 1; Unit 2 on hold
New York State Electric & Gas	Nine Mile Pt.	18	$382 million	$5.1 billion

Utility	Reactor	Share (%)	First Cost Estimate	Current Cost Estimate
Niagara Mohawk Power Corp. (N.Y.)	Nine Mile Pt.	41	$382 million	$5.1 billion
Ohio Edison	Beaver Valley	42	$321 million	$3.5 billion
	Perry 1	30	$632 million for both	$6.4 billion for both
	Perry 2	30		
Pacific Gas & Electric (Calif.)	Diablo Canyon 1	100	$620 million for both	$5.4 billion for both
	Diablo Canyon 2	100		
Pacific Power & Light (Calif. & Northwest)	WPPSS 3	10	stopped; 75% completed	stopped; 75% completed
Pennsylvania Power & Light	Susquehanna 1	90	$1.1 billion for both	$4.1 billion for both
	Susquehanna 2	90		
Pennsylvania Power Co.	Perry 1	5	$632 million for both	$6.4 billion for both
	Perry 2	5		
Philadelphia Electric	Limerick 1	100	$1.7 billion for both	$6.7 billion for both
	Limerick 2	100		
Portland General Electric (Oreg.)	WPPSS 3	10	stopped; 75% completed	stopped; 75% completed
Public Service Electric & Gas (N.J.)	Hope Creek	95	$600 million for 2	$3.8 billion for only 1
Public Service Co. of Indiana	Marble Hill 1	83	canceled after spending $2.5 billion	
	Marble Hill 2	83		
Public Service Co. of New Hampshire	Millstone 3	3	$400 million	$3.8 billion
	Seabrook 1	36	$900 million for both	$9 billion for both
	Seabrook 2	36		

[continued]

Utilities with Nuclear Power Plants under Construction—*Continued*

Utility	Reactor	Share (%)	First Cost Estimate	Current Cost Estimate
Public Service Co. of New Mexico	Palo Verde 1	10	$2.8 billion for 3	$9.3 billion for 3
	Palo Verde 2	10		
	Palo Verde 3	10		
Puget Sound Power & Light (Wash.)	WPPSS 3	5	stopped; 75% completed	
Rochester Gas & Electric (N.Y.)	Nine Mile Pt.	14	$382 million	$5.1 billion
Southern California Edison	Palo Verde 1	16	$2.8 billion for 3	$9.3 billion for 3
	Palo Verde 2	16		
	Palo Verde 3	16		
Texas Utilities	Comanche 1	88	$780 million for both	$4.6 billion for both
	Comanche 2	88		
Toledo Edison (Ohio)	Beaver Valley	20	$321 million	$3.5 billion
	Perry 1	20	$632 million for both	$6.4 billion for both
	Perry 2	20		
Union Electric (Mo.)	Callaway 1	100	$550 million	$3 billion
United Illuminating (Conn.)	Millstone 3	4	$400 million	$3.8 billion
	Seabrook 1	18	$900 million for both	$9 billion for both
	Seabrook 2	18		
Washington Water Power	WPPSS 3	5	stopped; 75% completed	
Western Massachusetts Electric Co. (Mass.)	Millstone 3	12	$400 million	$3.8 billion

Several other companies, hurt by unneeded nuclear projects, are developing sophisticated conservation programs to avoid building new generators. These include Pacific Gas & Electric of California, San Diego Gas & Electric, Northeast Utilities (a holding company for Connecticut Light & Power and Western Massachusetts Electric Company), Pacific Power & Light of Oregon, Public Service Company of New Mexico, Arkansas Power & Light, Florida Power & Light and Texas Utilities.

Several Wall Street analysts also prefer power companies that are diversifying into nonregulated, growth industries. The Southern Company, for instance, is investing in telecommunication ventures, while Montana Power owns several fuel subsidiaries.

Of the approximately 200 investor-owned utilities traded on the major stock exchanges, Wall Streeters are also willing to consider power companies that have recently completed power plants and plan to build no more, including Baltimore Gas & Electric, Dominion Resources (which owns the Virginia Electric Power Company), Florida Progress (which owns the Florida Power Corporation), Northern States Power (which operates in Wisconsin), Wisconsin Electric and Wisconsin Public Service.

INVESTING IN ELECTRIC ENTREPRENEURS

Selecting good investments among electric entrepreneurs requires some work. For the very large firms involved in cogeneration or conservation—such as General Electric, Johnson Controls or Fischbach—alternative energy remains a small portion of their overall operations. At the same time, most independent producers (such as Roger Sant's Applied Energy Services and Tom Casten's Cogeneration Development Company) remain privately held companies that rely on partners rather than stock sales to the general public. The number of pure electric entrepreneurs whose stock can be purchased on one of the national exchanges remains small.

Because these young firms have little history by which the management can be judged, the more you can learn about the company's products and markets, the better. Although most major brokerage houses now employ analysts who specialize in independent power production, they do not regularly issue reports on the industry or specific companies. Alternative energy is featured in few investment newsletters; one monthly advisory is *Sundex*, available for $130 annually from Energy Investment Research Group, P.O. Box 73, Glenville Station, Greenwich, CT 06830.

Below is a list of the publicly traded electric entrepreneurs as of late 1984, with each company's stock symbol and address. To receive more information about a firm, write to its financial officer and ask for the most recent annual and quarterly reports, as well as the company's 10K filing with the Securities and Exchange Commission (SEC).

Applied Solar Energy Corporation—SOLR (15251 E. Don Julian Road, P.O. Box 1212, City of Industry, CA 91749), a designer and manufacturer of photovoltaic products, is traded on the NASDAQ market.

Besicorp—BESIE (221 Canal Street, Ellenville, NY 12428) manufactures low-cost solar collectors, manages energy use in buildings and develops cogeneration projects. It is traded on the NASDAQ market.

Catalyst Energy Development Company (110 Wall Street, New York, NY 10005), develops, owns and operates cogenerators and small hydroelectric dams. In October 1984, it filed with the SEC to sell its shares on the NASDAQ market; its stock symbol is expected to be CEDC.

Chronar Corporation—CRNR (P.O. Box 177, Princeton, NJ 08540) produces systems to manufacture photovoltaic cells and is traded on the NASDAQ market.

Cogenic Energy Systems—CESI (127 E. 64th Street, New York, NY 10021), a manufacturer of packaged cogeneration equipment, is traded on the NASDAQ market.

Energy Conversion Devices—ENER (1675 W. Maple Road, Troy, MI 48084) develops amorphous materials and photovoltaic cells. It is traded on the NASDAQ market.

Energy Factors—EFAC (1495 Pacific Highway, Suite 400, San Diego, CA 92101) operates cogeneration systems and is traded over-the-counter.

Novan Energy—NOVN (1630 N. 63rd Street, Boulder, CO 80301), a small solar-collector company that manages energy use in buildings, is traded over-the-counter.

Spire—SPIR (Patriots Park, Bedford, MA 01730) manufactures photovoltaics and is traded over-the-counter.

Thermo Electron—TMO (101 First Avenue, P.O. Box 459, Waltham, MA 02254), a high-technology firm that develops engines and medical equipment as well as cogeneration systems, is traded on the New York Stock Exchange.

Time Energy—TIME (2900 Wilcrest Drive, Houston, TX 77042), an energy services company that manages almost 900 buildings, is traded on the NASDAQ market.

Ultrasystems—ULTR (16845 Von Karman Avenue, Irvine, CA 92714), is an engineering and construction company that builds defense systems, cogenerators and wood-fired power plants. It is traded on the NASDAQ market.

Vawtpower—VAWT (134 Rio Rancho Drive, Rio Rancho, NM 87124) is the only publicly traded wind electric company. It is traded over-the-counter.

SEC regulations restrict the advertising of many alternative energy investment opportunities. Rather than own shares of a company, some investors participate in an alternative energy project through a limited partnership. For as little as $5,000, they gain any appropriate tax credits and earn a share of the electricity revenues. Such projects are explained in detailed prospectuses prepared by the developers. To receive copies of new offerings for wind, cogeneration and other alternative energy projects, simply inform your stockbroker or financial adviser of your interest.

Some brokerage houses have developed their own mutual funds that invest in electric entrepreneurs and alternative energy ventures. For a $10,000 minimum investment, for instance, you can participate in Merrill Lynch's Liberty Equipment Investors Fund, which participates in a variety of independent energy projects. Kidder Peabody's Alternate Energy Investment Management Program, which is marketed to corporate investors able to contribute a minimum of $10 million, focuses on cogeneration and waste-to-energy projects. The New Alternatives Fund also invests in solar and alternative energy development and requires only a $2,650 initial investment. The advantages of these managed accounts are that individual investors can avoid the tedious research needed to track specific projects and receive the security of diverse investments.

More risky investments are possible in the venture capital market, where equity in a company can be purchased before the owners register the firm's securities with the SEC and make them available on public markets. To learn of such opportunities, alert your broker or investment adviser of your interest. Your broker can also direct you to one of the many investment organizations that regularly meet in most major cities to hear presentations by entrepreneurs; the MIT Enterprise Forum of Washington, D.C., for instance, maintains a mailing list and organizes regular seminars for area investors interested in venture capital opportunities.

Investing in corporate securities or projects, especially in an expanding industry like independent power production, offers both promise and risk. Be sure to thoroughly investigate the individual companies before you participate.

APPENDIX

The generators and suppliers of electricity have traditionally included two types of companies: private or investor-owned utilities and public or government-owned utilities. Each usually avoids competition by being the monopoly supplier of power in a particular community or region. Only 219 private companies generate 75 percent of the nation's total electricity capacity. The remaining quarter is provided by 2,195 municipalities, 929 rural cooperatives, 54 joint-action agencies and 12 federal power agencies. Actual control of the industry is even more centralized with only 9 investor-owned holding companies supplying 20 percent of U.S. electrical power.

In exchange for a monopoly franchise in a specific service area, utilities are required to provide an adequate and reliable supply of electricity at reasonable rates. To ensure private companies gain no undue profits from their monopoly power, state utility commissions review and approve rates and construction plans, as well as initiate financial and management audits of local utilities. Regulators are elected in 11 states and appointed by the governors or state legislatures in the other jurisdictions. Municipal systems are usually run by the city council or an independent board elected by voters or appointed by local officials. The Federal Energy Regulatory Commission oversees interstate electricity transactions; the President appoints its members.

Private power companies finance themselves by selling stock or by issuing bonds; they normally reward stockholders (who tend to be individuals rather than institutions) with dividends from the year's profits. Public firms issue tax-exempt bonds; they have no stockholders and make no profit. Wall Street investment bankers sell the stocks and both types of bonds on the market exchanges.

About 500 electrical equipment manufacturers supply utilities with generators, transformers, switch gear and other equipment. General

Electric and Westinghouse dominate the industry. Engineering and construction firms—such as Bechtel, Stone & Webster and Brown & Root—often build the power plants and transmission lines for utilities.

Power companies usually employ lawyers and lobbyists to represent their interests before state legislatures and regulatory commissions. In Washington, D.C., the Edison Electric Institute lobbies for private utilities, the American Public Power Association advances public firms, and the National Rural Electric Cooperative Association does the same for the co-ops. The Atomic Industrial Forum, the National Coal Association, the American Gas Association, the Solar Energy Industries Association and other trade groups promote the interests of fuel distributors or equipment manufacturers. A variety of other organizations represent large industrial users of electricity, state regulators, individual consumers and environmentalists.

Electricity is a premium, convenient and flexible form of energy. Although three units of fuel are needed to generate one unit of electricity, consumers have been willing to pay the price to light bulbs, run computers and power an array of appliances. The Department of Energy calculates that coal supplied 53 percent of U.S. electricity in 1983, while natural gas contributed 12 percent, nuclear 13 percent, hydroelectric dams 15 percent, oil 6 percent, and geothermal and other renewables 1 percent. Energy analysts believe the department's tabulations underestimate the contribution from biomass and other renewable resources.

The method of producing electricity has not changed dramatically since Thomas Edison's days, although generators have certainly become larger and more sophisticated. Typically, the process begins by burning oil, natural gas or coal, or by splitting atoms, to boil water. High-pressure steam spins a turbine that rotates a magnet inside coils of wire. (At a hydroelectric dam, falling water turns the turbine.) The motion of the magnetic field near the wire moves electrons inside the wire; this movement is electricity.

Transformers "step up" the power plant's output to the high voltages, or pressure, needed for long-distance transmission. More than 585,000 circuit miles of overhead wires carry high-voltage electricity to load centers across the United States, where other transformers "step down" the current into 4-million miles of distribution lines that connect with residences, commercial buildings and industries. The current entering a U.S. home is 120 volts, while a flashlight battery supplies about 1.5 volts.

Almost all U.S. electrical equipment uses an alternating current (AC) in which the electrons reverse directions. The number of times electrons move back and forth determines the current's frequency, which is normally 60 cycles per second (60 hertz or Hz) in this country. A direct current (DC), in which electrons move in only one direction, is delivered by most batteries.

Electrical equipment is very expensive. Today's large nuclear reactors average about $2,800 per kilowatt of capacity; a 1,000-megawatt plant, therefore, costs at least $2.8 billion. High-voltage transformers cost more than $2.5 million, while the pole-top units in your neighborhood run about $1,000. Transmission and distribution facilities typically represent half a utility's total investment.

Unlike other fuels, electricity cannot be easily stored. Its supply, therefore, must be instantaneously matched with the fluctuating demand from an array of consumers, or power outages may result. To fulfill the matching requirement, utilities operate three types of generators. "Base load" plants, usually the most expensive to build but the least costly to operate, run almost constantly, supplying the region's minimum requirements throughout the day. Cycling or intermediate plants, usually middle-aged and less efficient units, begin working when demand rises. Peaking stations, typically using the most expensive fuels, run only when consumption is at its highest. Normally, utility engineers want to maintain 15 to 20 percent more capacity than needed for the peak demand as a reserve margin to handle emergencies or to substitute for generators undergoing normal repair; in 1984, the industry's excess capacity reached almost 40 percent.

A power plant's percentage of time operating is expressed as its capacity factor. All generators must be shut down for regular maintenance, but the higher the capacity factor, the better the performance and the lower the cost of electricity. Nuclear reactors usually operate less than 60 percent of the time, while coal-fired plants enjoy an 80 percent capacity factor.

Electric power is measured in watts, named after James Watt, the 19th-century Scottish engineer and inventor (not Ronald Reagan's infamous secretary of interior). Most of us use 40-, 60-, 75- or 100-watt light bulbs. A rule of thumb holds that each person uses the output of a 1-kilowatt (1,000-watt) electric plant. Therefore, a 100-kilowatt (kw) power station (about the size of a small wind-energy machine) can serve a mid-sized apartment building or commercial complex. A 1-megawatt (mw) facility (producing 1,000 kilowatts) supplies approximately 500 homes. Today's biggest bruisers, 1,000-megawatt generators, power all the residences in a city the size of Sacramento, California, Fort Lauderdale, Florida, San Antonio, Texas, or Rochester, New York.

Each month, consumers are billed for the number of kilowatt-hours (kwh) they use. The difference between a kilowatt and a kilowatt-hour is roughly analogous to the difference between an automobile's speed and mileage. Power consumed over time—measured in kilowatt-hours—is recorded by your electric meter just like your car's odometer reports mileage traveled. Peak demand—measured in kilowatts—is similar to your car's speed at a given instant, as measured by your speedometer. A

100-watt bulb burning for 10 hours consumes 1 kilowatt-hour of electricity.

Electricity rates vary greatly among utilities. Residents of Noxon, Montana, serviced by Washington Water's hydroelectric dams, pay only 2 cents per kilowatt-hour. Consolidated Edison's customers in New York City, dependent upon many oil-fired boilers, pay eight times as much.

In 1978, Congress passed the Public Utility Regulatory Policies Act (PURPA) to encourage the development of cogenerators, machines that supply both heat and electricity, and equipment that taps solar, wind and other renewable resources. PURPA enables entrepreneurs employing these technologies to avoid costly regulations and to sell their electric power at reasonable rates to electric utilities. The law, upheld by the Supreme Court in 1983, allows independent power producers to compete in the electricity market.

ACKNOWLEDGMENTS

My debt to individuals is very great, for a book of this kind relies upon the cooperation of the participants in the story. More than 200 executives took time to explain their work and their perspectives on the transition within the electricity market. Among utility executives, those at Southern California Edison, Pacific Gas & Electric, Commonwealth Edison of Chicago and New England Electric System were most helpful.

I am grateful to the Edison Electric Institute (EEI), the American Public Power Association (APPA) and the National Association of Energy Service Companies for the help and hospitality offered at their annual conventions. Susan Farkas at EEI's library and Madalyn Cafruny of APPA's public affairs office deserve special thanks for generously providing access to publications and reports.

Among independent power producers, I especially appreciate Jan Hamrin of Independent Energy Producers, Mike Zimmer of the Cogeneration Coalition and Tom Gray of the American Wind Energy Association. In addition to explaining alternative energy technologies, they provided written materials and introductions to leading entrepreneurs.

Among utility critics, I thank Richard Morgan and Alan Nogee of Environmental Action Foundation for access to their extensive library and files. They often directed me to other sources that would provide a fresh perspective on a particular issue.

I have gained much from attending utility conferences and meeting with energy executives at their own offices or power plants. While traveling across the country, I have enjoyed the hospitality of Mary Squiers; Laurie and Ed Kurpis; my parents, Jay and Grace Munson; and my in-laws, Hugh and Ann MacEachern.

My great indebtedness to written sources appears in the notes to the book. I also appreciate the fine work of Congressman Richard Ottinger who, until his retirement in late 1984, chaired the Energy Conservation and Power Subcommittee of the U.S. House of Representatives and organized a series of thorough hearings on critical issues affecting the utility industry.

For their continued aid, I thank Marion and Warren Weber, Wade Greene, Alida and Mark Dayton, Donal O'Brien, Jr., and Elizabeth McCormack. Moreover, Tina Hobson and others at the Center for Renewable Resources kindly provided a foundation for my research.

Although writing a book is often a lonely task, I owe a great deal of thanks to editors and reviewers. Carol Hupping of Rodale Press gracefully demonstrated the wisdom of cutting a manuscript to solve structural problems. Peter Harnik recrafted sentences with skill and patience. Leona Schecter, my literary agent, provided advice and hope. Alan Miller, Kevin Finneran and Chris Flavin offered shrewd suggestions and comments. Ty Braswell, a friend and colleague, helped promote the publication. My deepest thanks goes to my wife, Diane MacEachern, for her constant support and encouragement.

NOTES

INTRODUCTION

Statistics on the utility industry's financial problems are recounted in a variety of published materials. A few of the most comprehensive include: "Are Utilities Obsolete?" *Business Week* special report, May 21, 1984; James Cook, "Nuclear Follies," *Forbes,* February 11, 1985; Scott A. Fenn, *America's Electric Utilities* (Washington, D.C.: Investor Responsibility Research Center, 1983); Matthew L. Wald, "9 States See Higher Rates Because of Nuclear Plants," *New York Times,* February 26, 1984; John Noble Wilford, "Laxity and Safety Rules Raise Expense of Nuclear Reactors," *New York Times,* February 27, 1984; Matthew L. Wald, "Despite High Cost, Some Utilities Feel Compelled to Finish Reactors," *New York Times,* February 28, 1984; Matthew L. Wald, "Utilities' Chapter 11 Prospects," *New York Times,* June 26, 1984; John R. Emshwiller, "Electricity Costs Rise Sharply as Utilities Add New Nuclear Facilities," *Wall Street Journal,* August 11, 1982; and Arthur A. Thompson, "The Strategic Dilemma of Electric Utilities," *Public Utilities Fortnightly,* Part I on March 18, 1982, Part II on April 1, 1982.

Several newsletters and magazines regularly cover the electricity industry. Those I found most helpful are: *Public Utilities Fortnightly* (published by Public Utilities Reports, Arlington, Va.); *Electric Utility Week* (published by McGraw-Hill, New York); *The Energy Daily* (published by the King Publishing Group, Washington, D.C.); *Energy User News* (published weekly by Fairchild Business Newspapers); *Inside Energy* (published weekly by McGraw-Hill); *Electric Light & Power* (published monthly by Technical Publishing, a company of Dun & Bradstreet, Barrington, Illinois); *Public Power* (published bimonthly by the American Public Power Association); and *Power Line* (published bimonthly by the Environmental Action Foundation).

Chapter 1. ON THE ROPES

My thanks to the Edison Electric Institute for the invitation to its 52nd annual convention, held at the Sheraton-Boston Hotel from June

226

18-20, 1984. Comments by Charles Dougherty and Tom Sullivan are from speeches given at the convention. Andrew Hines's statement is from his interview with the author, June 19, 1984.

Data on the utility industry's size drawn from a report by the U.S. Energy Information Administration entitled *Financial Statistics of Selected Electric Utilities* (Washington, D.C.: Department of Energy, February 1984); "Corporate Balance Sheet Scoreboard,"*Business Week*, June 25, 1984; and "Fixed Reproducible, Tangible Wealth in the United States," *Survey of Current Business*, August 1984.

A Troubled System

Information on the Washington Public Power Supply System drawn from "Whoops Fallout Plays Havoc with the U.S. Bond Market," by Kevin Finneran, *Financial Times Energy Economist*, September 1983; and "Money Meltdown," by Scott Ridley, *New Republic*, August 29, 1983.

Data on Public Service Company of Indiana from "PS Indiana Says It Won't Finish Nuclear Project," by Bill Richards, *Wall Street Journal*, January 17, 1984.

Early 1984 setbacks for the nuclear industry are outlined by Milton R. Benjamin in "Atomic Power Industry Jolted Anew," *Washington Post*, January 28, 1984.

The comment about shareholders losing money is by the former Edison Electric Institute chairman, Frank W. Griffith, in his "The Perspective of the Chairman," *Public Utilities Fortnightly*, May 13, 1982.

Information on AFUDC from "Electric Utilities," by Jean A. Briggs, *Forbes*, January 2, 1984. Complete data on utility financing from various publications by Merrill Lynch's Utility Research Group, including "Projected Construction and Internal Financing for Electric Utility Companies," June 1984. Comments about Standard & Poor's ratings from a speech delivered by Douglas Randall, Standard & Poor's vice-president, at the company's ratings seminar on January 28, 1985.

Statistics on the utility industry's woes are included in the publications listed above, as well as in "A Now-Wary Power Industry," by Robert D. Hershey, Jr., *New York Times*, May 22, 1984. See also testimonies by Douglas C. Bauer, senior vice-president for economics and finance of the Edison Electric Institute; and by Alan S. Miller and David Goldstein on behalf of the Energy Conservation Coalition, before the Subcommittee on Energy Conservation and Power of the House Committee on Energy and Commerce, February 7, 1984.

Too Bleak to Meter

I. C. Bupp's quotation is from "A Dark Time for Utilities," *Business Week*, May 28, 1979.

A good review of rising nuclear construction estimates is a report entitled *Prometheus Bound: Nuclear Power at the Turning Point,* by I. C. Bupp and Charles Komanoff (Cambridge, Mass.: Cambridge Energy Research Associates, November 1983). See also Christopher Flavin, *Nuclear Power: The Market Test,* Worldwatch Paper #56 (Washington, D.C.: Worldwatch Institute, December 1983). Richard Morgan's quotations and those of the Atomic Industrial Forum spokesperson are from Morgan's book, *Nuclear Power: The Bargain We Can't Afford* (Washington, D.C.: Environmental Action Foundation, 1977), as well as Morgan's numerous articles in *Power Line.*

Quotation by the *Wall Street Journal* from "James Klepper, Chief of NRC in Midwest, Is Beset by Problems," by Geraldine Brooks, *Wall Street Journal,* August 28, 1984.

Quotation by Carl Walske of the Atomic Industrial Forum from "Federal Agency Prods Nuclear-Plant Officials To Raise Performance," by Arlen J. Large, *Wall Street Journal,* May 10, 1984.

References from the studies by the Massachusetts Institute of Technology and the Congressional Office of Technology Assessment are reported in "Despite High Cost, Some Utilities Feel Compelled to Finish Reactors," by Matthew L. Wald, *New York Times,* February 28, 1984; and "Laxity and Safety Rules Raise Expense of Nuclear Reactors," by John Noble Wilford, *New York Times,* February 27, 1984.

Information about William Dickhoner of Cincinnati Gas & Electric from Geraldine Brooks's article, "Cincinnati G&E's Chief Draws Fire Over Stalled Zimmer Nuclear Plant," *Wall Street Journal,* January 18, 1984.

Criticism of labor union activities cited in "Nuclear Plant Workmanship Found Often Faulty," by Thomas O'Toole, *Washington Post,* August 2, 1984; and "Nuclear Crews Stretch Work, Up Costs," by Charles Komanoff, *Wall Street Journal,* March 19, 1984. Quotations by union official are from "LILCO Spent More, Got Less From Workers," by Stuart Diamond, *Newsday,* November 17, 1981.

Material on decommissioning power plants from "A Long-Term Problem for the Nuclear Industry," by Colin Norman, *Science,* January 12, 1982; and *Analysis of Nuclear Reactor Decommissioning Costs,* by David Greenwood, et. al. (Washington, D.C.: Atomic Industrial Forum, 1981).

For information on nuclear utilities' growing reliance on banks, see "Utilities With Troubled Nuclear Units Turn to Banks as Bond, Paper Ratings Fall," by Jeff Bailey, *Wall Street Journal,* January 20, 1984; and "Nuclear Utilities: Money Raising Is Disrupted by Industry Problems," by Robert L. Simison and Charles F. McCoy, *Wall Street Journal,* February 14, 1984.

A comprehensive study on reactor reliability has been done by Charles Komanoff. See *Power Plant Cost Escalation: Nuclear and Coal*

Capital Costs, Regulation and Economics (New York: Komanoff Energy Associates, 1981; reprint, Van Nostrand Reinhold, 1983).

Komanoff's estimates of nuclear power's financial damage from his conversation with the author, June 29, 1984.

Comments by Byron Lee of Commonwealth Edison from his interview with the author, April 24, 1984.

Comment by Jerry Klingher of the Nuclear Regulatory Commission and Philip O'Connor of the Illinois Commerce Commission from "Com Ed's Last Stand," by Harvey Wasserman, *Environmental Action,* June 1984.

Statistics about Commonwealth Edison from the company's "1984 Annual Report" and "1983 Marketing Program."

Quotation by New England utility executive from "Are Utilities Obsolete?" *Business Week,* May 21, 1984.

Rate Shock

Information about price hikes is drawn from many of the sources listed above, including Wald, Emshwiller and Hershey. Perhaps the most comprehensive review is *Rate Shock: Confronting the Cost of Nuclear Power,* by Alan J. Nogee (Washington, D.C.: Environmental Action Foundation, October 1984). Additional material about the Wolf Creek reactor from "Wolf Creek: The Bill Comes Due," by Nunzio Lupo, *Wichita Eagle-Beacon,* March 25, 1984. Information about Riverbend, Hope Creek, Nine Mile Point and Clinton from "The Nation's Nuclear Trials," by Henry T. Simons, *Financial World,* June 13-26, 1984.

An assessment of Shoreham's impact on Long Island's economy is contained in "Direct Testimony of Gregory A. Palast" before the New York Public Service Commission, PSC Case No. 27563, February 10, 1984. The impact on Missouri's economy is from "Testimony of Robert Klepper" before the House Consumer Protection Committee, Missouri General Assembly, January 18, 1974.

Quotation by Frank Jones, Suffolk County's deputy executive, is from "U.S. Trying to Revive A-Plant That State, County Believe Is Dying," by Dale Russakoff, *Washington Post,* May 6, 1984.

Comments about a "death spiral" are cited in testimony delivered by Amory B. Lovins and L. Hunter Lovins before the Subcommittee on Energy Conservation and Power, Committee on Energy and Commerce, U.S. House of Representatives, February 7, 1984.

Quotation by Steven Cooper of Touche Ross from his interview with the author, August 17, 1984.

In Transition

Comments by John Barr of Morgan Stanley from *Electric Utility Week,* October 10, 1983.

Reports by the Government Accounting Office are recounted in *Electric Utility Week,* August 15, 1983.

Quotation about the "greatest historical transition" by Douglas Bauer, executive vice-president of the Edison Electric Institute, during his interview with the author, January 6, 1984.

Chapter 2. CHOICES AND CONSEQUENCES

Losing the Nuclear Gamble

Information on Wilfred Uhl and LILCO was obtained from off-the-record interviews with LILCO employees and an excellent seven-part series of articles by Stuart Diamond of *Newsday,* first published in November 1981. (Diamond is now with the *New York Times;* Rick Brand continues *Newsday*'s coverage of the Shoreham reactor.)

First-rate articles on LILCO's attempt to avoid bankruptcy are: "U.S. Trying to Revive A-Plant That State, County Believe Is Dying," by Dale Russakoff, *Washington Post,* May 6, 1984; "New Lilco Chief Brings Blast of Aggressiveness To Floundering Utility," by Ron Winslow, *Wall Street Journal,* April 27, 1984; and "N.Y. Nuclear Plant Teeters on Brink," by Michael Isikoff, *Washington Post,* April 1, 1984.

Hearing a Different Drummer

Most information about and quotes by Guy Nichols come from his interview with the author, June 11, 1984. Data on New England Electric's alternative energy programs drawn from the company's reports and from the author's interviews with Fred Pickel, administrator of NEES's special energy projects, June 11, 1984, and with Linda Sanders of the utility's public affairs office, February 2, 1984.

Good articles on NEES and Nichols include: "NEES's Nichols: The Clever Kid in the Utility Class," by John McCaughey, *The Energy Daily,* January 17, 1984; "New England's Energy: How Long Overcapacity?" by Douglas M. Bailey, *New England Business,* February 20, 1984; "New England Electric Stock Hits New High," by Walter H. Crockett, Jr., *The Evening Gazette* (Worcester, Mass.), January 6, 1984; and "New England Electric: Discounting Rates to Heat Up Energy Use," in *Business Week,* March 21, 1983.

Chapter 3. PLANNING FOR UNCERTAINTY

Planning for What?

Quotations by Guy Nichols from his interview with the author, June 11, 1984.

The utility industry's demand forecasts are compiled by the North American Electric Reliability Council (NERC) of Princeton, New Jersey. An example of the group's many reports is "Electric Power Supply &

Demand 1984-1993." Michael Gent, NERC's president, spoke with the author, July 5, 1984.

A good overview of the power planning debate is given by Rochelle L. Stanfield in "Lights Out in the Year 2000?—It Depends On Whose Forecast You Believe," *National Journal,* April 4, 1984.

Quotation by Ernie Liu from "Electricity Output Rose 8.3 Percent in Year, Spurred by Economy and Bad Weather," by Ron Winslow, *Wall Street Journal,* June 20, 1984.

The Chiles Report is entitled *The Future of Electric Power in America: Economic Supply for Economic Growth* (Washington, D.C.: Department of Energy, 1983; DOE/PE-0045). Other forecasts of accelerated consumption include "Our Stake in the Electric Utility's Dilemma," by Peter Navarro, *Harvard Business Review,* May/June 1982; and "Dimming Our Electric Future," by John Siegel and John Sillan, *Wall Street Journal,* May 4, 1984.

Congressman Richard Ottinger (D-N.Y.) organized an excellent hearing on the Chiles Report and a critique by the Congressional Research Service on February 7, 1984, before his House Subcommittee on Energy Conservation and Power. Instructive testimony was given by Danny Boggs of the Department of Energy; Douglas Bauer of the Edison Electric Institute; Rene H. Males of the Electric Power Research Institute; Langdon Crane of the Congressional Research Service; Andrew Varley of the National Association of Regulatory Utility Commissioners; Alan S. Miller and David Goldstein on behalf of the Energy Conservation Coalition; and Amory B. Lovins and L. Hunter Lovins of the Rocky Mountain Institute.

Information on the Edison Electric Institute's advertisements is drawn from the trade association's campaign document, "Electricity: The Power of Choice." See also "Unwise Energy Blitz," by Richard Munson, *Christian Science Monitor,* March 12, 1984.

Information on the marketing and advertising efforts of utilities, including a quotation from a Pacific Power & Light executive (David Bolender), can be found in various issues of *Electric Utility Weekly* (especially March 7 and August 19, 1983); and "More Utilities Step Up Efforts in Marketing," by Bill Richards, *Wall Street Journal,* March 12, 1984.

Quotation by the ELCON official, Jay Kennedy, from his editorial, "A New Federal Push for Unneeded Nuclear Plants," *Wall Street Journal,* September 28, 1984.

Additional comments by Amory Lovins were gained during his interview with the author, February 7, 1984. Mr. Lovins has authored or coauthored a variety of books on energy policy, including *Soft Energy Paths* (New York: Harper & Row, 1979); *Least Cost Energy* (Andover, Mass.: Brick House Publishing Co., 1981); and *Brittle Power* (Brick House Publishing Co., 1982).

Good summaries of energy conservation activities are: Marc H. Ross and Robert H. Williams, *Our Energy: Regaining Control* (New York: McGraw-Hill, 1981); Howard S. Geller, *Energy Efficient Appliance$* (Washington, D.C.: American Council for an Energy Efficient Economy, 1983); and James J. MacKenzie, "Whipping Potential Electric-Power Shortages of the 1990s," *Christian Science Monitor,* March 12, 1984.

Planning by Whom?

The Solomon Brothers's report commenting on regional planning is entitled "Electric Power Supply and Demand—1983-93." It was published on June 29, 1983.

Ralph Cavanaugh provided detailed historical information on energy planning in the Pacific Northwest and the quotation, "Given the way the U.S. power pools are actually organized . . . ," during his interview with the author, May 4, 1984. He has also written "Electrical Energy Futures," *Environmental Law* (Northwestern School of Law of Lewis and Clark College, 1983); and "Stumbling Toward Utopia: The Implementation of the Pacific Northwest Electric Power Planning and Conservation Act," (report by the Natural Resources Defense Council, May 11, 1981). Mark Reis offered additional data during his interview with the author, October 27, 1983.

A concise argument for regionalization is provided by Mason Willrich and Kermit R. Kubitz in their article: "Why Not Regional Electric Power Generating Companies?" *Public Utilities Fortnightly,* June 9, 1983. Mason Willrich, now vice-president of Pacific Gas & Electric, explained his thoughts in more detail during his interview with the author, May 4, 1984.

Congressman Richard Ottinger organized comprehensive hearings on regional regulation before his House Subcommittee on Energy Conservation and Power on June 26, 1984.

Who Will Stop the Rain?

Information and quotations about acid rain derived from "Acid Rain Issue Prompts Self-Examination," by Douglas Martin, *New York Times,* February 26, 1984; "Widespread Ills Found in Forests in Eastern U.S.," by Philip Shabecoff, *New York Times,* February 26, 1984; and "Acid Rain: Push Toward Coal Makes Global Pollution Worse," by Joanne Omang, *Washington Post,* December 30, 1979.

The environmentalist's perspective is outlined in various policy papers by the Sierra Club and the National Clean Air Coalition. Also see Lewis Regenstein, *America the Poisoned* (Washington, D.C.: Acropolis Books, 1982).

The utility industry's view is presented in the Edison Electric Institute's publications, including "An Updated Perspective on Acid Rain," November 1981; and "Acid Rain Control Legislation," August 15, 1983. A brief overview of the contrasting viewpoints is offered by

Congressman Henry A. Waxman (D-Calif.) and Carl E. Bagge, director of the National Coal Association, in "The Battle Over Acid Rain Legislation," *New York Times,* October 28, 1984.

The most detailed government study on acid rain is by the National Academy of Scientists, *Acid Deposition: Atmospheric Processes in Eastern North America* (Washington, D.C.: National Academy Press, 1983).

Quotations by Richard Ayers of the National Clean Air Coalition from his interview with the author, July 5, 1984.

Comments by Alvin Vogtle, formerly with the Southern Company, from "Electric Utility Executives Forum," *Public Utility Fortnightly,* June 9, 1983.

Debates among the nation's governors are described by Jane Perlez in "Acid Rain Debate Divides Governors," *New York Times,* February 26, 1984.

Quotations from the Rev. Jesse Jackson delivered at the Acid Rain Convention in Manchester, New Hampshire, January 6, 1984.

Information on global warming can be found in: Stephen H. Schneider with Lynne E. Meisrow, *The Genesis Strategy: Climate and Global Survival* (New York: Plenum Press, 1976); William W. Kellogg and Robert Schware, *Climate Change and Society* (Boulder, Colo.: Westview Press, 1981); Walter Sullivan, "Study Finds Warming Trend That Could Raise Sea Levels," *New York Times,* August 22, 1981; Council on Environmental Quality, *Environmental Quality: Tenth Annual Report* (Washington, D.C.: Government Printing Office, December 1979); and National Academy of Sciences, *Changing Climate* (Washington, D.C.: National Academy Press, 1983).

The quotation, "What are utilities to do?" from the author's interview with Fred Sener of Cleveland Electric Illuminating, April 26, 1984.

What Price for Fuels?

A review of Big Oil's diversification is in "Competing for the Sun," by Richard Munson and Barrett Stambler, *Technology Review,* November/December 1982. See also Steven Greenhouse, "An Unsettling Shift in Big Oil," *New York Times,* March 11, 1984; Energy Action Foundation's "Where Have All the Dollars Gone?" June 21, 1981.

Diverse views on horizontal divestiture are presented in the transcripts of hearings before the Committee on the Judiciary, U.S. Senate, August 3, 1979; joint hearings before the Subcommittee on Antitrust and Monopoly of the Committee of the Judiciary, U.S. Senate, and the Subcommittee on Energy and the Environment of the Committee on the Interior, House of Representatives, June 28, 1978; and hearings before the U.S. Congress, Joint Economic Committee, Subcommittee on Energy, *Horizontal Integration of the Energy Industry,* November 19 and December 8, 1975.

Information and quotations about the pricing of Hoover Dam's power from Martin Tolchin's articles "House to Consider Dispute on Power" and "House Votes to Retain Cheap Sale of Hoover Dam Power in 3 States," *New York Times,* May 1, 1984, and May 5, 1984, respectively. The argument in favor of cost-based pricing is made by Carl Boronkay in "Hoover Dam Benefits Could Crumble for Southland," *Los Angeles Times,* April 19, 1984. The case for market-based pricing is made by Thomas J. Graff and David Marcus of the Environmental Defense Fund in their op-ed article, "Revenue Runoff from Hoover Dam," *Wall Street Journal,* March 30, 1984.

Comments by public power officials from Alex Radin's speech, "Meeting the Test of New Challenges," made before the American Public Power Association's annual conference on June 12, 1984.

Who Generates Power?

A review of the rise and fall of self-generation is presented in two books by David Morris of the Institute for Local Self-Reliance: *Self-Reliant Cities* (San Francisco: Sierra Club Books, 1982) and *Be Your Own Power Company* (Emmaus, Pa.: Rodale Press, 1983).

News about Ted Finch's windmill from: "State Tells Con Ed To Buy 2 Kilowatts—From a Windmill," by Linda Greenhouse, *New York Times,* May 6, 1977.

A critical analysis of President Carter's National Energy Acts can be found in Barry Commoner's *The Politics of Energy* (New York: Alfred A. Knopf, 1979).

For a review of Congressman John Dingell's (D-Mich.) early efforts to promote utility reform, see: 94th Congress, 2nd Session, "Electric Utility Rate Reform and Regulatory Improvement," hearings before the Subcommittee on Energy and Power of the Committee on Interstate and Foreign Commerce, House of Representatives, March and April 1976.

Testimony on PURPA is in: 95th Congress, 1st Session, "National Energy Act," hearings before the Subcommittee on Energy and Power of the Committee on Interstate and Foreign Commerce, House of Representatives, May 1977.

Other information on PURPA gained from interviews with Ross Aine, counsel with Van Ness, Feldman, Sutcliffe, Curtis & Levenberg, June 5, 1984; and Bruce Driver, counsel to House Subcommittee on Energy Conservation and Power, December 7, 1983. See also news items in *Electric Utility Week* throughout 1978.

Comments by Senators Dewey Bartlett and Howard Metzenbaum from *Electrical Utility Week,* October 16, 1978.

Chapter 4. THE INVENTORS

Thomas P. Hughes wrote one of the best books on early electrical developments, entitled *Networks of Power* (Baltimore: Johns Hopkins

University Press, 1983). Other good accounts include: Sheldon Novick, "The Electric Power Industry," *Environment,* November 1975; Martin Glasser, *Public Utilities in American Capitalism* (New York: Macmillan, 1957); Harold I. Sharlin, *The Making of the Electrical Age* (New York: Abelard-Schuman, 1963); Marc Messing, Paul Friesema and David Morell, *Centralized Power: The Politics of Scale in Electricity Generation* (Cambridge, Mass.: Oelgeschlager, Gunn, and Hain, 1979); and William Rogers, *Brownout* (New York: Stein & Day, 1972).

Thomas Edison has been the subject of several biographies. A few of the most interesting are: Robert Cornot, *A Streak of Luck* (New York: Seaview Books, 1979); Matthew Josephson, *Edison* (New York: McGraw-Hill, 1959); Robert Silverberg, *Light for the World* (Princeton, N.J.: D. Van Nostrand, 1967); Wyn Wachhorst, *Thomas Alva Edison: An American Myth* (Cambridge: MIT Press, 1981); Ronald W. Clark, *Edison: The Man Who Made the Future* (New York: G. P. Putnam's Sons, 1977).

A collection of Edison's writings appears in Dagabert D. Ross, ed., *The Diary and Sunday Observations of Thomas Alva Edison* (New York: Philosophical Library, 1948). The Edison Institute in Dearborn, Michigan, and the Edison Archives in West Orange, New Jersey, contain numerous pictures of and letters by the inventor.

Chapter 5. THE EMPIRE BUILDERS

A well-written biography of Samuel Insull is Forest McDonald's *Insull* (Chicago: University of Chicago Press, 1962). The Chief's selected speeches are contained in *Public Utilities in Modern Life* (Chicago: privately printed, 1924). Histories sponsored by utility companies or their suppliers include: James A. Cox, *Century of Light* (New York: Benjamin Co., 1979); Charles E. Neil, "Entering the Seventh Decade of Electric Power," *Edison Electric Institute Bulletin,* September 1942; and Paul W. Keating, *Lamps for a Brighter America* (New York: McGraw-Hill, 1954).

Many individual utilities have published their own histories; one of the best, which includes information about John Barnes Miller, is William A. Myers's *Iron Men and Copper Wires: A Centennial History of the Southern California Edison Company* (Glendale, Calif.: Trans-Anglo Books, 1983).

Quotation by Thomas Hughes from his book *Networks of Power* (Baltimore: Johns Hopkins University Press, 1983).

Data about utilities during the Depression was compiled by the U.S. Department of Commerce and can be found in Senate Document 124, 73rd Congress, 2nd Session.

Chapter 6. THE PUBLIC DEFENDERS

Information about rural electrification drawn from Clayton D. Brown, *Electricity for Rural America: The Fight for REA* (Westport,

Conn.: Greenwood, 1980); Jack Doyle, *Lines Across the Land* (Washington, D.C.: Environmental Policy Institute, 1979); Willard Luff, "Water Systems and Bathrooms for Farm Homes," *Rural Electrification News*, September 1940; and Robert A. Caro's excellent book, *The Path to Power: The Years of Lyndon Johnson* (New York: Alfred A. Knopf, 1982), which includes quotations by farm wives.

Mr. Democracy

Good biographies of George Norris include: Richard Lowitt, *George Norris: The Persistence of a Progressive, 1931-1933* (Urbana: University of Illinois Press, 1971); Alfred Lief, *Democracy's Norris* (New York: Stockpole Sons, 1939); Richard I. Neuberger and Stephen B. Kahn, *Integrity: The Life of George W. Norris* (New York: Vanguard Press, 1937).

Norris's own writings are contained in *Fighting Liberal: The Autobiography of George W. Norris* (New York: Macmillan Co., 1945).

Accounts of the early conservation movement are drawn from: Samuel P. Hays, *Conservation and the Gospel of Efficiency* (Cambridge: Harvard University Press, 1959); and Roderick Nash, *Wilderness and the American Mind* (New Haven: Yale University Press, 1967).

M. L. Ramsay writes an interesting review of the early battles between private and public utilities in *Pyramids of Power: The Story of Roosevelt, Insull, and the Utility Wars* (New York: Bobbs-Merrill Co., 1937). Also see Judson King, *The Conservation Fight* (Washington, D.C.: Public Affairs Press, 1959); and Matthew Josephson, *The Robber Barons* (New York: Harcourt, Brace & World, 1934).

The Federal Trade Commission's report, *Utility Corporations,* is contained in Senate Document 92, 70th Congress, 1st Session, 1928. A good summary, as well as independent analysis, is contained in Ernest Gruening, *The Public Pays: A Study of Power Propaganda* (New York: Vanguard Press, 1964).

Herbert Hoover is profiled by David Burner in *Herbert Hoover: The Public Life* (New York: Alfred A. Knopf, 1978).

Several books have been written about the Tennessee Valley Authority. One of the most interesting is by the organization's first director, David E. Lilienthal, entitled *TVA: Democracy on the March* (New York: Harper & Brothers, 1944). See also Preston J. Hubbard, *Origins of the TVA* (New York: W. W. Norton & Co., 1961); and William U. Chandler, *The Myth of TVA* (Cambridge, Mass.: Ballinger Publishing Co., 1984).

Chapter 7. THE GOLDEN AGE

Material on the visions of futurists drawn from "Whatever Became of the Predicted Effortless World?" by Sam Love, *Smithsonian,* November 1979.

Quotation by David Morris from his book, *Self-Reliant Cities: Energy and the Transformation of Urban America* (San Francisco: Sierra Club Books, 1982).

Private Power Endures

Philip Sporn supplies a utility executive's view of the "golden age" in his books *Energy—Its Production, Conversion and Use in the Service of Man* (New York: Columbia Graduate School of Business, 1963); and *The Social Organization of Electric Power Supply in Modern Societies* (Cambridge: MIT Press, 1971).

Information on Edwin Vennard from his books: *Government in the Power Business* (New York: McGraw-Hill, 1968); and *Management of the Electric Energy Business* (McGraw-Hill, 1979); and from an interview entitled "Edwin Vennard: Telling the Public," *Electric Perspectives*, Spring 1983.

Controlling the Atom

Several first-rate histories of nuclear power have appeared recently. They include: H. Peter Metzger, *The Atomic Establishment* (New York: Simon and Schuster, 1972); Walter C. Patterson, *Nuclear Power* (New York: Penguin Books, 2d edition, 1983); I. C. Bupp and Jean-Claude Derian, *The Failed Promise of Nuclear Power* (New York: Basic Books, 1978); Peter Pringle and James Spigelman, *The Nuclear Barons* (New York: Holt, Rinehart and Winston, 1981); Daniel Ford, *The Cult of the Atom* (New York: Simon and Schuster, 1982); and Mark Hertsgaard, *Nuclear* (New York: Pantheon Books, 1983).

A first-hand account of the Manhattan Project is Leslie R. Groves's *Now It Can Be Told: The Story of the Manhattan Project* (New York: Dial Press, 1977). For a description of Franklin Roosevelt's role, see: James MacGregor Burns, *Roosevelt: The Soldier of Freedom, 1940-1945* (New York: Harcourt Brace Jovanovich, 1970).

The Brookhaven Report is entitled *Theoretical Possibilities and Consequences of Major Accidents in Large Nuclear Power Plants* (Washington, D.C.: Atomic Energy Commission, 1957).

An authoritative look at the Atomic Energy Commission is: Richard G. Hewlett and Oscar Anderson, Jr., *A History of the U.S. Atomic Energy Commission*, 2 volumes (University Park: Pennsylvania State University Press, 1962). A first-hand account is offered by David Lilienthal's diaries, entitled *Journals of David E. Lilienthal*, Vol. 1: *The TVA Years, 1939-1945;* Vol. 2: *The Atomic Energy Years, 1945-1950* (New York: Harper, 1964).

Background on U.S. bilateral nuclear agreements with Euratom and other countries found in the Congressional Research Service's report for the Subcommittee on National Security Policy and Scientific Developments of the Committee on Foreign Affairs of the U.S. House of

Representatives, *Commercial Nuclear Power in Europe: The Interaction of American Diplomacy with a New Technology* (Washington, D.C.: Government Printing Office, 1972).

The Atoms for Peace speech is recounted in Dwight Eisenhower's memoirs, *Mandate for Change* (New York: Doubleday & Co., 1963).

Chapter 8. SHATTERED MOMENTUM

The Blackout: Niagara Falls, November 9, 1965

The most comprehensive book on the event (as well as a good review of the utility industry's development) is William Rodgers's *Brownout* (New York: Stein & Day, 1972). See also Peter Z. Grossman, *In Came the Darkness: The Story of Blackouts* (New York: Four Winds Press, 1981).

Magazine reports of the blackout include: "The Disaster That Wasn't," *Time,* November 19, 1965; "Working to Bar Another Blackout," *Business Week,* November 20, 1965; and "Whodunit?" *Newsweek,* December 20, 1965.

The Protests: Washington, D.C., April 22, 1970

Biographies of Edmund Muskie include: Theo Lippman, Jr., and Donald C. Hansen, *Muskie* (New York: W. W. Norton & Co., 1971); and David Nevin, *Muskie of Maine* (New York: Random House, 1972). See also Muskie's own book entitled *Journeys* (Garden City: Doubleday & Co., 1972).

Information on Earth Day from Garrett De Bell, ed., *The Environmental Handbook* (New York: Ballantine, 1970); *Christian Science Monitor,* January 22, 1970; *New York Times,* April 23, 1970. The author also benefited from discussions with Denis Hayes, coordinator of Earth Day in 1970, and now chairman of the Solar Lobby.

Data on the Clean Air Act drawn from: Charles O. Jones, *Clean Air* (Pittsburgh: University of Pittsburgh Press, 1975); Hazel Erskine, "The Polls: Pollution and Its Costs," *Public Opinion Quarterly,* Spring 1972; "Muskie Criticized by Nader Group," *New York Times,* May 13, 1970; "Pollution: Will New Laws Be Better Than the Old?" *New York Times,* September 27, 1970; and Office of Science and Technology, *Electric Power and the Environment* (Washington, D.C.: Executive Office of the President, October 1970).

For information on other protests, see Richard Morgan and Sandra Jerabek, *How to Challenge Your Local Electric Utility* (Washington, D.C.: Environmental Action Foundation, 1974); Harvey Wasserman, *Energy War: Reports from the Front* (Westport Conn.: Lawrence Hill & Co., 1979); Dean E. Abrahamson, *Environmental Cost of Electric Power* (New York: Scientists Institute for Public Information, 1970); *The Price of Power* (New York: Council on Economic Priorities, 1972); and Lee

Metcalf and Vic Reinemer, *Overcharge* (New York: David McKay Co., 1967).

The Embargo: Kuwait, October 1973

Much has been written about the rise of OPEC and the impact of the 1973 embargo. Three of the best books are: Anthony Sampson, *Seven Sisters* (New York: Viking Press, 1975); Robert Stobaugh and Daniel Yergin, eds., *Energy Future* (New York: Random House, 1979); and John M. Blair, *The Control of Oil* (New York: Pantheon Books, 1977).

A good review of the U.S. government responses to oil price hikes can be found in: Daniel Yergin and Martin Hillenbrand, eds., *Global Insecurity* (Boston: Houghton Mifflin Co., 1982).

The Missed Dividend: New York City, April 3, 1974

Leonard Hyman of Merrill Lynch offers a good overview of the industry's financial history in his *America's Electric Utilities: Past, Present, and Future* (Arlington, Va.: Public Utilities Reports, 1983).

Contemporary reports on Con Ed's actions include: "A Financial Crisis for the Utilities," *Business Week,* April 27, 1974 (contains comments by Charles Benore); "Con Edison: Archetype of the Ailing Utility," *Business Week,* May 25, 1974 (contains Marshall McDonald's quotation); "The Bills Are Electrifying," *Newsweek,* April 8, 1974; and "Shock from Con Ed," *Time,* May 6, 1974.

Comments by Donald Cook and *Business Week* in "Will the Light at the End of the Tunnel Go Dim?" *Business Week,* March 1976.

The Accident: Three Mile Island, March 28, 1979

Information on Three Mile Island and other nuclear accidents is included in many of the books mentioned above, particularly *Nuclear Power, The Nuclear Barons, Nuclear* (includes quotation by James Deddens), and *The Cult of the Atom* (contains comments by Donald Brand and an unidentified utility vice-president).

The Kemmeny Commission study is entitled *Report by President's Commission on the Accident at Three Mile Island* (Washington, D.C.: Government Printing Office, 1979).

A good review of the media's coverage of the TMI accident is "At Three Mile Island," by Peter M. Sandman and Mary Paden, *Columbia Journalism Review,* July/August 1979.

Information on other nuclear accidents drawn from: John G. Fuller, *We Almost Lost Detroit* (New York: Reader's Digest Press, 1975); and David Comey, "The Incident at Browns Ferry," from *Countdown to a Nuclear Moratorium* (Washington, D.C.: Environmental Action Foundation, 1976).

The Default: Pacific Northwest, July 25, 1983

Much has been written about the Washington Public Power Association. Some of the most comprehensive stories include: "Whoops," a four-part series by Chip Brown in the *Washington Post,* December 3-7, 1984; Peter W. Bernstein's "A Nuclear Fiasco Shakes the Bond Market," *Fortune,* February 22, 1982; Daniel Jack Chasan's series entitled "The Fall of the House of WPPSS," *The Weekly* (Seattle, Washington), October 1984; Thomas C. Hayes's "Washington Power's Problem," *New York Times,* February 15, 1983; and Philip Dion's "Whoops—Default in Northwest Has Muni Bond Market on Edge," *National Journal,* September 24, 1983.

Other data on the Washington Public Power Supply System is drawn from many of the articles mentioned above, particularly those by Finneran, Ridley and Miller/Goldstein, as well as the author's interviews with Ralph Cavanaugh of the Natural Resources Defense Council, May 4, 1984; and Mark Reis of the Northwest Conservation Act Coalition, October 27, 1983. Quotations by Mark Reis in "Whoops: A $2 Billion Blunder," *Time,* August 8, 1983. Quotation by Carl Halvorson in "The Fallout from 'Whoops,' " *Business Week,* July 11, 1983.

Congressman James Weaver (D-Oreg.) organized hearings on the default before his House interior subcommittee on mining, forest management and the Bonneville Power Administration on January 26, 1984.

Chapter 9. GOVERNMENT'S HELPING HAND

Deciphering the complex federal budget and tax code is both difficult and inexact. The most comprehensive reviews of federal payments to promote energy resources are: *An Analysis of the Results of Federal Incentives Used to Stimulate Energy Production* (Washington, D.C.: Battelle Memorial Institute for the Department of Energy, June 1980); Joseph Bowring, *Draft Report on Federal Support for Nuclear Power: Reactor Design and the Fuel Cycle* (Washington, D.C.: Department of Energy, 1980); Richard Morgan, "Federal Tax Subsidies to Electric Utilities," published by Environmental Action Foundation, July 1983; and Amory B. Lovins, "Note on Subsidies to U.S. Nuclear Power Systems," published by the Rocky Mountain Institute, October 19, 1983.

The author benefited from interviews with Richard Morgan, January 9, 1984; Amory Lovins, February 7, 1984; Jim Akers of the Edison Electric Institute, January 26, 1984; and Allan Richardson of the American Public Power Association, January 19, 1984.

A review of phantom taxes is found in *Power Line,* April/May 1984.

Analysis by Duane Chapman from his 1980 testimony before the California Energy Commission, entitled "Nuclear Economics: Taxation,

Fuel Costs and Decommissioning." See also his book *Energy Resources and Energy Corporations* (Ithaca, N.Y.: Cornell University Press, 1983), and his testimony before the U.S. House of Representatives' Subcommittee on Oversight and Investigations, "Hearing on Nuclear Policy," October 23, 1981.

Quotation by David Lilienthal from *Journals of David E. Lilienthal* (New York: Harper, 1964).

Material about regulatory burdens and the quotation from one critic are from the author's interview with Peter Navarro of Harvard University, September 5, 1984. Also see Mr. Navarro's article: "Our Stake in the Electric Utilities' Dilemma," *Harvard Business Review,* May/June 1982.

Complaints about regulations were a constant refrain from utility officers across the country. Some of the most helpful insights were gained from the author's interviews with Fred Sener, a systems planning engineer at Cleveland Electric Illuminating, April 26, 1984; Byron Lee, executive vice-president of Commonwealth Edison, April 24, 1984; Harold Finger, executive director of the U.S. Committee for Energy Awareness, May 25, 1984; and James Brennan, director of Pacific Gas & Electric's energy management department.

A Federal Bailout?

Information about Senator Alphonse D'Amato's subsidies for LILCO from "Tax Bill Allows Shoreham Bailout," by Ruth Caplan, *Power Line,* June/July/August 1984. A first-rate overview of the federal efforts to save Shoreham, which includes quotations by Frank Jones and the script of an anti-LILCO radio ad, is "U.S. Trying to Revive A-Plant That State, County Believe Is Dying," by Dale Russakoff, *Washington Post,* May 6, 1984.

Other material on a federal bailout includes: Matthew L. Wald, "Energy Department Is Making an Effort To Save Shoreham," *New York Times,* April 22, 1984; Arlen J. Large, "Reagan Will Press NRC, State Regulators To Accelerate Building of Nuclear Plants," *Wall Street Journal,* May 9, 1984; Dale Russakoff, "Hodel Sees DOE Role Aiding Nuclear Utilities," *Washington Post,* May 9, 1984; and Pete Early, "Nuclear Energy Office Diverts Funds to 'Generic Activities,'" *Washington Post,* September 24, 1984.

For information on the Rural Electrification Administration's massive loans for nuclear plants, see: "U.S. Rural-Energy Agency Finds Itself Tangled in Nuclear Problems," by Bill Richards, *Wall Street Journal,* February 9, 1984; and "Public Power Lost," by Daniel Deudney, *Working Papers,* September/October 1982.

Data on the size of bank loans to utilities from "Utility Stockholders: Little Guys Have the Most to Lose," *Business Week,* May 21, 1984.

Information on the Touche Ross study from the author's interview with Steven Cooper, an accountant with the firm, August 17, 1984; and "Should Utilities Go Bankrupt?" *Power Line,* June/July/August 1984.

Struggles for Preference

My thanks to the American Public Power Association for the invitation to attend its 1984 national conference, held at the Sheraton Boston Hotel, June 11-13, 1984.

Congressman Richard Ottinger organized a lively hearing on relicensing federal dams before his Subcommittee on Energy Conservation and Power, House of Representatives, May 17, 1984. Interesting testimony was provided by Frederick Mielke of Pacific Gas & Electric, Joseph Farley of Alabama Power Company, Alex Radin of the American Public Power Association, and Gordon Hoyt of Anaheim, California's municipal utility.

The public utilities' perspective is outlined in various publications by the American Public Power Association, including "Consumers, Competitive and the Public Interest, October 1983; "Questions and Answers," *Public Power,* March/April 1984; "Preference Principle Endangered," by Alex Radin, *Public Power,* July-August 1984. See also Tim Redmond's "They're Stealing Our Rivers!" *San Francisco Bay Guardian,* January 18, 1984.

The private utilities' perspective is contained within the Edison Electric Institute's brochure, "The Benefits to Consumers from Hydroelectric Projects Operated by Investor-Owned Utilities," 1983.

Material for this section was obtained from interviews with Frederick Mielke, chairman of Pacific Gas & Electric, June 18, 1984; Allan Richardson, vice-president of the American Public Power Association, February 12, 1984; Vic Reinemer, editor of *Public Power,* January 25, 1984; Robert Thomken, legislative assistant to Congressman Richard Shelby, February 12, 1984; Douglas Bauer, senior vice-president of Edison Electric Institute, January 6, 1984; Jim Akers, director of policy analysis, Edison Electric Institute, January 26, 1984; Don Van Raesfeld, city manager of Santa Clara, California, May 9, 1984; Jim Beck, electric utility manager, Santa Clara Municipal Utility, May 9, 1984; Dave Kaplan, general counsel, Sacramento Municipal Utility, May 8, 1984; Gordon Hoyt, manager of Anaheim, California, Municipal Utility District, May 11, 1984.

A comprehensive look at public power efforts is *Taking Charge,* by Richard Morgan, Tom Riesenberg, Michael Troutman (Washington, D.C.: Environmental Action Foundation, June 1976).

Chapter 10. THE NEW COMPETITORS

Data on California's independent power producers from Pacific Gas and Electric Company, *Small Power Production Quarterly Report,*

Fourth Quarter 1984, and similar reports by Southern California Edison and San Diego Gas and Electric.

A good, brief overview of small-scale power production is Christopher Flavin's "Electricity's Future: The Shift to Efficiency and Small-Scale Power," Worldwatch Paper #61 (Washington, D.C.: Worldwatch Institute, November 1984). For a regular update on this emerging industry, see *Cogeneration and Small Power Monthly* (Box 33458, Washington, D.C. 20033).

Text of the Kansas gas company's advertisement from *Electric Utility Week,* February 14, 1983.

Producing by Saving

Many books and articles have been written about the potential of energy conservation. A few that I found most helpful are: Marc H. Ross and Robert Williams, *Our Energy: Regaining Control* (New York: McGraw-Hill, 1981); Solar Energy Research Institute, *A New Prosperity: Building a Sustainable Energy Future* (Andover, Mass.: Brick House Publishing Co., 1981); John C. Sawhill, ed., *Energy Conservation and Public Policy* (Englewood Cliffs, N.J.: Prentice-Hall, 1979); Lee Schipper, "Raising the Productivity of Energy Utilization," in Jamck M. Hollander, ed., *Annual Review of Energy* (Palo Alto: Annual Reviews, 1976); Denis Hayes, *Rays of Hope: The Transition to a Post-Petroleum World* (New York: W. W. Norton & Co., 1977). Author benefited from his April 25, 1984, interview with Marc Ross, professor of physics at the University of Michigan.

Data on appliances drawn from: Howard S. Geller, *Energy Efficient Appliances* (Washington, D.C.: ACEEE, 1983); and Amory B. Lovins and L. Hunter Lovins, "Prepared Testimony on Long-Term Demand for Electricity," presented to the Subcommittee on Energy Conservation and Power, Committee on Energy and Commerce, U.S. House of Representatives, February 7, 1984.

Quotations by Joseph P. Kennedy II from his interview with the author, August 24, 1984. Other information on Citizens Energy Company from the author's interviews with Steve Rothstein, general manager of Citizens Conservation Corporation, July 31, 1984; and Joe Fitzpatrick, general manager of Citizens Heat and Power Corporation, August 24, 1984. See also Mitchell C. Lynch, "Another Kennedy Makes His Mark, But With Energy-Saving Programs," *Wall Street Journal,* December 14, 1981.

Other information about energy service companies from author's interviews with Bob Roche, senior vice-president of Time Energy, August 22, 1984; William Parks, technical representative with Johnson Controls, July 31, 1984; Bill Curner, Washington representative of Scallop Thermal, August 22, 1984; and Martin Klepper, principal with Lane & Epson, P.C., and counsel to the National Association of Energy Service Companies, September 12, 1984. The author also appreciates the association's invitation to its first annual conference, held in Washington, D.C., on October 15-16, 1984.

Business Week's projections in: "Energy Conservation: Spawning a Billion $ a Year Business," *Business Week,* April 6, 1981.

Industry's Bonanza

Good articles in the popular press on cogeneration include: Stuart Diamond, "Cogeneration Jars the Power Industry," *New York Times,* June 10, 1984; Stuart Diamond, "Do-It-Yourself Electricity on the Rise," *New York Times,* June 24, 1984; Scott Armstrong, "An Old Idea That's Generating New Energy," *Christian Science Monitor,* August 28, 1984; Tom Alexander, "The Little Engine That Scares Con Ed," *Fortune,* December 31, 1978; and Erik Larson, "Industry Examines Profit Prospects of Selling 'Cogeneration' Energy," *Wall Street Journal,* February 19, 1981.

Numerous studies have been completed on the potential of cogeneration. A few of the most illuminating include: *Industrial Cogeneration Potential (1980-2000) Targeting of Opportunities at the Plant Site (TOPS),* a five-volume report prepared for the U.S. Department of Energy, DOE/CS/40362-1; Office of Technology Assessment, *Industrial and Commercial Cogeneration* (Washington, D.C.: U.S. Congress, OTA-E-192, February 1983); Frost & Sullivan report discussed in "Cogeneration Jars the Power Industry," *New York Times,* June 10, 1984.

Author greatly benefited from his lengthy discussions with Mike Zimmer, executive director of the Cogeneration Coalition, January 24, 1984; and Glenn Lovin, president of the International Cogeneration Society, May 24, 1984.

Material on specific cogeneration projects drawn from the author's interviews with Ray Stagg of the Hotel del Coronado, September 17, 1984; Allan Christie of S&W Cannery, August 22, 1984; Robert Stewart of Procter and Gamble, September 12, 1984; and Roberta Williams of Texaco and Getty, August 27, 1984.

Information on the natural gas industry's interest in cogeneration from "Cogeneration Seen Boosting Gas Demand, Aiding Profits in Processing," by Rick Hager and Bob Williams, *Oil & Gas Journal,* September 24, 1984.

Data on and quotations by Roger Sant of Applied Energy Services, from his interview with the author, June 1, 1984. See also Sant's book (coauthored with Dennis W. Bakke and Roger F. Naill), *Creating Abundance: America's Least-Cost Energy Strategy* (New York: McGraw-Hill, 1984).

Quotations by Dick Nelson of Cogenic Energy Systems from his interview with the author, July 10, 1984. Other material gained from the company's reports.

Quotation by John Hopkins of the National Electrical Manufacturers Association from his interview with the author, May 24, 1984.

Quotation by Frank DiNoto of Hawker Siddeley Power Engineering from "Cogeneration Jars the Power Industry," *New York Times,* June 10, 1984.

Quotations by Paul Carroll of Fischbach & Moore from his interview with the author, June 15, 1984. Other data on Fischbach from the company's reports.

Quotations by Dave Wallace of General Electric from his interview with the author, August 31, 1984. Other data on General Electric's cogeneration activities from the company's numerous press releases, kindly forwarded to the author by Howard Masto, supervisor of General Electric's press relations.

The author also gained an understanding of the cogeneration industry from many interviews with industry leaders. A few of the most helpful include: Roy Alpur, president of Independent Power Corporation in Oakland, May 4, 1984; Tom Widmer, vice-president of Thermo Electron in Boston, June 14, 1984; Jerry Davis, president of Thermo Electron's Energy Systems Division, June 14, 1984; Dr. Ed Taylor, corporate energy manager for Louisiana Pacific in Samoa, California, August 22, 1984; Lee Roberts, counsel with Hannon & Morton in Los Angeles, August 22, 1984; and James Dunlop, vice-president of Brooklyn Union Gas, August 17, 1982).

Modern-Day Quixotes

Data on the number of wind-energy machines supplied by Tom Gray of the American Wind Energy Association, July 26, 1984 and Kathleen Gray of the California Energy Commission, September 17, 1984. Additional information from *The Solar Agenda—Progress and Prospects* (Washington, D.C.: Solar Lobby/Center for Renewable Resources, 1982).

Estimates about the 1985 cost of electric wind machines from the author's interview, November 13, 1984, with Emile Coulon, president of Enertech Corporation, and a November 12th interview with Gerry Alderson, president of U.S. Windpower.

Descriptions of the need for reliable maintenance of decentralized power applications are described by E. F. Lindsley in his article "Planning Practically for a Decentralized Electrical System: How Past Experience Can Guide Us," in Harold J. Brown, ed., *Decentralizing Electricity Production* (New Haven: Yale University Press, 1983).

Comment by Ed Blum of Merrill Lynch is from his interview with the author, July 6, 1984.

Information on U.S. Windpower is from "Private Investors Selling Wind Power to Utilities," by Wallace Turner, *New York Times,* February 14, 1983.

Data about the Jacobs Wind Energy Company is from the company's reports. Quotation by Paul Jacobs is from his interview with the author, July 25, 1984.

Resurgence of an Ancient Fuel

Information about Dow-Corning and quotations by Bernard Bartos from his interview with the author, August 21, 1984. The author also benefited from an interview with Tom Holliday of Consumers Power, April 23, 1984; and with Howard Warren of the *Detroit News*, April 16, 1984. Bartos's quotation, "I can see the reactor. . . . " from "Cogeneration Jars the Power Industry," *New York Times*, June 10, 1984. Other data on Dow-Corning's cogenerator from "Industrial-Strength Wood Power Is Back," by Barry Rohan, *Detroit Free Press*, March 20, 1984.

Three good books on renewable resources are: Daniel Deudney and Christopher Flavin, *Renewable Energy: The Power to Choose* (New York: W. W. Norton & Co., 1983); Denis Hayes, *Rays of Hope: The Transition to a Post-Petroleum World* (W. W. Norton & Co., 1977); and Solar Energy Research Institute, *A New Prosperity* (Andover Mass.: Brick House Publishing Co., 1982).

A report specifically dealing with wood and biomass is Nigel Smith's *Wood: An Ancient Fuel with a New Future,* Worldwatch Paper #42 (Washington, D.C.: Worldwatch Institute, 1981).

Data on Ultrasystems' power projects and the process of gaining fuel supplies from the company's annual reports and from the author's interviews with Ted Kingsley, senior vice-president, September 17, 1984; Mark Lyons, a wood supply specialist, May 14, 1984; and Robert Kennel, a vice-president, November 13, 1984.

Information on Hawaii's biomass efforts from "Hawaii: A Paradox in Paradise," by Richard Munson, *Solar Engineering & Contracting,* March/April 1983.

Data on San Diego's waste-burning project from the author's interview with Dick Hopkins, resource recovery manager with Thermo Electron, June 14, 1984.

Rivers of Energy

Information on United American Hydropower's Mohawk River project and quotations by David Goodman from "New York Investors Go With the Flow," by Edward A. Gargan, *New York Times,* March 11, 1984.

For an optimistic view of the hydro gold rush, see "Minihydro," by John McPhee, *New Yorker,* February 23, 1981.

Quotations by Leslie Eden from her interview with the author, June 14, 1984. Ms. Eden also kindly supplied several issues of Hydro Consultants' informative newsletter, *Hydrowire,* and magazine, *Hydro Review.*

For different perspectives on the potential of hydropower, see: William A. Loeb, "How Small Hydro Is Growing Big," *Technology Review,* August/September 1983; and Dan Gillmar, "Outlook Called Dim for Hydro Power," *New York Times,* September 6, 1982.

Other data gathered from the author's meeting, November 13, 1984, with David Bristol, vice-president of HYDRA-CO Enterprises; Richard Roos-Collins of Friends of the River Foundation; and George Lagassa of Mainstream Associates; as well as the author's interview, August 28, 1984, with Mark Henwood, president of Henwood and Associates.

The Electric Inferno

Information on Hawaii's geothermal efforts from "Hawaii: A Paradox in Paradise," by Richard Munson, *Solar Engineering & Contracting,* March/April 1983.

Comments by John Shupe of the Hawaii Natural Energy Institute from his interview with the author, January 10, 1983.

The most comprehensive review of this resource is: Interagency Geothermal Coordinating Council, *Geothermal Energy Research, Development and Demonstration Program, Fourth Annual Report* (Washington, D.C.: U.S. Department of Energy, June 1980). See also Vasel Roberts, "Geothermal Energy," in Peter Aver, ed., *Advances in Energy Systems and Technology,* Vol. RF (New York: Academic Press, 1978).

Tapping the Sun

Data on the number of solar-energy collectors supplied by Carlo LaPorta of the Solar Energy Industries Association.

Quotations in this section are from interviews with the author: Kevin Finneran, July 13, 1984; Peter Barnes, May 3, 1984; and Amory Lovins, February 7, 1984.

The history of solar energy, including Socrates' quote, is well recounted by Ken Butti and John Perlin in *A Golden Thread: 2000 Years of Solar Architecture and Technology* (New York: Van Nostrand Reinhold Co., 1980).

A first-rate review of modern architecture and passive solar designs is "The American House," by Philip Langdon, *The Atlantic,* September 1984.

Information on solar cells drawn from: Christopher Flavin's *Electricity from Sunlight: The Future of Photovoltaics,* Worldwatch Paper #52 (Washington, D.C.: Worldwatch Institute, December 1982); Paul D. Maycock and Edward N. Stirewalt, *Photovoltaics: Sunlight to Electricity in One Step* (Andover, Mass.: Brick House Publishing Co., 1982); and Richard Munson and Barrett Stambler, "Competing for the Sun," *Technology Review,* November/December 1982.

Quotation by Paul Gray of the Massachusetts Institute of Technology from his speech to the 1984 convention of the Edison Electric Institute, June 20, 1984.

A review of the utility industry's interest in centralized photovoltaic applications from "Solar Photovoltaic Power Systems: An Electric Utility R&D Perspective," by Edgar A. DeMeo and Roger W. Taylor, *Science,* April 20, 1984.

Information about Stan Ovshinsky and Energy Conversion Devices from the company's reports and the author's interview with Lionel Robbins, ECD's vice-president, March 20, 1984.

Chapter 11. THE OTHER PLAYERS

The Financiers

Quotations by Del Ferris of First Interstate Bank and Susan Morse of PruCapital from their interviews with the author, May 14 and May 10, 1984, respectively.

For a review of alternative energy financing, see Martin Klepper, *Innovative Financing for Energy Efficiency Improvements* (Washington, D.C.: Lane and Edson, three-report series, 1982-83). Information on utility financing for energy conservation from Amory B. Lovins and L. Hunter Lovins, "Electric Utilities: Key to Capitalizing the Energy Transition," Mitchell Prize 1982 Competition Winner; and Mr. Lovins's "Saving Gigabucks with Negabucks," *Public Utilities Fortnightly,* March 21, 1985.

Information on North Carolina's electricity tax from "North Carolina's Alternative Energy Corporation Is Pursuing Energy Efficiency for the State," by Sanford Lakoff and Jon M. Viegel, *Energy Conservation Coalition Bulletin,* December 1982.

The quotation by Leonard Hyman, vice-president of Merrill Lynch, is from his book, *America's Electric Utilities: Past, Present, and Future* (Arlington, Va.: Public Utilities Reports, 1983).

The author also benefited from lengthy interviews with Leonard Hyman, July 11, 1984; Ed Blum of Merrill Lynch, July 6, 1984; Richard Baker of the Bank of America, May 3, 1984; Jeffrey Whitehorn of Dreyfus, July 9, 1984; Tom DePre of A. G. Becker Paribas, July 10, 1984; and Paul Bjorn of Price Waterhouse, April 27, 1984.

The Politicians

The Battelle study is entitled *An Analysis of the Results of Federal Incentives* (Washington, D.C.: Battelle Memorial Institute for the Department of Energy, June 1980).

Quotations by Jan Hamrin of Independent Energy Producers from her interviews with the author, May 7, August 21, and September 17, 1984. Other information gained from the association's reports.

The Utilities

Early articles about relations between utilities and entrepreneurs include: Dick Kirschten, "What Role Will the Utilities Play in Harnessing the Sun's Energy?" *National Journal,* October 6, 1979; and Robert D. Hershey, Jr., "Utilities Oppose Buying Electricity Others Produce," *New York Times,* September 12, 1982.

Judge Harold Cox's decision is *State of Mississippi v. FERC,* Civil Action No. J79-0212 (c), U.S. District Court, Southern District of Mississippi, February 19 and February 27, 1981. A report of the Supreme Court's decision is in "Alternative Power Gets a Lift," by Steven J. Marcus, *New York Times,* June 11, 1983.

Specific PURPA regulations are outlined in "Small Power Production and Cogeneration Facilities: Regulations Implementing Section 210 of PURPA" (Final Rule: Federal Energy Regulatory Commission), 45 *Federal Register,* 12214, February 25, 1980.

David Morris wrote a first-rate review of PURPA provisions in his book, *Be Your Own Power Company* (Emmaus Pa.: Rodale Press, 1983). See also *Promoting Small Power Production* (Washington, D.C.: Center for Renewable Resources, 1981).

Quotations by James Bruce of Idaho Power Company from his interview with the author, June 19, 1984. See also Mr. Bruce's comments from "1984 Electric Utility Executives' Forum," *Public Utilities Fortnightly,* June 21, 1984.

Comment from the Idaho Public Utility Commission from *Electric Utility Week,* January 10, 1983.

Quotations by Don Von Raesfeld of Santa Clara from his interview with the author, May 9, 1984.

The comment, "public power companies have not developed . . . ," made by Mark Henwood, president of Henwood & Associates, during his August 28, 1984, interview with the author.

A favorable view of the utility industry's interest in independent power producers is offered by Douglas Cogan and Susan Williams in their book, *Generating Energy Alternatives at America's Electric Utilities* (Washington, D.C.: Investor Responsibility Research Center, 1983).

Information on Southern California Edison's alternative energy program from William R. Gould's October 1980 statement, "One Utility's Path to Renewables."

The utility industry's statistics and its projections about future capacity are from "35th Annual Electric Utility Industry Forecast," *Electrical World,* September 1984.

Quotations by Glenn Lovin of the International Cogeneration Society from his interview with the author, May 24, 1984. Other material gained from *Cogeneration World,* the bimonthly publication of the society, and Mr. Lovins's speech, "Cogeneration: A Year After the Supreme Court's Decision," May 9, 1984.

An understanding of the utilities' perspective on negotiations with entrepreneurs was gained from scores of interviews with power company officials. Among the most helpful officials were: Joe Meyer of Pacific Gas and Electric, May 4, 1984; Sebastian John (Bash) Nola, Southern California Edison's cogeneration and small power production manager, May 11, 1984; Fred Pickel, New England Electric's special energy projects manager, June 11, 1984; Robert Ruscitto, head of Boston Edison's economic development division, June 14, 1984; and Richard Choguoji, assistant engineer at the Los Angeles Department of Water and Power, August 29, 1984.

Chapter 12. STRENGTH THROUGH DIVERSITY

Fortune magazine's listing of the largest industrial corporations by sales begins with the July 1955 issue. An additional ranking of utilities, according to their assets, begins on July 1956.

For a review of ten new directions transforming our lives, see John Naisbitt's *Megatrends* (New York: Warner Books, 1982).

A New Generation of Executives

Quotation by *Fortune* magazine from its November 1969 issue.

Comments by John Bryson of Southern California Edison from his interviews with the author, May 15 and July 17, 1984. His article (written with William Brownell) is entitled "Deregulation and the Efficiency of the Electric Power Industry" and is included in *Electric Power Strategic Issues*, James Plummer, Terry Ferrar, and William Hughes, eds. (Arlington, Va.: Public Utilities Reports, 1983).

The American Public Power Association offers a thoughtful analysis of changes needed within the utility industry in its booklet, *The Next 10 Years* (Washington, D.C.: APPA, 1984).

Public Utilities Fortnightly annually presents "The Electric Utility Executives' Forum." One of the most insightful visions is offered by Robert H. Short, chairman of the Portland (Oregon) General Electric Company, in the June 21, 1984, issue.

Information and quotations about Cool Water's gasification process are drawn from "Coming of Age at Cool Water," by Marie Mastin Newman, *Electric Perspectives*, Spring 1984.

Criticism of utilities' research efforts from speech by Massachusetts Institute of Technology president Paul E. Gray before the Edison Electric Institute's convention on June 20, 1984.

Material on fuel cells drawn from "Fuel Cells: Space Age Technology," *Electric Perspectives*, Spring 1984; and "A Rebound for Fuel Cells," by Stuart Diamond, *New York Times*, September 6, 1984.

Information on Solar One from Southern California Edison's annual reports; author's interview with Phil Martin, a SCE senior vice-president, May 14, 1984; and "Steam from the Sunshine," *Newsweek,* December 13, 1982.

Data on computer energy controls drawn from "Telecommunications: A Trillion Dollar Dividend for Electric Utilities?" by Alan J. Nogee, *Power Line,* June/July/August 1984.

A well-written account of environmentalists' efforts to have Pacific Gas & Electric implement conservation programs is David Roe's book, *Dynamos and Virgins* (New York: Random House, 1984).

Information on load management from Alan S. Miller and Irving Mintzer, "Evolving Load Management Technologies: Some Implications For Utility Planning and Operations" (Washington, D.C.: World Resources Institute, July 1984).

The quotation, "We are mining energy . . . ," is by Grant N. Horne, vice-president of Pacific Gas & Electric, and is cited in "Adding Power But No Plants," by Matthew Wald, *New York Times,* July 6, 1984.

Material on the Port Hood conservation experiment drawn from David B. Goldstein's "Hood River Progress Report: January 1984" (published by the Natural Resources Defense Council); and "BPA Launches the Hood River Conservation Project," an "Issue Alert" by the Bonneville Power Administration, November 1983.

Quotation by the General Accounting Office from *Electric Utility Week,* July 11, 1983.

Reconsidering Electricity

A first-rate collection of articles on diversification is contained within: James Plummer, Terry Ferrar, and William Hughes, eds., *Electric Power Strategic Issues.* The quotation, "We are in a critical financial condition . . . ," is by Terry Ferrar of the Dallas-based Central and South West Corporation and is included in "Utilities Search for New Revenue Sources," *Electrical World,* July 1981; see also "Utilities Strengthen by Diversity," *New York Times,* May 4, 1981; and "Fighting Insull's Ghost," by Allan Dodds Frank, *Forbes,* February 1, 1982.

Comment by Don Frisbee of Pacific Power & Light from "A High-Risk Era for Utilities," *Business Week,* February 23, 1981.

A good review of utilities' telecommunications efforts is supplied by Alan J. Nogee in "Telecommunications: A Trillion Dollar Dividend for Electric Utilities?" *Power Line,* June/July/August 1984.

Quotation by Senator Alphonse D'Amato from *Electric Utility Week,* March 14, 1983.

The quotation, "Every time we try . . . ," from the author's interview with Guy Nichols of New England Electric, June 11, 1984.

Quotation by David Owens of Edison Electric Institute from his interview with the author, November 13, 1984.

Fears about the monopolization of solar energy are expressed by Ray Reece in his book, *The Sun Betrayed* (Montreal: Black Rose Books,

1979). See also *Power and Light: Political Strategies for the Solar Transition,* by David Talbot and Richard E. Morgan (New York: Pilgrim Press, 1981).

Comments by Peter Barnes of the Solar Center from his interview with the author, May 3, 1984.

Comments by Chris Burke of Trident Energy from his interviews with the author, February 13, May 7, and September 5, 1984. Other information on CP National supplied by the company's reports.

Advancing Competition

Two first-rate anthologies have been published on deregulation and competition: *Electric Power Strategic Issues,* James Plummer, Terry Ferrar, and William Hughes, eds. (Arlington, Va.: Public Utilities Reports, 1983); and Howard J. Brown, ed., *Decentralizing Electricity Production* (New Haven: Yale University Press, 1983).

Comments by Richard Tabors of the Massachusetts Institute of Technology from his interview with the author, June 13, 1984. See also his paper, coauthored with Bennett W. Golum, Roger E. Bohn and Fred C. Schweppe, "An Approach for Deregulating the Generation of Electricity," in *Electric Power Strategic Issues.*

Detailed studies of deregulation include: *Deregulation of Electric Power: A Framework for Analysis,* prepared by the Massachusetts Institute of Technology for the Department of Energy, September 1982; *Alternative Models of Electric Power Deregulation,* prepared by the Edison Electric Institute, May 1982; "Proceedings of the MITRE-Edison Electric Institute Conference on Deregulation in the Electric Power Industry," November 16-17, 1982; and Irwin M. Stelzer's "Electric Utilities: Next Step for Deregulators," *Regulation,* July/August 1982.

Two good reports in the popular media are: Tom Alexander, "The Surge to Deregulate Electricity," *Fortune,* July 13, 1981; and John Emshwiller, "Debate Heats Up on Merits of Deregulating Utilities," *Wall Street Journal,* June 2, 1981.

Quotation by American Electric Power officials, Joseph Dowd and John Burton, from *Public Utilities Fortnightly,* September 16, 1982.

Comment by Matthew Holden of FERC from *Public Utilities Fortnightly*'s special issue on deregulation, September 16, 1982. Quotation by Paul Levy of the Massachusetts Commission from his article, "The Road to a New Monopoly," *New York Times,* July 5, 1981.

Information about the Florida power broker gained from the author's interviews with Michael Gent, president of the North American Electric Reliability Council, July 5, 1984; and Andrew Hines, chairman of the Florida Power Corporation, June 19, 1984.

One of the best articles on promoting competition in the electricity market is by Arthur A. Thompson, Jr., a professor of economics and business administration at the University of Alabama. The piece is entitled, "New Driving Forces in the Electric Energy Marketplace—To a 'Death Spiral' or Vigorous Competition?" *Public Utilities Fortnightly,* June 21, 1984.

Opening the Grid

Comments by Charles Ross cited in "Transmission Lines Must Be Fairly Shared," by Chapman (Chip) Stockford, *Public Power,* May-June 1984.

A typical criticism of wheeling by a utility executive is offered by Paul Ziemer, chairman of Wisconsin Public Service Corporation, in "Interview with New EEI Chairman: Paul Ziemer," *Electrical World,* May 1984.

William States Lee's atypical quotation favoring an open grid is from "Duke Power Succeeds Building Nuclear Units Without Outside Help," by Ed Bean, *Wall Street Journal,* October 17, 1984. Lee is the chairman of Duke Power.

American Public Power Association has prepared many reports on gaining access to power. Perhaps the most succinct summary of the group's position is "Transmission Lines Must Be Fairly Shared."

The Supreme Court's decision on wheeling is: *Otter Tail Company v. United States,* 93 S. Ct. 1022 (at 1035), 1973.

Comment by Don Von Raesfeld of Santa Clara from his interview with the author, May 9, 1984. Other information supplied by Jim Beck, Santa Clara's electric utility manager, on the same day.

Information on Electricity Consumers Resource Council supplied by John Anderson, ELCON's executive director, during his interview with the author, September 7, 1984.

Data on Lukens Steel, including the quotation from the administrative judge, from *Electric Utility Week,* June 27, 1983.

Comments by Michael Lofker of Renewable Energy Ventures from his interview with the author, August 17, 1984.

Comments by Dudley Pratt of Hawaiian Electric Company from his interview with the author, January 1983.

Information about California legislation supplied by Jan Hamrin of Independent Energy Producers, interviewed on May 7 and August 21, 1984; Diane Fellman of the California Public Utilities Commission, interviewed on May 9, 1984; and Mike Garland, California's energy and resource manager, interviewed on May 8, 1984.

Quotations by Bash Nola of Southern California Edison from his interview with the author, May 11, 1984.

Unresolved Issues

Information on Financial Corporation of America drawn from "Fincorp Sheds Light on Dark Side of S&L Deregulation," by David A. Vise, *Washington Post,* September 2, 1984.

Quotations by Dina Beaumont of the Communications Workers of America and James Olson of AT&T are from "The Painful Downsizing of AT&T," by Merrill Brown, *Washington Post,* September 2, 1984.

Comments by Tom Casten of Cogeneration Development Corporation from his interview with the author, July 10, 1984. Those by Roger Sant of Applied Energy Services from his meeting with the author, June 1, 1984.

Quotations by Charles Harnarch of Cleveland Electric Illuminating from his interview with the author, April 23, 1984.

Information on unheated residences gained from "Study Says 1.5 Million Homes to Be Heatless," *Washington Post,* December 18, 1981.

Jan Hamrin's quotations from her interview with the author, May 7, 1984.

The quotation, "The vision has faded . . . ," by Roger Pollak from his article "Solar Power: The Promise Fades," *Progressive,* September 1984.

EPILOGUE

What's in It for Me?

Hundreds of articles have been written in local newspapers about pending rate shocks. The most comprehensive review of the dispersed phenomena is provided by Alan J. Nogee in his report, "Rate Shock: Confronting the Cost of Nuclear Power" (Washington, D.C.: Environmental Action Foundation, October 1984). Three other good overviews are: Matthew L. Wald's "9 States See Higher Rates Because of Nuclear Plants," *New York Times,* February 26, 1984; "Prometheus Bound: Nuclear Power at the Turning Point," by I. C. Bupp and Charles Komanoff (Cambridge, Mass.: Cambridge Energy Research Associates, November 1983); and James Cook's "Nuclear Follies," *Forbes,* February 11, 1985.

Most brokerage firms publish reams of reports on energy company stocks and bonds. Particularly helpful were comments and studies provided by Leonard Hyman and Edward Blum, both of Merrill Lynch.

INDEX

Boldface page numbers indicate entry in chart. Page numbers in *italic* indicate photographs.

255